# Glimpses of Hindu Astrology
# &
# Some Aspects of Indology

Sri Garib Das Oriental Series No. 173

# Glimpses of Hindu Astrology & Some Aspects of Indology

**S.R.N. Murthy**

**Sri Satguru Publications**
*A Division of*
**Indian Books Centre**
Shakti Nagar, Delhi
INDIA

*Published by :*
**Sri Satguru Publications**
Indological and Oriental Publishers
*A Division of*
**Indian Books Centre**
*40/5, Shakti Nagar,*
*Delhi-110007*
(INDIA)

First Edition : Delhi, 1993

ISBN 81-7030-383-4



PRINTED IN INDIA

**Dedicated to;**

*Veda Brahma Sri Ahobala Shbashtry my respected grand father who initiated me to Hindu Astrology & Professor B.V. Raman, Editor, The Astrological Magazine, Bangalore who created a forum for these articles of mine.*

# Foreword

Dr. S.R.N. Murthy is a well-known scholar in geology and has many papers on the subject to his credit. He has, with this background of geology, delved deep into allied areas of knowledge in ancient Indian literature and as a result of his studies, has written extensively on a variety of connected topics in the pages of The Astrological Magazine. His articles are not only of academic interest being incisive, indepth and analytical but can also be of practical import if applied suitably.

The present volume is a collection of articles he has written for us since the last twenty years. He deals with an unusual versatility with the abstruse topic of the evolution of time, comparing time with space and clubbing the two as a uni-dimensional force. His thoughts on the fourth-dimension foray into ancient Hindu literature on the subject.

Dr. Murthy is also well-grounded in Astrology. Some of his articles depict clearly the rationale of Astrology, judicial astrology and how it fits with Einstein's Theory of Relativity. He has dealt with matters relating to Kalpas or Time Cycles, the Hindu Calendar, Indian Chronology, movements of Mars, Saturn, Mercury and Venus and how they affect human affairs, the topic of Ayanamsa, economy and planets, Vastu principles, ground water, gems, sound, and many other interesting topis. He also proves with relevant evidence the geological reality of the now invisible Saraswati river and that the so-called Aryans were local, not outsiders. Incidentally I have always emphasised that the term *Arya* does not have a racial connotation as made out by some European indologists and their Indian counterparts. The term Arya means *noble* and Aryans were the original inhabitants of Bharata Varsha. Dr. Murthy's papers on earthquakes deserve serious attention by the seismological department.

It is a matter of gratification these brilliant papers by Dr. S.R.N. Murthy will now be available in a book-form. I commend this volume to all those genuinely interested in the pursuit of knowledge and lovers of ancient Indian wisdom.

Bangalore
15th April, 1993

**Dr. B.V. Raman**

# Preface

'Astrology' the Vedic science of stars/time gained a status of science (Shāstra) in the East, especially in India as an undivided part of the Vedas (Vedanga) while it did not gain such a position in the Western civilisation even to this day. While astrology and astronomy were developed side by side in the Orient, only astronomy was developed in the occident to the exclusion of astrology. This fact has remained even to this day and many Nobel Laureates have condemned astrology while they praise astronomy, specially in the Western scientific groups. In the Indian context, it is difficult to separate the two disciplines and almost all activities of Hindu society is controlled by them since ages. That Hindu Astrology has its roots in the Vedic literature is very well known. Several of the Rg. Vedic hymns have been devoted to the description of the luminaries and the planets as well as distant starṣ While the luminaries are described in the Soura and Pavamāna sooktas, the latter have their own student seers who have composed - rather seen (Mantra drashtārās)-the latter ones have been described by the Graha Yagnya and nakshatreshthi mantras, drawn from various sooktas of different Mandalas of the Rg. Veda respectively. Thus the Vālmiki Rāmāyaṇa statement that;

"ĀMNĀYĀNĀM AYOGENA SHĀSHTRAM PRASHI-THILĀMIV"

meaning that without the application of the Vedas the sciences get into disuse, the science of time practiced since the time of the Vedas is growing from strength to strength over the millenia in India as a very important discipline of science being taught under the title "Jyouthishā" in almost all Sanskrit Pathashālās. It has not been included in the curriculum of modern colleges since they are offshoots of Western thinking which has prejudiced opinion about Astrology. This is not without reason. The Western astrology even to this day has many ambiguities and has distorted roots in the Oriental scriptures. They do not know their exact origins and have been mixed up and do not yield proper results as a result many cannot claim faith in this field. But Hindu astrology has a firm foundation in the Vedas and has been developed on the question of mathematical basis over many many thousands of years and when put to test has been yielding correct results, either in mundane or in human astrology. Thus, this science is in thorough practice by many in this land even to this day.

Astrology has been the life and breadth of India. From time reckoning, to the conduct of any festive to the ceremonies of birth to death, each Hindu is enjoined to consult astrologer and the whole country has in that way has a strong cultural, living foundation of astrology. It was practiced by royalties in the middle ages for the determination of the future of many nations, war, famine, drought, etc. But then it also practiced human astrology since āyurveda claimed the corresponding close relationship between the Piṇdāṇda (human embryo) and the Brahmānda (the cosmic field). It did go a long way to master the techniques of what is called the special field of astrology namely 'Nādi' systems.

Thus the science of astrology has retained its scientific outlook inspite of many shortcomings. Research in Hindu astrology has taken a backseat since a long time. Even to this day the rules or principles of Hindu astrology are old and many are still giving correct results. The amount of literature that has developed in this field in India is something superb and tremendous. There are numerous texts in each of the triskandha jyoutisha namely astronomical, horoscopical and interpretational fields. The many siddhāntās that are available to us from the time of Lagadha-the first Vedic astrologer are many; similarly the text on Hindu horoscopy and texts on interpretation. It is simply impossible to have a mastery over all such texts and the learned depend upon few exceptional ones which are time proven.

In this book 'Glimpses of Hindu Astrology', I have carefully selected some 45 of my contributions to the world famous "The Astrological Magazine", edited by Professor B.V. Raman over the years. Some of the articles presented herein stress on the scientific basis of the subject to start with and then the evolution of the Hindu Calendar. Then some seven articles deal with the mundane aspects followed by a discussion on the vexed question of ayanāmsha. Then the applications of astrology to national problems have been presented, followed by their civil engineering aspects, gemmology, sound vibration etc. Then some articles are presented on the vexed problem of predictive seismology with many of the author's observation; finally with a couple of articles on esoteric astrology.

Most of the almanacs in India spell out the annual rainfall, crop pattern, climate, vegetation, calamities, etc. of the specific regions to which they serve. This type of literature is unheard of or conspicuous by their absence in the Western countries. The daily weather forecast given in the televisions make their observations only for the next 24 hours. But in India the climate for the year, the rains, the crops that can grow well etc. are given in advance for a year in these almanacs. People can judge by a study of these almanacs their superiority and serviceable nature, inspite of abandoning research in these fields from long ago due to historic reasons.

As mentioned earlier, it is next to impossibility to present all the principles of Hindu astrology and their many applications in a small volume like this. The theoretical and applied Hindu Astrology is a fertile field of research for the students of the Earth as well as the general public. In this connection the reader is referred to a book 'An Integrated Theory of the Earth' by the present author. It is the earnest hope of the author if the reader gets a glimpse of Hindu astrology - as the very title makes it clear by going through this volume.

**S.R.N. Murthy**

# Acknowledgements

In this connection it is my duty to thank Professor B.V. Raman, Editor - The Astrological Magazine, Bangalore for giving me permission to present these articles in a book form and also for writing a suitable foreword. I cannot fully express my hearty thanks to Professor V.N. Jha, Director, Centre of Advanced Study in Sanskrit, University of Poona, Pune-7 for evincing keen interest in the material and recommending the same to my publishers. My most grateful thanks are due to Messers Indian Books Centre, New Delhi-7, specially to Sri. Sunil Gupta and Sri. Naresh Gupta for immediately undertaking for publishing the book in a neat and elegant form in these days of increasing cost of publication.

The author is thankful to his life partner Mrs. Leela and children Prasad, Bansi and Meena who cooperated with him throughout the writing of these articles at a time when he should have devoted the same to their happiness.

# Contents

# 1

# The Evolution of Time

The evolution of time forms the tersest chapter in the book of philosophy, *i.e.,* pursuit of truth or the real. It is a challenge to the subtlest of minds and the sharpest in intelligence. Time is something which is ordinarily indescribable. The fraction of time called second or its multiplication, *i.e.,* the actual continuation as minute, hour, day, week, month, year, etc., refer to the same kind of object, whose dimensions are linear or unidirectional. The unidimensional motion of space itself most probably appears as time, hence the space-time continuum in curve gains gravity. Thus the materialisation of space co-evolves with time. Then the nature of time is dependent on the nature of the evolution of space, especially into a specific material object gaining certain force of gravitation. Therefore, the nature of time depends on the nature of gravitation of an object which influences its surroundings. Hence an understanding of time gives us a clear knowledge of the universal evolution. Since the visible universe is but the evolution of time-space curve, the materialism of life and its relation will bring us closer to the true principle of existence.

Past, present and future are successive sections of the unidimensional time. A clear understanding of the present with a specific context to the past naturally reflects as future when considered in unidimensional analysis.

The fractions of time as seconds, minutes, hours, etc., are arbitrary units and the time necessary for light to propagate through a distance equal to the diameter of an elementary particle is taken as unit. The diameter of the elementary particle is given to be about $3.10^{-13}$ and the velocity of light is $3.10^{10}$ cm/sec. This unit of time would be $10^{-23}$ sec. The present stage of universe is speculated by various means on radioactive age determination of oldest rocks and minerals is of the order of $10^{-17}$ sec. or $5.10^{-9}$ years. The unit of time sec. has a ratio with the age of the universe $10^{17}$ sec., which is of the order of $10^{40}$ which is noted to be not a constant but is variable. This ratio is of much significance; the electromagnetic interaction has the same ratio to the gravitational interaction. The electromagnetic interactions are stronger by $10^{40}$ times that of the gravitational interactions. This means that the gravitational interactions between gravitons, *i.e.*, the energy of gravity quanta is very very weak and the gravitons are given to have a spin twice that of photons, *i.e.*, the energy quanta of light, and are probably of the nature of nutrinos which have extremely low probability of absorption.

Similar to the electromagnetic waves produced by an oscillating electromagnetic charge are the gravity waves produced by the oscillation of a body of object. These gravitational waves are noted to carry extremely low energy and their measurement is a problem. However, there is interaction between gravity waves, and the gravitons of a particular object react with those of the other. The positive reaction of the gravitons of two cellestial bodies can be taken to be sympathetic while the negative reaction are asympathetic.

The evolution of time is in cooperation with the evolution of space as has already been noted for, together they form a unidimensional force. Therefore, the unit of time $10^{-23}$ sec may also be considered the unit of space, unless there is any difference that could be found out and the energy quanta of space, *i.e.*, spaceton is accepted. The ratio between the unit of time and the age of the universe is ($10^{40}$ ratio) also arbitrary on the unit of time we have considered. The properties of space will remain the same but differ in its character within and surrounding the area of celestial objects producing gravitons of different character in combination, or structural arrangement.

In the organic world, the living thing made of non-living stuff differs from the non-living only in its complexity and set of organisation, as understood from Oparin searching for the origin of life. Accordingly, the organisation of its molecules confers on the system the properties we recognise as life. If that is so, it is much easy to explain the interaction of gravitons of a particular wave of specific celestial body on the complex structure of the non-living stuff forming the basis of life, however negligible that force of interaction be.

The space occupied within and between the tissue of a particular nature by the specific organisation of non-living material in organism with life does react in a significant way with the spatial surrounding characterised by specific reactions of the gravitons. It is no matter of scientific investigation to say that because it is now not possible to exactly ascertain the reaction relationship between such interactions that one should overlook or show ignorance about the existence of such a relationship for want of a clear understanding about the subtleties of nature. The organic cells which go to form various parts of the human body are different and the special cells forming the brain are capable of reacting significantly with the spatial changes in its surroundings. It is only a question of evolution of the complexity of the organic structures and their relationship to the whole life.

The mind is a force developed due to such an organisation of non-living matter within the organic bodies and is capable of reacting with the external world influenced by the surrounding space. Thus time is inherent with the universal evolution and relates life with the entire universe.

"The entire fabric of astrology rests on the broad principle of evolution in Time," observes Prof. B.V. Raman in his introduction to the booklet, *Astrology for Beginners*. He continues that "Every object, mineral, vegetable and animal, must pass under the rule of nature through all stages. A scientific investigation of Time gives us a clue to attempt future predictions". Thus, a scientific analysis of life in relation to the universe does not accept any alleged relationship between the life and celestial bodies but it is with a clear proof beyond all uncivilised arguments.

The ratio that the microcosm bears to the macrocosm, *i.e.*, $10^{40}$ is noted to be a variable and not a constant. This is sufficient proof to say that the formation and deformation of the visible universe is not conforming to any constant or else our mathematical acumen to understand the principle has not been sufficient. Within the scope of mathematical knowledge, an explanation for this variability has not been possible and the mathematical reasoning ends at this boundary.

The variability of such a phenomenon has since been established, it may be anything and difficult to grasp within the ambit of human conception, and the limitations of the human senses. The individual has to surrender to the universal environ and the field beyond is tread by yogic experience and the power of prayer to the super-human, super-universal principle, call it by any name.

The Rigvedic hymns describing many natural forces as gods enjoin that one who prays to such and such a one will become so and so. They, *i.e.,* the different natural forces, are all called gods because they have been endowed with powers which are super-human. Take for example, fire, water, etc., and they work simultaneously in many individuals while an individual entity like human or any organism is capable of doing the things at a single place only. Since the nature is endowed with such super-human powers, they are referred to as gods and the Vedic hymns describe many such. When we enter the Vedantic discourse and understand the purport then we are given to feel that all the gods are one and the same (*Ekam sad viprah bahudhā vadanti*). Microcosm bears the same relation to the macrocosm as an entity bears to the whole, which is the same as "ātmavat sarvabhūtani".

If we have to recognise clearly the relationship between the microcosm and the macrocosm, we have to have a complete knowledge about time, since it is the one factor which gives us a clear picture of the universe surrounding us. This is referred to as *kāla* or *vidhi* in Sanskrit suggesting something which is not possible to overcome ordinarily. Time, as we have referred to earlier, co-evolves with the universe and is something of an indescribable force of exactitude associated with the constant change in manifestation.

In deciphering the relationship between the microcosm and macrocosm, the manifestational units of time, *i.e.,* the celestial objects, referred to as Grahas, Nakshatras, etc., are takn into consideration. The planets referred to as Grahas are self-meaningful in Sanskrit. Graha means to draw or to pull, *i.e.,* grāhati or karshati. The understanding about the force of attraction by planets is as old as astrology itself in Sanskrit.

Prof. B.V. Raman quotes Sri O'Neil in his book *Astrology for Beginners* (p. 16), as having stated that the earth travelling in its orbit around the Sun produces gravitational waves of about the same magnitude of light year that travel through space with the same velocity of light, and there would be four crests of such a gravitational earth-wave in space between us and the nearest star which is about four light years away. The gravitational waves may have any wavelength, from smallest found in light waves, which are fractions or parts of a billionth of an inch to ones far longer than any radio-wave ever produced by man, i.e., billions of billions of miles length.

A scientific analysis of life in the universe, therefore, does not accept any alleged relationship between them but a sound underlying principle. The more this principle is realised the better one can understand the reaction between the life and its environ, in the past and future. There can hardly be any other subject worth its study as the science of astrology with such a fundamental basis, the understanding and exposition of which calls for rare devotion, supreme sacrifice.

The interaction of gravitons of specific planets with others can be considered and the effect of such an interaction on the specific environs on the earth. With the unit distance, *i.e.*, astronomical unit of the mean distance from the earth to the Sun as 149.5 million km. as equivalent to 8 minutes of the velocity of light we can see that a gravity wave produced by the earth will reach the Sun (or the reverse) within 8 minutes as the gravity waves have the same velocity of light. Taking this as a unit, one can multiply this time factor by the astronomical unit for other planets and arrive at the time required for the gravity wave of particular planets at the Sun (or the reverse). For example, the unit time 8 minutes multiplied by 0.39 for Mercury, 0.72 for Venus, 1.52 for Mars, 5.20 for Jupiter, 9.54 for Saturn, 19.19 for Uranus, 30.07 for Neptune and 39.52 for Pluto will give us the time required for the travel of gravity waves of these planets in unidimension. Of course for the Moon, this time interval may be very little, *i.e.*, about within two seconds.

The composition of the planets varies and their physical properties exercise full control over the characters of the gravitons of specific gravity waves. During their motion around the Sun, the planets' gravity wave interact as a result of which the events will take place on the earth, subject to the local environment's modification.

There are a hundred or thousand variable in this process to ascertain the exact fact, a complex as an event which happens on this earth. Not only the laws of pure celestial mechanics may be required for their eluciadation, but of magnetohydrodynamics, fluid dynamics and possibly what may be referred to as psycho-dynamic (in case of evolved organic systems) are required. This entire complex is further modified from extra-solar gravity waves from other planetary system and celestial objects. It is hard to realise whether there is any subject of science which can really tackle this problem even in its infancy.

In this connection, it may be recalled that the text of *Tattwasiddhānta* in Sanskrit gives us some idea. The text gives us an idea that there is a rhythm in time, referred to as Yama in Sanskrit, the author observes that the are 8 Time Waves in the interval between successive sunrisings. Each Time Wave of three-hour duration, of 90 minutes rise 90 minutes fall. The duration of rise fall of a Time Wave is characterised by planets as follows:

| *Tattwa* | *Duration (minutes)* | *Planet* |
|---|---|---|
| Ākāsha | 30 | Jupiter |
| Vāyu | 24 | Saturrn |
| Āgni | 18 | Mars |
| Apah | 12 | Venus |
| Prithwi | 6 | Mercury |

The difference observable in the data given above and the duration of gravity waves of planets given earlier may require justification. This would be obvious in view of the modifications needed in the light of complexity.

Thus the evolution of time traces the evalution of space into matter. The material universe was recognised by the Hindu sages spacio-temporal entity and it was clearly pressed that it is not the real form but attended upon instant change, hence called Jagat. This also forms the crux of Indian Philosophy, as the wave of creation, *i.e.*, the evolution of space into matter and the dissolution of matter into space is inherent with the evolution of time; it is not the real but something apparent. They referred to this principle of creation as Brahma or the creator which means that which evolves or brmhate. *Om iti brahma prasouti*-says the Upanishad, meaning that the space evolves as the sound of Om, as sound is the property of space, while that of Vāyu is sparsha, *i.e.*, touch; that of Agni is rūpa, *i.e.*, form; that of Āpah is rasa, etc., taste, and that of Prithwi is gandha *i.e.*, smell.

Therefore, it is clear that everything is present in space and can be produced subject time. The material is fresh in āroha teja or rising Time Wave and old in avaroha tejatattwa or falling Time Wave. That is a spacio-temporal entity. While the active force is called Brahma, the existence is referred to as Vishnu, the kalpa of which adorns the deity with the conch and the circular weapon in hands, suggesting the evolution (as the sound of conch) and the maintenance of the evolved in the of the circular weapon (maintaining the sence of universe). The destructive force, of course, is referred to as Maheshwara, the dissolution of the evolved material universe in a form, really and understandably, the reality of Hindu myth.

Right time for right thing is well known. Carry out some work in advance keeps it mature while delay is death. The desired results are perfect only when done in right me. To find the proper or appropriate time or a thing to be carried out is one of the most important subjects of astrology. A study gives us a clue to push the situation into the natural spacio-temporal wave which makes the desired object being realised with least effort. Otherwise, a lot of energy, time, effort and many other things go waste. This is true in planning an individual's history or of a country's.

Take for example the economic planning of a nation on its developing programme. This is one of the most important and vital affairs of the state. Herein one has to arrive at the reaction of the birth chart of the state with the planetary cabinet during the period of planning. Subject to the state chart, the most favourable and strong planet's Dasa Bhukti should be considered for a healthy and unsullied development plan. One should not, even though temporary approval is there, undertake developmental planning and implementation during the adverse Dasa Bhuktis, especially of the lord of the 8th, the 6th or the 12th bhava-lords. For the annual receipts of tax and revenue, one has to look into the strength of the 2nd house and the 2nd lord; the 4th house and its lord for trade and agriculture; the 6th and its lord for raising loans; the 10th house and its lord for foreign trade, export revenue, etc. The aspectual strength goes a long way to fulfil the funds for the plan. A favourable Dasa Bhukti of the lord of the 4th house and the 3rd house would see the development of the nation in its education, landed estates, communication, and general prosperity and happiness of the people. The budget for the annual programme can have the best advice from the planetary cabinet. In a year, if the lord of the 2nd house is the lord of the year, the state is assured of good finance, subject to other conditions. The taxes can be levied on the section of the public which is ruled by such a planet for additional receipts for planning. That section of the public will be capable of meeting the receipts. If the burden of tax falls on the section of the public whose lord is debilitated and weak and finds no place in the annual cabinet of that year, they feel not only extremely burdened but finally the receipts planned on that section drops off affecting the planning adversely. States may have to draw overdraft, where such are available, and that may also be affected if the lord is adverse or the house is weak.

Such is the knowledge of the science whose foundations are basic and most fundamental. Ignorance of such a science will only keep the student poor for such advantageous, and away from the advice 'fore-warned is fore-armed', and an inadequacy to deal with the problems. An adviser of state should have these norms understood, otherwise the rulers will be misguided and the state left in misery. The science of time alone is the best weapon and the best of all the branches of knowledge-30.

# 2

# The Fourth Dimension

Of the three dimensions of space and the time, *i.e.,* the fourth dimension, the last one is of critical importance. The physicist has come to appreciate the grip of time only when it became necessary to determine the speed of light. Einstein took special note of it when he formulated the Special Theory of Relativity, which can be generalised in the statement that two observers in uniform relative motion, as a result of their relative speed, will be unable to detect any difference in the physical laws governing matter, motion and light.

Atomic theory did not appreciate the entry of gravity in its considerations but discussions of astronomical problems and movements of large-scale electrically uncharged bodies demanded the influence of the gravity factor. Validity of the uniform gravitational field at greater distances has been questioned. The General Theory of Relativity states that in a specific frame, fixed relative to the observer, the observer finds all the bodies falling subject to a particular gravitational pull and in a frame with the scale of the speed of light which undergoes accolerated fall relative to the observer the efect of gravitation will be nil. Therefore, respecting the specific frame of reference, it may be generalised that gravity starts influencing on the frames of reference other than that of light.

Time is a function of light and has evolved from space. Amplitude of space wave varies from zero to that of sound waves. With the increase of amplitude the Ultra-violet and the components of the spectrum result to end the Ultra-red, all falling within the physical nature of light. Time originates with the component of light which has a determined velocity of 1,86,000 miles per second. Now it has been proved that the space bends inward if the amount of the three angles in a triangle is more than $180^0$ and outward if it is less than $180^0$; this is very relevant to consider the fact that space also tends to be wavy. Further, the mind waves are so large that they can easily govern entire range of waves from the Ultra-red to that of the unqualified space. Hence it can comprehend the whole range and is of practical importance in colour-therapy.

Gravity also originates with time from light. At the velocity of light gravity is nil. Short of the velocity of light energy results in matter, and gains light and is reckoned with time.

When the unqualified space starts evoking into sound, light and matter it undergoes a dramatic disturbance which is generally referred to as creation. This harmony is dissolved at the start of an asystematic disturbance with disharmony referred to as destruction. Considering the Hubble's constant for the generation of the galaxies to be approximately $9 \times 10^9$ years, the velocity necessary to escape exceeded by their separatist tendency, *i.e.*, the expansion limits, the gravitational restraint to quantity of intergalactic material not more than seven times the mass of the galaxies.

The psychological phenomenon of thought is a harmonic wave vibration of the mind. When the vibrations have completely ceased operate, the medium of mind, governing to cosmic activity, dissolves within it the unified space.

Interfering with the other vibratious of sound, light, heat, etc., of the physical nature the medium of mind is struck up. Although time and gravity have no direct effect over mind medium, they strike an indirect impact when the mind medium reacts to the physical existence within the range of light and the vibrations. The polarised vibrations of the medium do not get affected by time and gravity and a continued practice relieves the mind wave from the effect of light vibrations also to make finally dissolved in the unqualified space.

The unqualified space is itself a constant and has the capacity to evolve and dissolve, the evolution to attain the constancy. Since it is evolves into physical universe, and is comprehended by the medium of mind, the mind being subtler than the unqualified space. Since the unqualified space is indestructible the medium of mind also is devoid of destruction, annihilation. The control for the polarising of the mind is exercised by the subtler medium which is a cosmic constant. This is the subtlest of the mediums known to the best knowledgeable sources and is self-effective most unqualified, the nature and character of which is incomprehensible by the medium of mind.

It is well known that time in the presence of red light passes quicker than in presence blue light. In other words the flow of time regulated by the wavelength of light. Variations of time is directly proportional to the wave-length of light. Whether the same relation is true with regard to gravity also is not certain. However, it can be noted that gravity increases towards the shorter wavelength end of the spectrum. Hence, gravity is inversely proportional to the wavelength of light. Therefore, time and gravity show opposite relationship.

Sense of time and consequently the day is different from planet to planet in the solar family depending upon the spin of the planet and on the Earth itself from the equator to the poles. If the appearance of the Sun is the criteria for the day fixation it is at an interval of 24 hours at the equator and six months at the poels. Therefore, the Hindus referred to the day for the people at the poles as being equal to one year of the people living at the equatorial regions. Therefore, 360 years of the equatorial people constituted one year for the people at the pole and called Deva Varsha. Such 12,000 Deva Varshas constituted one Divya Yuga or Maha Yuga. 71 such Divya Yugas formed one interval of Manu or Manvantara. Hence, 306,720,000 equatorial years or 852,000 Polar years will make one interval of Manu. With the precession of equinoxes amounting to 54" year over a maximum of $27^0$ *Surya Siddhanta* states that one Maha Yuga will require 600 repetition of the $108^0$ movement of the $27^0$maxima to and from the Vernal Equinoctial point. Although a lot of controversy prevails about the consideration of the precession of the equinoxes and some advocate even to do away with it and follow the Sayana system of the Hindu Almanacs, since the best observatory value for it now is 50" 26 year amounting to 25,735 years instead of 25,920 years based on the *Surya Siddhanta* to complete one cycle of $360^0$, the geochronologists have to observe that the value of solar years contemplated by the *Surya Siddhanta* for the present wave of creation being 1955,885,068 solar years till 1967 almost agrees with the nine periods of mountain formation at interval of about 200 X $10^4$ years and vies with the best radio-active dating quoted earlier.

A Kalpa is referred to as being of the order of 4320 x $10^6$ solar year making a day of the Creator, *i.e.*, the evolutionary force of the Cosmic Constant; it is equal in amount to a night, a day forming a period of 8640 x $10^6$ years, the time now contemplated for the galactic generation. Dissolution of galaxies removes huge Universal lamps from the Cosmic scene which determine time for us. Since the process of creation and dissolution is likely to have been balanced by the Cosmic Constant, dissolution of the galaxies gives place for the formation of new galaxies and the process has no end hence no beginning. Such is the function of time, revelation of the truth.

## References


1. *Surya Siddhānta,* by Kashi, Sanskrit Series, No. 144, 1946.
2. *Astronomy,* by Baker, R.H, Van Nostrand/East West Press, 1964.
3. *Internal Constitution of the Earth,* by B. Gutenberg, Dover, 1951.
4. *One Two Three Infinity,* by Gamow G., Bantom Books, 1965.
5. *Frontiers of Astronomy,* by Hoyle, F. Mentor Books, 1957.
6. *Pear's Cyclopaedia,* 1964.
7. *Geology of India and Burma,* by Krishnan, M.S., Higginbothams, 1965.
8. "The Hindu Calendar," by Murthy S.R.N., The Astrological Magazine, Vol. 56, No. 7.

"The Vexed Question of Ayanamsa-A Symposium," by various authors, The Astrological Magazine, Vol. 51, No. 8 onwards.-336.

# 3
# Rationale of Astrology

Astrology is the science of foretelling events by stars according to one dictionary. Prof. B.V. Raman defines astrology as "the philosophy of discovering and analysing past impulses and future actions of both individuals and nations" (P. 43, *Astrology and Modern Thought,* 1965). The logic pertaining to stars is astrology. Is it necessary to call for any more relationship that exists between the starry heavens and the terrestrial things, animate and inanimate, than to understand that the terrestrial things are part of the vast Universe around us? It is but commonsens to feel that, we, the living beings on the earth are in direct connection with the whole of the Universe. If any one denies this, it is only to be observed that such a denial is most unscientific and accounts for ignorance. How the stars can influence the animate and inanimate objects is slowly being studied by modern science. The history of the earth is part of the history of the Universe and the evolution of the man on earth is part of the evolution of the earth and Universe. Man has been trying to unravel the relationship that exists between himself and the vast Universe from the dawn of civilisation. His great achievement is that he slowly understood the motions of the earth and the planets around the Sun and expanded his mental horizon to realise that forces like gravity exist to hold the celestial bodies in their positions. He advanced in his understanding to know that the whole Universe is based on space-time continuum and is relativistic in its outward behaviour. In his pre-occupation with external knowledge he has spent little time to unravel the relationship between himself and the Universe. This has been accomplished by the subject-matter of Astrology. It would be easier to establish the relationship that exists between the celestial and terrestrial objects now onwards as most of the terrestrial-extra-terrestrial relationship has been formulated.

The eovlution of life is directly related to the evolution of the Earth and in turn to the evolution of the Universe. It is one of the most fundamental steps of the science of the earth, to have established this relationship and to have brought the life closer to the Universe. The geological control of climates and the climatic control over the life need not be emphasised. In spite of such direct relationship it is hard to ignore the effect of Cosmos on the life.

To know the motions of the celestial objects alone and leaving the subtler relationships is like enjoying the interest leaving the principle without being fully exploited. The modern astrophysics is like utilising the interest alone. The more fundamental and subtle truth has not been understood so far and it amounts to leaving the principle unexplored. It is more a relativistic knowledge one possesses after the study of modern science leaving the more useful and grand principles of the Universe.

When it has been understood that there is a fundamental rhythm in the Universe, the application of such a rhythm to the more subtle principle of existence like life should be examined. For the scientist who is more interested in the husk it may of be little value to taste the grain. Superficial knowledge will be of less utility but of much danger.

The human life or life in general is a physico-chemical entity. The life force in the body frame is accommodated only when conditions of living are satisfied. The life force is expressed well in the organic framework better than the inanimate objects. It is only a degree of subtler or refined conditions. Similarly in the living body, mind is nourished only under special conditions and its development and evolution is a part of the evolution of the living world. This reasoning leads us to connect the life and thought direct to the Cosmos and it is no exaggeration to state that Cosmos is reflected in the human life in a most perfect way. In Hindu astrology, therefore, Brahmāṇḍa and Pindāṇḍa relationship is taken into consideration and equated.

A statement in astrology like 'Chalannivāsam kurute pumāsam pātālashāli nalinīvilāsi' (meaning that the Sun in the nadir at the time of birth makes the person to have moving house) is as good as a theorem of Pythagoras. Pythagoras theorem has been tested and examined or Pythagoras proposed the idea after long observation that $3^2+4^2 = 5^2$. Similarly after examination and observation of several life sketches, the proposition has been instituted and it is for the student to examine and confirm or reject it. Since it requires longstanding observations and time consuming study one should not reject the truth of a statement unexamined. However, each case has to be examined in its own framework and each case is to be treated separate, though a certain degree of statistical approach is allowed.

Study of natural science subjects clearly indicates the difficulty in understanding the varied aspects of nature. Take for example the nomenclatare of rocks. No two specialists would like to agree in naming a particular sample of rock by the same name. There will be differences between specimen and specimen or sample and sample. However, observations that the granitic batholyths are uniform throughout their length and breadth are common. Similarly no two interpretations of geological structures by specialists can be possible for, the degree of experience, background of work and other factors differ from person to person. Given such arguments, astrological literature can be proved beyond doubt that the principle enunciated in the well established texts are true to times and not conjectural.

As we can predict the crop of a particular seed on the basis of the soil, climate and rainfall during a particular period and the time of its harvest, so we can decide with a certain degree of approximation the trend lines of the events of a particular life born under a given time. Based on the stellar motions and a clear understanding of the evolution of time, the astrologer equipped with superior thinking and full of experience can interpret the nature and extent of events bound to the birth of a particular life entity. Sociological and collective principles can hardly be defined with mathematical clarity. Moods of a government, deliberations of an assembly, fury of a mob, etc., are ruled by no mathematical rule. Scientists should accept the limitations of mathematics and mathematical reasoning.

The validity of inference and other indirect evidences equally reveal truth where direct evidences are not available. It is not necessary for a deep examination to know that smoke indicates fire. If one sees smoke one infers the presence of fire there. Truly the presence of the Sun or Mars in the ascendant of a particular birth indicates that the person will be a kharvāta-baldy, unless otherwise the rule is modified due to other aspects. The value of evidence may, at times, not be true even if ti is seen by eyes as for example the mirage. Even though it is pratyaksha one cannot certify that it is true. Similarly scientists who insist on pratyaksha pramāṇa-eyewitness evidence-can take it only for granted, for what they observe may be beyond the ken of the real.

Astrological reasoning is based mostly on facts of longstanding observations and dependent on time. Whether the Himalayas were present when the earth was formed cannot be said by anybody for nobody was present when the Himalayas appeared. But, the principles of science make it clear to us that the Himalayas have been a very recent mountain chain, not even sixty million years old, based on a study of its rocks. This is purely an inference. Whether the earth is expanding or was it originally contracting is nothing but pure conjecture! Therefore, the degree of truth of one or a body of evidences differs and a scientist should consider these things and then judge. Kepler, (*Quarterly Journal of the Royal Astronomical Society*, Vol. 13, No. 3, London, 1972) believed that Astrology contained only conjectures. He also believed that the doctrine on the motions of the planets was immutable and was established by the highest principles. Kepler should have lived to see the Euclidian principles being devoured by the laws of relativity, and to ponder on the greatest conjectures of the science like expanding or steady-state Universe theories. Moreover, mathematical foundations of science have not been able to bring out the true, solid and lasting principle of Nature.

Numbers are arbitrary, measures are arbitrary and the thoughts have been moulded to advance on these narrow lines. Hence, we are obliged to arrive at arbitrary conclusions, more or less relativistic. No one knows why numbers were introduced. having been largely used by traders the numbers have brought us to narrow lanes. Thinking in broad terms of the Vedic order has been lost, and there are people who believe that in numbers lay the secrets of natural truth.

If only one accepts the direct relationship that exists between the man and the Cosmos, it does not necessitate further proof to make one comprehend the rules of astrology. It would be a worthy attempt of examine the rules of astrology then and to conclude if they are conjectures on valid inferences to inform one in advance of the events that are to take place. To live up to the ryhthm of the Universe or the man of Cosmos is the perpetual wish of the Veda Purusha as depicted in the *Purusha Sookta.* To ignore such a sublime principle is to invite trouble. Life with its underlying principle is superior to anything in the Universe. To adjust one's life to the order of the Universe makes life smooth-flowing and worthy. This programme can only be drawn and the blue print prepared when the harmony of life and Cosmos is understood. This is the aim of astrology which is not a bundle of superstitions, taboos and conjectures. Realisation of such a close relationship between the animate and the inanimate is the rationale of astrology and no branch of modern science has so well established these principles than Astrology.-53.

# 4

# The Astrological Control

It is evident that all the events that take place in the universe are connected by time. The time-based science of astrology reveals the characteristics of each and every event regarding its past and future with an observational record of the motion of the objects of centres of attraction, mathematically divined and basically prompted by the power of intuition, the nature's harmonious way of expressing things to the refined senses. Realisation of this natural vibration gives a farsight into the shape of things that are expected and measures its amplitude of effect. Thus it appears to be that a fundamental control operates over the living and the non-living universe alike and the realisation of such a control is as essential as realising the self itself, towards consciousness.

How does this astrological control operate in practice? Consider on the mundane plane; the economic, social, temporal, etc., controls can be read in the context of the planetary disposition prevalent during the entry of that land into the New Year. Things almost unexpected at the commencement of the year may take place during the course. The behaviour of population of a particular soil as depicted by the Moon in the chart of that land changes according to the changing environment that the Moon keeps tracing with reference to the other members of the solar family. A note in advance about the favourable or other trends controlled by the unknown time factor is very much necessary. The learned Editor of THE ASTROLOGICAL MAGAZINE interprets that in India during 1969 there will be scarcity of rains, grains will be destroyed and according to Garga, terrific storms will blow, creating fear in the mind of people and bringing destruction to the crops just before they deliver the yield. This is based on certain observations made by Garga. A statistical approach might have been there over a long stretch of the interval but the power of intuition is behind the formulation of the principle respect in the natural harmony.

The existence of such a control can be examined on the basis of a study of the climatic, geological and geographical, etc., controls. The seasonal regulation of climate of a particular land is controlled by its co-ordinates on the surface of the earth and its motion on its orbit. When the motion is controlled by time, it is better to read the time as related to the events.

Superior forces enforce the astrological control. Motion of the objects being inherent in the Universe, it is noted that the velocity is proportional to the angle by which the space-time axis has turned. At the same time, no object can move with the velocity of light or a velocity greater than light. Thus the angle by which the space time axis has turned varies from nil in the case of stationary objects (stationary is used in its bearest meaning denoting that the object is not characterised by either time or, fundamentally speaking light) to the maximum in the case of light. It follows that events under similar circumstances and in all respects should have this time space axial angle the same. But, it is everyone's experience that no two events are similar in the

Universe, although there appears to be almost about 60% overlap, in respect of 'similar events'. Thus events of cyclic or periodic nature should have almost the same space time axial angle under motion and the degree by which they depart from the absolute similarity is a measure of fundamental distortion.

Since the velocity angle of the space time axis of objects under motion is referred to that of light, transformation of energy into objects like the celestial bodies demanding their motion has been noted to set them in orbital motion which is the geodiscal path rather than the one explained earlier through the law of Universal gravitation. In the case of the earth, the electromagnetic core transforms into gravitational one from the mantle and upwards approaching the gross or inert lithophile section. A similar set can be presumed in other units of the Universe. Since energy in the form of light heat or electricity are interconvertible it is to be contended that the velocity decreases with the objects of grosser material. Thus the universal motion varying from the inert to the light, falling short of the velocity of light assumes inertia and gets into motion. Hence the shapeful and shapeless universe appears to be an agitation the amplitude of which varies from nil in the case of light to the maximum in the case of inert bodies.

Motion of the objects in its fundamental nature being related to the light, the light controls the former on the visual plane, described as velocity, which is but a measure of the agitation the light has suffered. Thus, the events said to have been connected in the fourth dimension, really are subjected to the agitation of space rather than light, for we expect that the medium in which light itself moves should be more fundamental, giving rise to light at one end and inertia (or possibly equatable to darkness) at the other end.

Then it follows that by understanding the relatively unagitated light-end, the vagaries of the more agitated inert-end can easily be deciphered. Jyothi, meaning thereby light, the science which considers the light as the basis of interpretation is the more perfect subject, and the objects of the manifest universe being the relative inert things controlled by the light, it is clear that there exists the Astrological Control.

It is said that:

*Trikālagnyo bhavejjīve swāmshe mridwamsha samyute,*

*Gopurādyāmshake vāpi shubhāmshe shubha veekshite;*

meaning thereby that Jupiter's disposition in the horoscope is important for one to keep aware of this principle underlining the Astrological Control, for, this is possible only when Jupiter is in his own amsa or mridwamsa or gopurāmsa or is being aspected by other shubha grahas or benefic planets. This will enlighten the person about the nature and operation of this control, since he would be a Trikalagnāni (a seer into the past, present and future) who aligns himself parallel to the natural harmony.-191.

# 5

# Approaching the Third Approximation

Vedic astronomers noted that the members of the Solar System originate at the below mentioned arc of the constellasions:

| *The constellation* | *The Arc* |
|---|---|
| Krittika | 26° 40' to 40° 00' |
| Uttarabhādra | 333° 20'-346° 40' |
| Mrigasira | 53° 20'-66° 40' |
| Poorvābhādra | 320° 00'-333° 20' |
| Bharani | 13° 20'-26° 40' |
| Jyeshta | 226° 40'-240° 00' |
| Swati | 185° 40'-200° 00' |

Centres of attraction would fall into the arc indicating the commencement of

| | |
|---|---|
| Vaishāka Māsasya Sita Tritīya | Treta Yuga |
| Navamyasou Kārtika Shuklapakshe | Krita Yuga |
| Nabhasya Māsasya ca Krishnapakshe | Kali Yuga |
| Trayodashi Panchadashi ca Māghe | Dwapara Yuga |

When these centres of attraction fall in the below given arcs at the eud of the successive seventy first cycle, commence the Manvantaras. They are-

| | |
|---|---|
| Āswayuja Shukla Navami | Swāyambhuva |
| Kārtika Dwādashi Sita | Swārohisha |
| Tritiyā Caitramāsasya | Uttama |
| Sita Bhādrapadasya ca | Tāpasa |
| Phālgunasyātwāmāvāsya | Raivata |
| Poushsyekādashi sita | Cākshusha |
| Āshadhasyāpi Dashami | Vaivaswata |
| Māghamāsasya Saptami | Suryasāvarṇi |
| Sravanasyāshtami Krishna | Indrasāvarṇi |
| Āshadasyāpi Pournima | Brahma |
| Kārtiki Pancadashi Sita | Rudra |
| Phālguna Pancadashi Sita | Daksha |
| Caitri Pancadashi Sita | Rouchya |
| Jyeshte Pancadashi Sita | Bhoutya |

Thus ends a Kalpa. An equal interval of time is noted for the systematisation of the Universe. This repeats, the commencement and the end are unknown. Departure from this cycle by Patanjala Yoga or 'Living true to this existence Unattached-Jeevanmukti' is advocated by the Hindu Philosopheres. Monism prefers the latter. Holding the mind to the back and withdrawing from the energy-mmatter-spirit interaction, thus keeping immune to the effects of the temporal situation avoiding self-annihilation using Patanjala Yoga results in the smooth way of departing from this cycle.

Study of astrology gives insight into the results in advance, and enables one to self-evaluate the extent of what may be referred to as the standard deviation from the Principle of

Absolute Truth and the path one has to pursue to be nearer and closer to that Principle, and finally realise it.

The centres of attraction going under the names Venus, Saturn and Mercury show some commonness during their motion drawing the spirit interested in them interacting on the space time plane. Similarly commonness is observed among the other centres of attraction described as the Sun, Mars and Jupiter. Based only on these it is difficult to evaluate a certain situation, constructive or destructive, as described in the *Gita:*

*Kim Karma Kimakarmeti Kavayópyatra Móhitah*

The astrological insight helps a clear appraisal which is not possible by any other observation exceepting the Yoga *i.e.,* the union of the mind with the Absolute. The latter is difficult of normal possession. This necessitates the study of and practicing Astrology.

None of the above two groups of centres of attraction have established the true path of interaction. Study of astrology gives the advance note of the interaction of all the centres of attraction on a particular origin of thought vibration regarding its nature, variation, extent and dissolution and tries to establish the golden mean position in the activities of the spirit.

How the mental vibrations react when these centres of attraction transit certain portions of the ecliptic arc during their motion, form the basic principles of astrology. The spirit strives to gather the beneficial rays and reap the good relative to its counterpart, and to have a smooth way close to the path of the Absolute Truth. In nature it is true that destruction is the rule and preservation, the exception. Truth itself can never be destroyed, hence an astrological approach.

Hindu Almanacs record that the following segments of arc on the ecliptic are characteristic of destructive vibrations, possibly the approximate uniformity of the directions of the powerful radio wave sources (*Frontiers of Astronomy,* page 250). The works of Ryle and others give a list of over 1,800 discrete sources of radio waves. Although these radio wave sources were found almost equal in all directions, the approximate uniformity of their directions would preclude the distant sources before the argument held by Gold. Gold's argument that the majority of the discrete sources were simply galaxies other than our own, the view upholding the uniformity of directions of the discrete radio wave source has been accepted by astronomers.

Given in the ecliptic arc:

11° 06' 40" to 12° 02' 00"

18° 40' 00" to 19° 33' 20"

33° 20' 00" to 34° 13' 20"

42° 00' 00" to 42° 53' 20"

56° 06' 40" to 57° 00' 00"

72° 13' 00" to 73° 06' 20"

86° 40' 00" to 87° 33' 00"

98° 06' 40" to 99° 20' 00"

113° 46' 40" to 114° 40' 00"

126° 40' 00" to 127° 33' 20"

137° 46' 40" to 138° 40' 00"

150° 40' 00" to 151° 33' 20"

164° 26' 40" to 165° 20' 00"

177° 46' 40" to 178° 40' 00"

189° 46' 40" to 190° 40' 00"

203° 06' 40" to 204° 00' 00"

215° 33' 20" to 216° 26' 40"

229° 46' 40" to 230° 40' 00"

244° 26' 40" to 252° 26' 40"

258° 40' 00" to 259° 33' 20"

271° 06' 40" to 272° 00' 00"

282° 13' 20" to 283° 06' 40"

295° 33' 20" to 296° 26' 40"

310° 40' 00" to 311° 33' 20"

323° 33' 20" to 324° 26' 40"

338° 40' 00" to 339° 33' 20"

353° 20' 00" to 354° 13' 20"

Therefore to enjoy the best of the situations and with beneficial rays, the above arcs of the echiptic should be avoided for any kind of commencement, notwithstanding the correction to safeguard against various other undesirable effects or doshas.

Sharp balance' tween virtue and vice is the result of normal appraisal and the "Absolute" is revealed under such sharpness demands greatest research which would be equally deep and penetrating as well as august. Thus astrology is a science par excellance.

# 6
# The Indian Chronology

The Indian chronology owes its origin to the Vedic astronomy. According to Shankara, the greatest exponent of the monist (Advaita) school of philosophy in India, the Vedic compositions expound the truths perceived by the sages at the superconscious plane, hence are eternal. Since the date of the Vedic perceptions are not fixed, the date of the Indian chronology also cannot be definitely ascertained.

Following the Vedic astronomy, various texts on Indian astronomy appeared like *Sāmrāt Siddhānta, Sarva Siddhānta, Siddhānta Sārabhouma, Sundara Siddhānta, Sūrya Siddhānta, Āryabhatta Siddhānta, Siddhānta Siromaṇi, Brahma Siddhānta, Vateshwara Siddhānta* and others amongst which *Sūrya Siddhanta* is the one the application of which is honoured even to this day in the Indian Ephemeris.

*Sūrya Siddhānta* commands highest authority in Indian Astronomy. Attributed to the authorship of Maya, there is reference in it for division of time from 1/3240000 fracrtion of a second to 8640 X $10^6$ X 360 X 100 solar years, the latter being called the life of Brahma. During the Brahma day takes place the creation, while dissolution of the Universe follows during the Brahma night. A Brahma night and day are each equal to 4320 X $10^5$ years.

According to *Sūrya Siddhānta* 195880000 years have been elapsed to the date of commencement of the Kaliyuga, *i.e.*, 18th February 3102 B.C. This is largely reflected in the age of the earth being of the order of some 1770 X $10^6$ years, given by A. Holms based on the radioactive method.

The Indian chronology and the geochronology appear to be complimentary to each other. The Indian chronology chiefly based on the incessant motion of the heavenly bodies has been able to impress and record on the rock pages of the sedimentary book of the earth the changes that have accompanied the large-scale evolution of the earth. The rock pages of the sedimentary book of the earth remain torn and mutilated for a perfect reading by the stratigrapher who has been able to reconstruct the history of the earth.

The parallel evolution that the history of the earth bears to the Indian chronology can be proved by a close study of the two records. The Indian chronology appears to be more perfect than the geochronology and is based on an observational record spreading over several thousand years, the august and dynamic characters of which is exceptional.

The Indian chronology is essentially based on the strong foundations of astronomy. For its construction the average rate of precession of equinoxes given in *Surya Siddhanta, i.e.*, 54" per year, is taken. It is stated in *Sūrya Siddhānta* that the point of equinox moves slowly 27° east of the vernal equinox and back 54° to move again 27° east completing a cycle of 108°. 600 such cycles will constitute one Mahāyuga equivalent to 4.32 X $10^6$ years.

One-tenth of a Mahāyuga is called 'Kaliyuga'

Two-tenths of a Mahāyuga is called Dwāparayuga

Three-tenths of a Mahāyuga is called Thretayuga and

Four-tenths of a Mahāyuga is called Kritayuga

71 such Mahāyugas make one Manvantara and there are 14 Manvantaras in one Kalpa, consecutive Manvantaras being joined by a period equivalent of one Kritayuga. Hence a Kalpa=

$$\frac{(4.32 \times 10^6) \times 71 + (4.32 \times 10^6) \times 4}{10} \times 15 = 4320 \times 10^6$$

solar years or one thousand Mahāyugas.

There are five ways of reckoning the time in the Indian chronology. They are given below:

1. Nākshatramāna,
2. Souramāna,
3. Chāndramāna,
4. Sāvanamāna and
5. Bārhaspatyamāna.

The arc of the ecliptic obtained by the division of the period of the earth's complete rotation around the Sun by the period required for one complete rotation around the earth by the Moon is called one Nakshatra extending 13° 20':

$$\frac{\text{Rotation period of the earth around the Sun}}{\text{Rotation period of the Moon around the earth}}$$

$$= \frac{365.25}{27.32} = 13^\circ 20'$$

Hence, there are 360/13° 20' = 27 Nakshatras

Reckoning of time based on these Nakshatras is the system of Nākshtramāna.

The Sun's northerly and southerly positions with reference to the earth divide the ecliptic into two and a further division was based on the seasonal changes into three each, called the ayana (solstice) and ritu (season) respectively. Each rtu constitutes two luni-solar months, the basis of such a division being effected on the successive Full Moon days and named after the respective constellation in which the Full Moon occurred. Thus the division of the zodiac into twelve came to be systematised.

With the Sun's transit of the vernal equinox as the beginning of the year, the system of Souramāna reckons the time of one sidereal year given in *Sūrya Siddhānta, i.e.*, 365.258756484 dividing it into 12 divisions.

Chāndramāna is actually a luni-solar system of measuring the time. The Moon's motion around the earth takes place once in 27.55459 days according to *Sūrya Siddhānta.*

Sāvanamāna system recognises a 360 days year and reckons the time accordingly.

Bārhaspatyamāna is based on the motion of Jupiter. On an average, Jupiter completes the revolution of the zodiac once in about twelve years. Five Jupiterian rotations will equal about two Saturn's revolutions. Hence a 60 year cycle was instituted, the system of which is also in vogue.

The waning and waxing periods of the Moon correspond to the two fortnights of the lunar months and the weekdays have been named after the successive fourth planet in series, the Moon, Mercury, Venus, the Sun, Mars, Jupiter and Saturn. Number four in the given succession is equatable with the constant of the empirical series in the Bode's law, which will actually complete the true series. The Bode's law is:

| *Mercury* | *Venus* | *Earth* | *Mars* | *(Vacant)* | *Jupiter* | *Saturn* |
|---|---|---|---|---|---|---|
| 4 | 4 | 4 | 4 | 4 | 4 | 4 |
| 0 | 3 | 6 | 12 | 24 | 48 | 96 |
| 3.9 | 7.2 | 10 | 15.2 | ... | 52 | 95=Actual distance |

In the series given above for the construction of the weekdays, the Moon is introduced in the first place since it is the nearest and the Sun in the place of the earth since the bearing is from the earth.

A day used to be reckoned from sunrise to the following sunrise comprising 60 ghatis of 24 each. Each ghati was further divided as given below:

| | |
|---|---|
| 1 ghati=60 palas | 1 lava=60 renus |
| 1 prana=10 palas=60 leekshakas | 1 renu=60 thrutis |
| 1 leekshaka=60 lavas | 1thruti=1/3240000 second |

Now looking at the geochronology one finds the history of the earth being divided into Eras, Periods, Epochs and Ages. This is based on a study of the bedded or the sedimentary rocks. The process of sedimentation in the sinking basin of the narrow seas is effected by the activities of the geological agents. Processes like weathering, denudation and deposition are involved and the sinking basins are the forerunners of prospective mountain systems, due to the process of orogeny. These mountain systems give rise to the land masses and the formation of continents is by the process of epeirogeny. Thus orogeny and epeirogeny are mechanical cyclic processes. The time required for the stratified rocks has been computed for the age of the earth.

A second method was based on the scale of organic evolution based on the fossils occuring in the stratified rocks.

A third method was based on the annual increase of salt in the oceanic water based on the assumption that the first formed seas were freshwater ones.

Other methods based on the internal heat and rate of cooling of the earth, the tidal retardation of the earth's rotation and origin and age of the Sun's heat-all give empirical values for the age of the earth. However, the radioactive method of determining the age of the earth has been in vogue and the age of the earth thus arrived may stand any where from 3300 to 4500 million years. Therefore, geochronology has to tread a long way for perfection.

A study of the stratified rocks indicates that the earth has not suffered large-scale changes since it got solidified and the geological record shows that conditions as normal as exist to this day. The cycle of orogeny and epeirogeny is continuing since the earth system was standardised. This evidence supports the basic view of the Indian chronology to consider the value of the average rate of the precession of equinoxes as 54" per year even though there occur slight variations in the long ages. Thus the Indian chronology has attained reliable perfection on scientific basis, is simple, equally dynamic, practicable and most natural.

There is agreement among the geologists, although not complete, as to the geological time since the Cambrian period, *i.e.*, about 600 million years. The geochronologists disagree regarding the time elapsed prior to the Cambrian period and the origin of the earth to the various stages of Archaen period. Holmes assigned a time varying from 1000 to 1070 million years. The age arrived at by Holmes is at wide variance with the determination made in recent times. The rater values may stand anywhere from 2000 to 3300 million years. The age of the earth accordingly has been computed to be of the order of 4500 million years.

One of the most important observations made by the geochronologist is the periodicity of the mountain building. Stratigraphical record shows the evidences of such cycles separated by an interval of about 200 to 250 million year.

Indian geochronology is as given below:

| *Group* | *System* | *Time Scale (in million years)* |
|---|---|---|
| Quaternary | Rcccnt | 0.01 |
| | Pleistocene | 1 |
| Tertiary | Pliocence | 12 |
| or | Mlocene | 25 |
| Kainozoic | Oligocane | |
| | Eocene | |
| Secondary | Cretaceous | |
| or | Jurassic | |
| Mesozoic | riassic | |
| Primary | Permian | |
| or | Carboniferous | |
| Palaeozolc | Devonian | |
| | Silurian | |
| | Ordovician | |
| | Cambrian | |
| Precambrian | Vindhyan | |
| | Delhi (=Cuddapahs?) | 735+5 |
| Archaean | Satpura | 955+40 |
| | Eastern Ghats | 1625+75 |
| | Dharwar (Aravalli) | 2300+100 |

Indian chronology is as given below:

Pārthiva
Kūrma
Pralaya
Anantha
Swetavaraha 1. Swāyambhuva
Brahma 2. Swārochisha

| | | | |
|---|---|---|---|
| Savitri | 3. Uttama | | |
| (*Kalpas*) | 4. Tāpasa | | |
| | 5. Raivata | | |
| | 6. Chākshusha | | |
| | 7. Vaivaswata: 28th of the 71 nos. of Mahāyugas: | | |
| | 8. Suryasāvarni | | |
| | 9. Indrasāvarṇi | 1. | Kritayuga |
| | 10. Brahmasāvarṇi | 2. | Tretayuga |
| | 11. Rudrasāvarnl | 3. | Dwaparayuga. |
| | 12. Daksha sāvarṇi | 4. | Kaliyuga is running from |
| | 13. Rouchya | | 18-2-3102 B.C. |
| | 14. Bhaitya | | |
| | (*Manvantaras*) | | |

The age based on the Indian chronology gives the value 1972.944 million years as the age of the earth. However, *Sūrya Siddhānta* effects a correction equivalent to 17.064 million years to the above value which view is not supported by the later authority of eminence, Bhāskarāchārya.

The calculations of the Indian chronology is given below:

One Mahāyuga = 4.32 million years

One Manvantara = 71 Mahāyugas + Kritayuga

One Kalpa = 14 Manvantaras + 15 Kritayugas

6 Manvantaras = 71 X 6 Mahāyugas + 7 Kritayugas

| | | |
|---|---|---|
| | | = 1852.446 M |
| 27 | | = 116.640 M |
| 28th | Krita | = 1.728 M |
| | Treta | = 1.296 M |
| | Dwapara | = 0.864 M |
| | Total | = 1972.944 M |

Correction effected by the *Surya Siddhanta* = 17.064 M
Thus the age of the earth = 1955.880 M
to the 18.2.3102 B.C. (M = million years)

A correlation between the Indian chronology and Indian geochronology reveals that the below given periods of the geochronology can be equated with the beginning of the various Manvantaras.

| *Manvantaras* | *Time of Commencement (in million years)* | *Periods* |
|---|---|---|
| Vaivaswata | ... 122.256 | Cretaceous/Jurassic |
| Chākshusha | ... 430.704 | Cambrian/Ordoviclan |
| Raivata | ... 739.152 | Delhis |
| Tāpasa | ... 1047.600 | Satpuras |
| Uttama | ... 1356.048 | ??? |
| Swārochisha | ... 1664.496 | Eastern Ghats |
| Swāyambhuva | ... 1972.944 | Dharwars |
| *Sūrya Siddhānta* correction | ... 17.064 | |

Age of the earth-... 1955.880 to the 18.2.3102 B.C.

Excepting the Permo-Carboniferous haitus and the shortage in the duration of the Dharwars being not reflected properly, there can be little doubt in recognising from the above table of correlation that the commencement of each Manvantara coincided with a specific cycle of orogeny.

It is relevant here to recall that according to modern astronomers the Sun is about 30000 light-years away from the centre of the galaxy Milky Way. Moving at a rate of about

296 km./second the Sun with the system goes round the centre of the galaxy once in 200 to 250 million years. However, it is not certain whether it requires 200, 250 or 300 million years.

According to the Indian chronology the Sun is the chief reckoner of time and is the maker of the Manvantaras. It is clear that the Sun's completion of a single circuit of the galaxy accounts for one Manvantara. Since the commencement of the successive Manvantaras coincided with the cycles of orogeny, the period of interval would be rather ($4.32 \times 10^6$) X 71 = 306.72 million years with a quiescent period of one Kritayuga = 1.728 million years. Hence it follows, that the Sun's revolution around the centre of the Milky Way possibly causes the accumulation of stresses required for the orogenic activities. Therefore, it is worthwhile investigating the sensitive arc of the Sun's orbit capable of effecting the geotectonic activities:

Considering the above problem, it is possible to determine the position of the Sun at the time of commencement of the Manvantaras. The Sun is located at $147^0.5$ from the centre of the galaxy Milky Way with reference to the 1950 equinoxes. Calculating for the period since the commencement of the current Manvantara it is obtained as given below:

| | | |
|---|---|---|
| Referred to 1950 equinox = | | 1950 |
| | | 3102 |
| Commencement of the | | 5052 |
| current Manvantara | = | 122256000 |
| | Total = | 122261052 |

| | |
|---|---|
| One Manvantara = <br> $71 \times 4.32 \times 10^6$ = | 306.72 million years |
| One Kritayuga = <br> $0.432 \times 10^6 \times 4$ | 1.728 million years |
| | 308.448 X 106 years |

for 308.448 X 106 years = 360°
for 122261052 years= 143°

Therefore, deducting 143° from the location of the Sun, *i.e.*, 147°.5 it is arrived at 4°.5 position of the galaxy. Thus, it can be generalised that the Oh. 18m. position from the centre of the Milky Way is a very sensitive point, the transit of which by the Sun allows the major changes in the disposition of the features of the earth to take place. Therefore, the Oh. position of the galaxy + 18' is justified for being set as the reference meridian.

The above considerations suggest that the geochronology can be read easily in terms of the Indian chronology. This enables the stratigrapher to have what can be referred to as a 'Rock-Hour' unit which is of easy comprehension and a standard reference irrespective of the destruction of the rock book of a particular area. Thus, the rocks of the Trichy area in Madras can be called: Rocks of the 7th Cycle 18 minutes.-307.

# 7
# Mundane Astrology

Scientifically speaking the subject of Mundane Astrology is that branch of knowledge which investigates into the events of the material world. Those events, so far as they affect humanity in a particular state or nation are of utmost importance, as such it has come to mean as state or national astrology. This field of study helps us in predicting general events like wars, plagues, pestilences, revolutions, earthquakes, fires, submergence and such calamities. Celestial events indicative of terrestrial changes which affect in a collective manner are also considered here such as the formation of governments, socio-political and environmental transformations, maintenance of peace, etc. Prof. B.V. Raman has been an advocate of astrological bureau to advise the people in power in evaluating such events and in his words "it could give the governments enough insight into future complications with foreign powers, that would be worth untold millions even if this supposed Bureau made only 60 per cent correct predictions". He also remarks that it is too much to expect in the present state of Mundane Astrology for this Bureau to be always correct as extensive researches are very necessary.

People who wish to live a democratic way of life express themselves in electing representatives who steer the wheels of government and serve the people to the best of their capacity. Democratic way of life is inherent to the people of India. However, the machines of the government have become so complex that it has been difficult to effect a smooth and effective activity. A simpler and more elegant form of government would be desirable and to this end composition of a simpler body is presented herewith based purely on astrological considerations.

Since the twelve houses of the zodiac govern various aspects of the state, it is easier to have a ministry each for the zodiacal house which enables to view things in proper perspective. They can be enumerated as below:

| *Significance of* | *Ministry of* |
|---|---|
| First House | Home |
| Second House | Food |
| Third House | Communications |
| Fourth House | Geology |
| Fifth House | Education |
| Sixth House | Defence |
| Seventh House | Foreign Policy |
| Eighth House | Health |
| Nine House | Law |
| Tenth House | Industries |
| Eleventh House | Finance |
| Twelfth House | Planning |

The above could be applicable to a state, nation or the world at large. If it could be formulated the administrative channels could be clear at all levels and flow easily. Since the ascendants of various states, nations and the World Organisations differ, the above port-folios change with reference to the ascendant. As for India, however, Virgo has been considered to be the ascendant. With the sign Virgo as the 1st house, the federal administrative body will have a composition depicted in the mundascope as given hereunder:

<table>
<tr><td>VII<br>Foreign<br>Policy</td><td>VIII<br>Health</td><td>VII<br>Law</td><td>X<br>Industries</td></tr>
<tr><td>VI<br>Defence</td><td colspan="2" rowspan="2">Prime Minister's<br>Cabinet</td><td>XI<br>Finance</td></tr>
<tr><td>V<br>Education</td><td>XII<br>Planning</td></tr>
<tr><td>IV<br>Geology</td><td>III<br>Communications</td><td>II<br>Food</td><td>I<br>Home</td></tr>
</table>

**Mundane Astrology**

A tentative composition of various ministries for a federal administrative body with Virgo ascendant has been suggested in the above mention'ed chart. The portfolios transform as the change in the ascendant takes place consequent upon the entry of a particular body of administration into power. The ministries sugested in the chart conform to the natural traits of particular houses which enable the work of the house to be carried out with least duplication, and with greater co-ordination and deeper effect. This would make the administrative body ideal, conforming to natural order.-20.

# 8

# Ādityachāra

The Sun, one of the millions of celestial bodies of tremendous energy in the vast Universe, has been praised by the enlightened, both in the field of ancient science of astrology and the modern disciplines of science. The Vedas, the authoritative religious texts of the Hindus, have devoted several sections in praise of that Source of Light singularly and in unparalleled tone as The Soul of the Universe. That Source of Incomparable Energy has been responsible for the creation, existence and dissolution of the material Universe in the sense that it forms the great principle underlying the visible material Universe. The living and non-living at large exists due to the Sun and the Sun controls and alters the Universal scene. The change that attends upon the motion of the Sun is surmised herein, notwithstanding the latest belief in the modern science.

Defining the effects of the Sun during his journey through the heavens *Brihatsamhitā's* author states that if the Sun does not enter Makara (Capricorn) Rasi but turns southwards, the life in the west and south suffers destruction. Similarly if the Sun turns back northwards not entering Kataka (Cancer) Rasi the life in the east and north suffers destruction. Darkness on the face of the Sun during the time other than that of eclipse indicates famine, destruction of holders of authority and power, accidents due to fire and weapons. Based on the shape of the darkness, like that of crow, headless man, sword, etc., on the face of the Sun during eclipse the nature heralds destruction of humanity in the form of storms, thunderstorms, earthquakes, etc. If the darkness on the face of the Sun resembles a stick then the chief will be killed; if that of headless man indicates sickness to people; if that of crow fear of theft and if that of a sword famine, etc. From those countries where these bad signs are seen, learned and pious people flee with children and become immoral. The money of the pious will be stolen away by the wicked in such countries. Rains will be cut short and people meet with destruction.

If the shadow on the Sun resembles that of an umbrella, flag, etc., recognised to be insignia of royalty, then change of royalty is indicated. If the shadow is due to smoke then people will suffer. The red Sun in Grīshmaritu is productive of fear in the mind of the people. In Varsharitu the dark Sun suggests shortage of rains. Straw yellow Sun in Himantaritu is indicative of sickness to people. During the rainy season if the Sun shines with the reflection of Sirish flower there will be rains the same day, and if he shines with the reflection of the feather of peacock then there will be no rains thenceforth for a period of twelve years. If the Sun shines with the colour of clouds harm from insects and pests is sure and a smoky reflection indicates harm from the neighbouring countries. With the colour of the Moon, resemblance to that of a pot, with a band of thin clouds encircling the Sun generally indicates change of administration. The constellation in which the Sun suffers such a shadow is sure to remove him that is born in the constellation from the world scene, and the nakshatras are noted to get purified from the rays of the shining Sun.

Some of the notes in *Brihatsamhita* may seem questionable for statements like that the Sun if he turns without entering Makara Rasi heralding no Uttarāyaṇa brings destruction to life in south and west. This is just in conformity with the ideas of the drifting continents well known to the geologists. Topsyturvying of the poles of the earth as a consequence of the drifting of the land masses demanded by the convection currents slowly but steadily will certainly reflect the motion of the Sun as reversed to the people observing from such moving continents. Because such occasions are generally rare and unthinkable during normal times, the statements by early observers have lost significance. It is equally certain the results of such a motion for many destructive forces also manifest on the land masses under movement and cause destruction of life.

How is this movement affected in nature? Is it ever possible for the land masses to move? These are generally questions arising in the minds of people who declared the earth as stable. Modern science upholding the early observations has corrected such an opinion of the majority of the people and declares that the earth is unstable.

Natural currents of electricity flowing through the crust of the earth are referred to as telluric currents and regarded as of solar origin. The normal voltage of these currents is several millivolts per km. and undergo a diurnal cycle of amplitude and direction. They are stronger on the daylight hemisphere of the earth. These telluric currents are related to the geomagnetic field variations and have proved to fluctuate during the variations of solar flares-induced cosmic radiation. Strong geomagnetic storms are correlated with high potential telluric currents of the order of several volts per km.

Occurrence of sunspots and solar winds are quite significant when the relation that exists between the telluric or earth currents and the solar effects are understood. In the light of the observations made by *Brihatsamhita* on the shadows appearing on the Sun and the effects on the surface of the earth the observations stand clarified from the scientific angle.

The effect of the Sun on the life is more significant. The induction of the white light on the brain cells resulting in the thought vibrations will be affected during the disturbed solar activity. The geomagnetic field is understood to get generally compressed to half of its normal distance during the period of the solar wind, being pushed by the energy particles streaming from the Sun on the sunlit hemisphere while in the dark hemisphere the field may extend as far as the path of Saturn around the Sun. Such a change being further altered by the presence of other members within the solar system tell adversely on the life.

Apart from the effect of the Sun on the living and non-living earth presently, the overall changes have been noted for the entire existence of the earth in astrology. The Sun's rotation around the centre of the galaxy causing a Manvantara and the changes that may be expected in the early or distant future have been clearely given by the Hindu astrology. Modern science is slowly coming to appreciate the established truths of astrology and it must be realised that the Sun and Time are one and the same.-201.

# 9

# Movements of the Moon

Selenologists have started dissecting the Moon for information employing the same usual methods of analysis. We hear that over hundred and sixty laboratories the world over are engaged in going deep into the rock samples collected from the surface of the Moon by the Apollo-11 expedition, and scientists are likely to discuss the aspects of selenology in the early January of 1970. Astrologers wait to see the extent of truth their scientific brothren are going to glean after the deliberations.

The physical Moon can give us information regarding the nature and type of rocks or other material constituting the Moon at surface and selenological structures may suggest the activities of the selenological agents. The selenological map, to be as complete as or even more than that of the earth, likely to be prepared in the early future and analyses of samples from various parts of the Moon's surface may also reveal important things beyond the ken of scientific analysis.

The importance the astrologer attaches to the moon is not comparable, for the position of the moon in any chart is the first key which unfolds his field of investigation. To an astrologer, the moon is the sole representative of mind and the situation of an event. The moon is described as

Jalapindātmaka meaning 'of water or liquid constitution'. The movement of the moon through the zodiac and its dynamic influence on the nature of living and non-living world is a very important and interesting study. Varāhamihira, the doyan of Indian Astrology of medieaval times, observes thus in Brhatsamhita: when the moon transits the constellations Jyestha, Moola, Poorvāshādha and Uttarāshādha through their southend then seeds, plants in water and forests meet with destruction. When it moves through their northend, the above receive improvement. Similar is with the arcs of Vishākha and Anūrādha when he becomes bad he gives non-benefic results. One important peculiarity of the transit of the moon with certain constellations is that the effects may be felt of the following constellations even before he transits them as in the case of Revati, Aswini, Bharani, Krittika, Rohini and Mrigasira.

The effects will be felt after he transits half the arc of the constellations Āridra, Punarvasu, Pushya, Āslesha, Makha, Pubba, Uttara, Hasta, Chitta, Swati, Visākha and Anūrādha. After the complete transit by the Moon of the arcs of Jyeshta, Moola, Poorvashādha, Uttarashādha, Sravana, Dhanishta, Satabhisha, Poorvabhadra and Uttarabhadra constellations are the results effected. This has been described as Anāgath, Madhyasamyogi and Atikrānth or Ardhabhogi, Adhyardhabhogi and Samabhogi also. Based on the disposition of the Chandrashring the observations are given as below:

The rising of the Moon with a horn rised resembling an yacht referred to as nau is indicative of trouble to sailors but is good to others.

If the Chandrashring is half-rised it goes under the name *laangal* suggestive of troubles to farmers but indicative of friendship between rulers without any apparent reason.

When the Chandrashring is half-rised in the south, it goes under the name *dushtalaangal* and indicates death of a Pāndyan king (of the present Tamil Nadu) and work of the armies.

When the Chandrashring is of equal rise going under the name *Sámashringachandrodaya,* the Moon foretells happiness and contentment everywhere. There will be welcome rains.

If the moonrise is of dandākāra there will be troubles to cattle and the rulers assume powers of severe punishment.

The disposition of the moonrise resembling that of bow it is called *Karmukha* and indicates war and the king of the land lying to the side of the bowstring will win. When the bow is north-south oriented it is called yugam, occasioning earthquakes. In the yugam if the south horn is a little rised over the other it is called *parshwashayee* that portends death of rich business magnets and destruction of rains. By the rise of one horn if the other faces downwards referred to as *āvariita* it is indicative of famine. When the complete line of circumference of the Moon is seen during the moonrise it goes under the name *kunda* and suggests stripping off of the offices of important ministers and countries. Uttarashringachandrodaya indicates improvement, contentment and happiness as well as rains. The reverse is for famine and fear. If one of the horns of the crescent Moon is directed downwards or unseen then one of the onlookers will be removed from the world scene.

If the Moon size is small at the time of rising, such a Moon is indicative of shortage while a large size suggests plenty. medium size indicates fear and hunger, as also increased activity for rulers.

Influence of Mars on Chandrashring destroys bad rulers and rulers in the West or the mleccha desa; being influenced by Saturn the crescent Moon suggests hunger and injury by weapons; influenced by Mercury rainlessness and hunger; by Jupiter death of pious rulers by weapons; by Venus unimportant rulers; and all these happen with widespread effects during the bright half and with local effects during the dark half. Influence of Kethu on the rising Moon is said to be benefic and destroys thieves. Fall of merteors on the eclipsed Moon indicates the death of the ruler born in that constellation.

In horoscopy Lagna indicates body and the Moon the mind. Life spirit of the body and the mind characteristic of the body go together. The body may exist without the active mind as a person is unconscious. But without the body there will be no way to hold the medium of mind. The medium of mind is just like any other medium with qualities describable by the concept of field theory, and coloured by the influence of many other factors, notwithstanding the peculiarities of the system particularising it. But why this medium of mind is represented by the Moon on the rationale of astrology belongs to the field of better observations and subtler perceptions. The Hindu religious texts, *i.e.,* the Vedas proclaim *Chandrama manaso Jatah* meaning that the Moon was born out of the mind of Supreme Purusha. It was stated in The Astrological Magazine-April 1943-that 'All diseases and more especially skin diseases, insanity and epilensy were believed to be subject to the influence of the Moon... we know as a matter of experience that these diseases get more virulent in their effects at the time of the New Moon'. One psychiatrist is said to have observed that "somnambulism is more prevalent during the Full Moon but the sexual organs are stimulated more during this period than at any other time both in beasts and homo-sapiens' (*Astrology and Modern Thought* by Prof. B.V. Raman, p. 87).

All activities have their birth in the mind of personalities and the mind is the enjoyer of all enjoyable things or otherwise. Thus the thought receptacle is mind and more fundamental is intelligence. Intelligence, Wisdom, etc., are just qualities colouring the medium of mind based on the constitution of a particular system of organic composition with life spirit, characteristic of the individual or accumulated by the family, *i.e.*, heridity.

*Manasastu parā buddhir yo buddhéhparatasthu saha*

*Evam buddhéhparam budhwa . . .*

states *Bhagavad Gita* meaning that the starter in the mind is superior and the Supreme Purusha is superior to that starter. Hence the mind is just a medium and this medium has to do with the Moon since the above Vedic injunction makes it clear that the Moon was born out of the mind of the Supreme Purusha.

What accrues to an individual by the transit of the Moon is given by the formula:

*Janma-sampat-vipad-kshema-pratyak-sādhana-naidhanam*

*Maitram-parama maitram cha . . . . . .*

meaning that the Moon transiting one's Janma Nakshatra will not give benefic results, transiting the second gives money, valuables, etc., the third star, troubles and accidents, etc.; the fourth happiness and enjoyment; the fifth no good: the sixth success; the seventh generally untoward; the eighth and ninth beneficent. This will recur and is periodic subject to the influence of other planets and the Dasa Bhukti notwithstanding the strength of the birth chart. These are day-to-day observations and can be tested.

The strength of the Moon is very essential to start any work. Chandrabala and Tarabala, *i.e.*, the constellational support are very important. To know in advance the nature of the trend of work is not known to modern science. Sanmukha chandrama and Dakshinasthita chandrama are noted to give benefic results, while Vāmasthita chandrama and Astasthita chandrama are said to produce bad results. The Moon transiting the arcs of Mesha trikonas, Vrishabha trikona, Mithuna trikona and Kataka trikona are referred to as the east, south, west and north respectively and travel is to be undertaken when either the Moon is facing the traveller or is to his right.-322.

# 10

# Movements of Mars and Mercury

Mars is stated to have five types of appearances: ushnamukha, ashrumukha, vyālamukha, rudhirānana and asimusala. If Mars retrogrades in the 5th, 7th or 9th star from the star in which he rises, he will be called ushnamukha and is supposed to affect the community who earn their livelihood by fire, *e.g.*, goldsmiths, foundry engineers and foundry workers, metallurgists in the modern steel mills, etc. Mars called ashrumukha, when he retrogrades in the 10th, 11th or 12th star from the star in which he rises and affects the community by installing poison in the natural juices important for life thus increasing unhealthy trends. He is supposed to cut short rains. When Mars retrogrades in the 13th or 14th star from the star in which he sets he will be referred to as vyālamukha and is stated to affect wild animals adversely and bring relief from famine to the community. After setting if mars retrogrades in the 15th or 16th star, he is hailed as rudhirānana who brings relief from famine but at the same time creates fear in the 'minds of the community and also inflicts skin diseases to such whose horoscope warrants. Mars retrogrades in the 17th or 18th star from the one in which he sets when he will be named asimusala and the community is stated to be affected by thieves, famine and fear of weapons.

Rising in the Phalguni (both) star if Mars retrogrades in Uttarashadha and then sets in Rohini, the adverse vibrations thus created affect all life.

Rising in Srvana if Mars retrogrades in Pushya he creates troubles to kings, elders and ruling class in general. Mars is stated to bring destruction to those sections of the community ruled by the specific stars when he rises in them. If Mars retrogrades in Makha, then transiting in the middle, he is uspposed to bring end to the rulers of Pandya kingdom, fear of weapons and famine due to shortage of rains. If he transits the midle of Makha and later does so in Vishākha he bringe famine. Transiting Rohini he brings destruction to community. If Mars transits in the south of Rohini, there will be shortage of rains and increase in the price of commodities. If Mars is seen with smoke covered, then people of Pāriyātra mountain suffer.

Destruction of clouds is to be apprehended if Mars traverses Rohini, Sravana, Moola, Uttaraphalguni, Uttarabhādra, Uttarāshādha or Jyeshta, in the absence of his adverse vibrations being removed or compensated by the association or aspects of other planetary vibrations. Traversing and rising in the sectors of Sravana, Makha, Punarvasu, Moola, Hasta, Aswini, Poorvāshādha, Visākha and Rohini, Mars vibrates favourable to the community and gives agreeable and best results.

Clear, shining like the slight pink flower, of a beauty like the metallic copper, Mars traversing in the north brings immense happiness to rulers and kings and prosperity to the community.

Mars produces one of the strongest vibrations in the cosmos around us during his transit almost comparable to that of the Sun. Above is given the effect harmonious and otherwise of his vibrations based on the text *Brihatsamhita.* The relationship of the earth with its members of the system is very essential to plan out thc annual programmes. All the programmes either of the individual or of the community should take note of these effects.

Any investments on industries controlled by martian vibrations like the foundry, steel and other metallurgical production, railways, production of war weapons, underground mining especially for metallic minerals, etc., should seek guidance from the annual martian transits. Adverse transit of Mars unaspected or modified by other favourable vibrations is sure to affect the undertaking badly and unprofitably defeating the purpose. Such sections of the community should be strengthened by martian people and they will be able to guide the industry, technological skill for such, etc., being vested in them by nature.

It is stated that Mercury rises with adverse effects. If the situation is normal he is noted to influence it in an abnormal way and if abnormal he brings normalcy.

Mercury's transit in the middle of Sravana, Dhanishta, Rohini, Mrigasira or Uttarāshādha causes shortage of rains and inflicts famine. Transiting Āridra, Punarvasu, Pushya, Āslesha and Makha, Mercury is noted to cause war, hunger, diseases, shortage of rains and sad affairs. When Mercury transits in the middle of the yogatāra of the constellations Hasta, Chitta, Swāti, Visākha, Anūrādha, and Jyeshta he causes many a type of food grains to be produced in plenty and increase in the price of oil, ghee, juices, etc. Transiting in the middle of Uttaraphalguni, Krittika, Uttarabhādra or Bharani Mercury is noted to affect adversely the constitution of living world. Transiting in the middle of Aswini, Satabhisha, Moola or Revati he is stated to cause destruction to people of business, doctors, navigators, horses, pearls, fishes, salt, etc. Transiting in the middle sector of

Poorvaphalguni, Poorvāshādha, or Poorvabhādra Mercury causes fear of weapons, hunger and diseases.

It is stated that there are seven types of movement of Mercury as per *Parāsaratantra.* They are enumerated as given here-Prākrita, Vimishra, Samkshipta, Teekshṇa, Yogāntaka, Ghora, and Pāpa. They denote Mercury's movement in the below given arcs:

| | |
|---|---|
| Prākrita = Swāti, Bharani, Rohini or Krittika | 40 |
| Vimishra = Mrigasira, Āridra, Makha or Āslesha | 30 |
| Samkshipta = Pushya, Punarvasu, Poorvaphalguni or Uttaraphalguni | 22 |
| Teekshna = Poorvabhādra, Uttarabhādra, Jyeshta, Aswini or Revati | 18 |
| Yogāntaka = Moola, Poorvāshādha or Uttarāshādha | 9 |
| Ghora = Sravana, Chitta, Dhanishta or Satabhisha, and | 15 |
| Pāpa = Hasta, Anūradha or Visakha | 9 |

and the numbers indicated against the respective types of motion suggest that Mercury if he rises with the characteristic motion he will seen rising or setting for so many days.

Mercury of Prākrita motion causes healthy trend in the community and increased crops; in Samkshipta motion mixed effects; and in the other motions he causes bad effects.

According to Devala, Mercury is stated to have four kinds of motion. They are Rijwi, Ativakra, Vakra and Vikala. They last 30, 24, 12 and 6 days respectively from the day of Mercury's rise or setting. Excepting Rijwi motion all other kinds of motion of Mercury is noted to cause undesirable effects.

If Mercury rises in Pushya, Āshādha, Sravana and Makha months he causes fear and anxiety in the minds of the people but causes desirable effects when he sets. If Mercury rises in the months of Āswayuja or Kārtika he causes fear of weapons, fire, thieves, water and famine. The city which will be surrounded by armies at the time of setting of Mercury will be relieved at the rise of Mercury.

Shining like gold, with the colour of parrot, and of large reflection Mercury if seen is noted to give all happiness and prosperity to the community.

Mercury is quick by action. He is mentioned to toe the situation. He is a friend of the Sun and Saturn, the worst enemies. He is a natural benefic although the last in the list of them. The harmonic vibrations he produces in the gravity field of the Solar system is not so much pronounced as that of the outer planets or even Mars and Venus, but are conspicuous by effect.

He is the yuvarāja in the planetary cabinet. He owns two mixed Rasis, one even and the other odd. He is neutral and kāraka for intelligence. He is all the more soumya. Though inconspicuous in body, he is representative of the all-powerful Vishnu. Thus he has been described in *Ramayana* war between Rama and Ravana as Budhāngārakayoriva, with Rama standing for Mercury.-74.

# 11

# Jupiterain Movements

Jupiter-benefic *par excellence* of the planetary cabinet, virtue personified, manly and wise, adviser to the seekers of truth and real, the sea of happiness-causes vibrations of decisive significance on the mundane plane. Next only to the Sun he is very massive in the solar family and causes gravitational vibrations of long lasting influence.

Disposed in the first amsa of Dhanishta star when he rises in Māgha masa (month), the year Prabhava commences, *i.e.*, meaning thereby that a new personification of time is born after the old cycle ends in Kshaya year. This calendar after Jupiter is the one followed in India comprising of sixty years. The sixty-year period is divided into twelve sections of five years each.

Varahamihira gathers from earlier observations that in the year Prabhava characterised by shortage of rains at places and excess at others, fire accidents, gales, etc., people will not experience any grief, while the natural and social affairs improve gradually during Vibhava, Shukla, Pramoda and Prajotpatti years, following successively. People will be happy and prosperous during the next three years Āngīrasa, Srīmukha and Bhāva, while unsatisfactory rains, sickness and war are experienced during the following two years Yuva and Dhātu. Then Īswara and Bahudhānya are stated to be very good while Pramādi is of ill-effect. During Vikrama and Vishu plenty and sufficient rains will be there but people suffer from fear and sickness. In the fourth section of the five years, Chitrabhānu is a year of plenty and happiness while Subhanu is less so and many people will be removed from the world due to illness during Tāraṇa. During Pārthiva ruling section will be happy and the lands improve much due to rains while Vyaya year causes many marriages. Excepting the year Sarvadhāri, the rest in the next five-year group, *i.e.*, Sarvajitu, Virodhi, Vikriti, Khara are stated to keep the community in fear. In the sixth five years Nandana. Vijaya, and Jaya are noted to be favourable for happy life while the year Manmatha is less so. Durmukhi is declared to cause undesirable things. Excessive rains and plenty of sickness rule Hevilambi while less crops and unhealthy nature prevail during Vilambi. Vikāri receives much rains, Sarvan gets famine, while in Plava people will be happy; these five yers form the seventh section. In the 8th five-year Sóbhakritu and Subhakritu bring joy to the community, Krodhi causes unhappiness while Viswāvasu and Parābhan are of mixed nature, especially fire accidents and injuries from weapons that characterist the latter. People experience many difficulties during Plavanga, while Keelaka and Soumya are happy years. Sādhāraṇa receives less or no rains and diseases kill the people while Virodhikritu causes scattered rains though sufficient crops are assured; these five years form the period of the nine section. In the tenth five years, during Pareedhāvi the mid-country will be destroyed, kings will die, less rains and fear of fire will be experienced while inactive people-people of fighting nature, trees of red flowers and red seeds will be destroyed during Pramādeecha. People will be happy during the year Ānanda while during Rakshasa and Nala years wheat and cereals grow more and incerdiary attitude will increase in the community respectively. Excessive rains, fear of thieve, cold waves prevail during the Pingala year, many kinds of grief during Kālāyukti year many favourable and welcome improvement during Siddhārthi; destruction of people during Roudri year; and medium rains in Durmati year comprise the five years of the elevent section. In the 12th five years, extremely rid crops will be produced during Dundubhi with destructive rains and death of kings happen in Rudhirodgāri. Rakthākshi causes fear of animals and sickness while people will be given to anger in Krodhana. The year Kshaya sees to the end of the force born in Prabhava.

Thus the twelve five-year periods are known to be ruled by Vishnu, Brihaspati, Indra, Agni, Prajapati, Ahirbudhanya, Pitru, Vishwedeva Soma, Indrāgni, Ashwinikumara and the Bhaga respectively. The five years in the sections ruled by Agni, Surya, Chandra, Prajapati and Shiva respectively are called Samvatsar Parivatsara, Idāvatsara, Anuvatsara, and Idvatsara respectively.

If Jupiter is of the colour of fire then it is suggestive of fear of fire, light yellow of fear of sickness, light dark colour of war, green colour of fear of thieves, red colour of fear of weapons and smoke colour of no rains. If seen in daytime the head of the State will die. Seen in clear sky in the night with pure golden reflection Jupiter confers happiness and prosperity on the community.

Commencing from Krittika star Jupiter transiting every two stars is supposed to make twelve years similar to the twelve months, with the fifth, the eleventh and the twelfth years having three stars each. Kartika year is unfavourable for taxi, auto-rickshaw, and engine drivers and pilots as well as goldsmiths, foundry engineers, etc. Many cattle will be destroyed and people suffer from diseases. Red and yellow flowers grow plenty. Mārgasira year records less rains, destruction of crops due to insects and wild animals, fear of sickness amongst people and enmity between friendly rulers. During the Pousha (Pushya) year heads of the State will be friendly, price of the commodities will double or treble but people will improve their health. Māgha notes increase in the worship of elders, happiness all over the earth, greenery and gain of friends will be the rule. Phālguna year records auspicious celebrations and rains at places; increase in the number of widows, powerful robbers and āngry rulers. Chaitra year may see enjoyable food grains, less rains, but welfare of the community and happy friendship amongst heads of the Stae are ensured. However, people of beauty and corpulence will suffer. People without fear enjoy happiness with the heads of the State respecting law and order and perform concious celebrations: all crops will record maximum production in Vaisākha. In Ashādha there will be rains at places as also crops and normalcy is maintained in all walks of life. The cruel community will suffer and all days record good produce during the Sravanayeas. In the Bhādrapada year cereals and crops the seeds of which are sown earlier to the commencement of the year grow ripe but close sown after will not grow and the community will enjoy plenty only at places. Plenty of rains, happy community, life with full of strength and excessive crops result in Āswayuja year.

When Jupiter transits in the north of the stars he causes improvement while adverse effects are realised when he transits south of them. If Jupiter transits within the span of a year two stars he causes favourable results but transiting more than the arc of two stars, *i.e.,* about 27° orbit he will cause destruction.

Jupiter is the consciousness itself and principal kāraka for the life. Having Jupiter even as maraka in a nativity is essential to receive his benefic aspects. Jupiter is the most unselfish causer and the best conferror of lasting happiness. His disposition in the ascendant is highly desirable and his full aspect on the Moon from a place of his own or the house of exaltation or a friendly. Rasi keeps the mind above fear, wise and full of conscience. Jupiter is the teacher, the justice, the adviser, the virtuous funds and the 'live and let live' principle of nature. He gives the astrologer the importance of an unselfish reader of future and gives him the purity of tongue. He is the divine language Sanskrit and the Satyam, Shivam, Sundaram principal of philosopher.-73.

# 12

# Venus in Marriage

The disposition of Venus commands the supreme importance in predicting marriage. Venus is the owner of the 2nd and the 7th houses of the zodiac, hence owns the portifolio of matrimony. The position of Venus and the aspects he receives, especially with reference to the Ascendant and the Moon whichever is stronger, indicate almost decisively the issue of marriage. One may be lucky to have a companion of opposite sex entirely favourble to him or her, while the other may lack in the respect. One may get married early while the other may get married late. One may get married more than once or one may restrain from marrying at all. All these and many more can easily be deciphered from a proper evaluation of horoscope.

Venus, lord of the 7th house, the planets posited in the 7th house, the interaction amongst them as also the support they have on their and in the Navamsa Kundali, all matter when we have to deal with the issue of marriage. However, the position of Venus and his relationship with the Lagna or the Moon-the stronger of the two, give half of the clue to the problem. The remaining points are to be derived from the other items mentioned above and the composite picture should be referred to the Dasa Bhukthi and the timing or otherwise of the issue to be give notwithstanding be effects from Gochara.

Venus in deep exaltation and with digbala for in a Dhanur (Sagittarius) Lagna-born will select marriage during his Dasa or Bhukhti when he is not disturbed by others, especially by the unfavourable vibrations. For the Mithuna (Gemini) Lagna-born his disposition in the fourth in debility may effect the marriage subject to other conditions but the degree of effect is far less. In the 10th, he loses digbala though he may be endowed with the power exaltation for the Mithuna-born. Venus in Thula (Libra) for Kataka (Cancer) may stand in the degree of effectiveness of marriage next in importance only to the above case first. For Makara (Capricorn) born, his transit of Mesha (Aries) may have an effect just opposite to the case of his emplacement in Thula for Kataka. For Kumbha (Aquarius), he is the good lord of the 4th and the 9th and the best Yoga-Kāraka although lord of the 9th for a Sthira Lagna - a dusthanadhipati. His situation in Vrischika (Scorpio) for Simha (Leo) born is not so effective as he would be in Kataka for the Mesha (Aries) born. Thus the degree of marriage effectiveness can be gauged based on the exaltation/debilitation strength coupled with the digbala for other Lagnas as well.

In the 7th house, situation of Mercury is supposed to bring in early marriage while that of the Sun delays. The rays of Saturn aspecting the 2nd, the 7th and the 12th houses may cause delay in marriages. His adverse rays on the lords of those houses and upon Venus by his lordship of owning certain houses which have to do with marital happiness may completely deny one of it.

Some are of the opinion that the arc of distance from the Sun to Venus decides the issue of marriage, and is directly proportional to the value thus arrived at proportionately equating the life-span to the full arc. This idea cannot be relied upon in cases where the longitude of the Sun and Venus are same or close lending to an interpretation for the combustion of Venus which is contested.

Venusian strength of a horoscope is the vitality of the native. It is the green vision of the personality and his outlook towards acquiring a companion for life or otherwise based on the interaction of the Venusian vibration with the others on his mind. Favourable Jupiterian and conformable Saturinine vibrations react and produce an outlook which will last long, also attach deeper values. Martian vibrations colour it for temporary enjoyment thus attach little importance. That of the Moon is very fickle. Unfavourable interactions adversely affect the harmony of matrimonial relations.

Sukrācārya (Venus) can be said to indicate the period of marriage in the horoscope. This period unknowingly may reflect in getting good and delicious meals, self-decoration, enjoying trips and attending marriages and other happy celebrations, vehicles, dance, drama, music, paintings, visiting beauty spots, etc.

One's own inclination to get married is a sure sign of Sukrāchārya. When it gets coloured by Jupiter one will attach a religious importance to marriage, seek a virtuous companion, have his passions tamed and get married at the right time, only when the colouration is conformable. Hindrances to marriage especially from Brahmins, teachers and other respectable persons in the society, false pride attached to marriage, acquiring an ugly partner, are to be expected when one's Venus is badly coloured by Jupiter. Vibrations from Saturn if favourable alter one's outlook towards marriage for a deep and steady companionship which will last long. May be a reserved outlook but a thin, beautiful, active, steady partner is sure to give company. There may be relatively a little delay in marriage, even when he is exalted and betows friendly and unstained cooperation. His adverse rays give one bad or quarrelsome companion of urgly habits and nature, always uncompromising. Rahu and Kethu influence the Venusian vibrations only for shadowy enjoyment, or else remove a number of partners from the scene, only to make the native's morality questionable. Mars colours Venus to be always with the other partner and when favourable, a brave and beautiful partner may give company. A quarrelsome, manly, overpowering partner is indicated for unfavourable Martian colouration rendering at the same time the native highly passionate. Mercury influences Venus for a quick and intelligent partner but when unfavourable the partner will become unsteady and hasty. The Moon is supposed to colour Venus for a charming companion but the rays being generally disturbed, influences the mind for changing faith often. The Sun's vibrations are usually uncompromising with those of Venus, hence almost neutral, although highly passionate. The partner may come from a royal family in the case of the Sun and the Moon influencing Venus, from family of fighters or mechanics in case of mars, from teachers or writers in case Mercury, from vaidic or priests and teachers and justices family in case of Jupiter, from civilians with responsibility or cobler in case of Saturn. The social status and temperament can be determined by the strength and aspects of the planets.

Short time or prolonged acquaintance between persons of opposite sex or entering into some sort of a civil agreement to spend a part of life together, even approved by social sanction does not possibly comprehened the full meaning of marriage as understood from the Hindu texts. The medium of mind is the common platform for all persons to meet and Venus of compatible temperament influences at the level when he takes over the person during his Dasa Bhukthi. When persons of opposite sex join at the level of mind and decide to pursue the path of realisation of the truth, that is defined by the term marriage. Possibly the sage Yāgnyvalkya and his spouse Maitreyi stand as typical example from the Upanishadic times as also Vasistha and his wife Arundhati in Vedic time and Savitri and Satyavan in Pourāṇic times. Every Hindu strives to atain to that status of being a grihastha (house-horder). The medium of mind does not separate the persons of different sexes except in the form and the rise of Venusian vibration permits its subsidence between persons of opposite sex of compatible temperament, which permits peace, progeny, progress in pursuit of the real. Unless there is complete faith and full understanding between the parties it can never be certified as 'married'. Thus, originate law, order, society etc., to maintain peace and harmony of the society, the essential thing for the realisation of truth by one and all. Sex is secondary in the Hindu comprehension of marriage. Devotion to each other even above life is stressed, which permits one to appreciate life in its fuller expression, especially at the physical plane. This is law of nature as such. is a sure indication of impure Venus which creates imbalance in the society. Hindu comprehension of marriage demands as understanding that the creation of male and female has no meaning in the mental field that supporting the Samkhya philosophy of Kapila. Venus can be read as nature's dispositor of male thatwa by way of giving veerya. Female being the miniature prakriti embodied to receive it for continuance of life. Therefore, it is justified that Venus assumes full hold regarding the aspects of marriage - 128.

# 13

# The Planet Staturn in Astrology

Saturn is the planet number six in the Solar family being at a distance of about 886 million miles from the sun. A planet with mean orbital velocity of six miles per second is the least of the six planets, hence befitting his name in Sanskrit Manda meaning slow. It has a sidereal period of 29.46 years and is about 765 times more voluminous than the earth. Though it is 95.2 times more massive than the earth, it has only 0.71 density and has ten satellites christened as Mimas, Enceladus, Tethys, Dione, Rhea, Tital, Themis, Hyperion, Japetus and Phebe, all of them far smaller than the Moon. His characteristic rings are noted to consist of myriads of tiny satellites or meteors.

Saturn is described to posses deep eyes, skeletal body; is tall, lazy, dark coloured, sickly, stingy, a spoiler of superiors of thick nalls, cruel, dirty, angry, old and liking dark cloths. He is westerly faced, ruler of Gurajat, of Kashyapa clan, son of the Sun, lord of Makara (Capricorn) and Kumbha (Aquarius), sectors of the Zodiac, friend of Mercury and Venus, enemy of the Sun, the Moon and Mars, lord of the western direction and liking iron. The enmity or friendship may be taken as incompatible and compatib'le planetary vibrations. He is noted to be most democratic and a strong leader of labourers,. All undesirable and dirty places, unclean and dark section of the humanity, illiteracy and ignorance, delay and death to such dark facets of life are stated to be generally governed by Saturn.

Saturn is exalted at Libra 20°. He is in moolathrikona position from 1° to 20° acquarius and is kāraka for the span of life. In gochara, in one's own star, he is noted to give sickness and difficulty; in the second star good and auspicious celebrations in the house and success in any undertaking; in the third star, sickness and fear of defamation; in the fourth star, advancement in undertaking by efforts; in the fifth star sickness, expenditure and differences with others; in the sixth star, respect and success in undertakings; in the seventh star doubt about success in undertakings and loss of health; in the eighth star success in undertakings and improved finance; in the ninth star difference with friends and difficulties; the 10th star fear from enemies; in the star good health of the family and success undertakings; in the 12th star diseased mind and fear of defamation; in the 13th star proved finance and health; in the 14th star destruction of undertaking and fear of enemy; in the 15th star health of the family and happiness; in the 16th star fear from authority, expenditure and weakness; in the 17th star differences with others and fear of sickness in the 18th star travel, expenditure and trouble in undertakings; in the 19th star fear of enemy and troubles to the family; in the 20th star favourable happenings and happiness of the home; in the 21st star ill-health and difficulty in undertakings; in the 22nd star favourable undertakings and profit cloths; in the 23rd star respect and advancement in undertakings; in the 24thstar respect of friends and auspicious celebrations; in 25th star enmity of people in power, travel, laziness; in the 26th star fearlessness, health, family and in the 27th star short of comfort and travel in foreign lands.

He is the king of oil lord of the poor. His vehicle is noted to be crow. He is the weakest planet due possibly to his distance from us but he is most effective, sure and steady. He is exact and his effectiveness will be due to reason that even though he is distant, he has a very appreciable degree of angular momentum, specific and full, and has be seen below:

| *The Planets and the Sun* | *Full Angular Momentum* | *Spefified Angular Momentum* |
|---|---|---|
| *The Sun* | *not more than 20* | |
| Mercury | 0.03 | 0.61 |
| Venus | 0.69 | 0.83 |
| Earth | 1.00 | 1.00 |
| Mars | 0.13 | 1.23 |
| Jupitar | 725.00 | 2.08 |
| Saturn | 294.00 | 3.08 |
| Uranus | 64.00 | 4.38 |
| Neptune | 95.00· | 5.48 |
| Pluto | 1.00 | 6.09 |
| Total | 1,181 | |

Excepting the angular momentum of Jupiter, Saturn's is to be reckoned with and anybody can see for himself as to why people ask for Gurubala (Strength of Jupiter) and Sanibala (strength of Saturn) in preference to all others.

Saturn is exalted in Libra for he is the planet of justice. Neither Jupiter nor the owner of that house Venus (Sukra) are elevated to that position. Even if they indicate in a horoscope a position of justice for the native, Guru and Sukra are more beneficial by nature and when such justices dispense justice, there will be an element of favouritism while Saturn is most impartial, for he has least attachment.

Saturn causes one of the Panchamahāpurusha yogas, i.e., Shasha Yoga when disposed in his own or exaltation house from the lagna or the Moon, in angles. He opposes royalty, pomp, etc., and wants to normalise excessive concentration. He represents civil servants and servants, without the knowledge of whom one can hardly approach higher levels and get the work done. Similarly, unless one has got Saturn in favourable positions in the horoscope, one can hardly realise the soul. He is the servant of Grahaloka (the world of planets) and the Sun representing the Ātma will never be realised without the help of Saturn. People who are interested in realising the greatest truth or the real, the crux of philosophy, will have to have Saturn in a congenial position. In association with the Moon, Saturn is supposed to give seriousness and exactitude although at the cost of sacrifice of a great thing. Such a disposition during the seven and half year period, Saturn is supposed to achieve the desired results, and hatha yogis are known to wait for the period and get success in their work. No doubt, Varāhamihira states for attaining mukti, one has to have exalted Jupiter in the 1st, the 4th, the 7th, 8th, the 10th or the 12th. This is verily subject to the disposition of Saturn for the required sharpness of penance.

Saturn in a favourable position is a great asset. Excepting for Vrishabha, Thula, Dhanus, Makara, Kumbha and Meena positions, he is not hailed as good in any other Ascendant. Rather he is noted to bring ruination. For Thula (Libra) and Vrishabha (Taurus), he is yogakāraka during his Dasha-Bhuktis. Since Jupiterians are most virtuous and fearful of wrongdoing, being very much dharmic, they are perhaps excluded from the evil effects of Ascendant Saturn in Dhanus (Sagittarius) and Meena (Pisces). Makara (Capricorn) and Kumbha (Aquarius) are his own and being the Lagna lord, he is not bad in Lagna. However, for Kumbha he is supposed to be bad, for he owns the 12th also and readers are having many interesting discussions about that enigmatic house in the various issues of the astrological magazine. While for Vrishabha he is the sullied lord, for he owns the 9th for a sthira rasi, for Thula he is the unsullied lord.

Exalted Saturn in Ascendant or Chandra Lagna is a great source of strength. Mahatma Gandhi is a typical example. He did with his physical and mental qualities exemplify the most exalted Saturn. His discipline, his steadiness, his passivity, his most powerful tools Ahimsa, his simplicity, his justice, his way of reaching the end by proper means, his unfailing faith in the Almighty are all due to exalted Saturn, which enabled him to lead the millions to shake off centuries of foreign yoke. His way of living, simplicity personified, is the essence of the law of nature which the Hindu sages expounded long back as in "Mā gridhakasyasiddhanam" meaning one should not covet other's things.

Although the same exalted Saturn was disposed in the 4th with other four planets in exaltation, and with the Moon in his own house in the case of Sri Rama (as given in THE ASTROLOGICAL MAGAZINE, Vol. 60 No. 10, pp. 948), such a thing is not coveted. One can easily hold him (Saturn) responsiblefor the demise for Rama's father on account of his direct aspect on the exalted Sun, for his banishment from the empire (for it is said that Saturn's aspect is bad as also Jupiter's placement) for 14th years, for his great travels in the Dandaka forest, for his disrupted family life, for his sick mind and for his suspicious as to his wife's character shattering his family happiness completely. If exalted Saturn could do this inspite of the toning effect by other exalted aspects, one can only imagine the plight of the natives with such and other dispositions in debilitation. In Tretayuga, when 3/4 of Dharma existed, Rama suffered due to the disposition of exalted Saturn in the 4th house. Rama's personality was influenced by Saturn in this way. Rama says:

*Laxmīschandrādapevadwā himavānawāhiman thyajet,*

*Ateeyāt sāgaro velām na pratignyām aham pituhu*

meaning that let wealth or laxmi leave the Moon, let snows render the Himalayas completely naked, let seas swell and submerge the lands-I will not leave the vow of father, i.e., the vow enjoined by Dasaratha being that of Queen Kailkeyi's instance Rama be banished to wilderness for 14 years and the kingdom passed to his younger brother Bharata. His seriousness in transactions, his formidable mind, his readiness to suffer for the sake of his father's words, are all due to Saturn's influence on his personality. Neither Jupiter, nor the Sun, nor Mars could have ever been able to make the Moon of Rama influence like that excepting for the powerful 10th house aspect of exalted Saturn. True to the words *Ātmāvy putra nāmāsi* - the son is himself - Rama, the virtue personified (Jupiter's exaltation), did not finch from sacrificing the empire and adopting a hermit's life in the thickest jungles. His empire, when it was restored to him, was hailed as Rama Rajya extoled by Valmiki in superlative terms.

Rama's education in Dhanurvidya or archery (Dhanus being the sign of Saturn in graha pūja) and especially his prowess with Siva dhanus with Akashaya tuneera, all show clearly that Saturn in the house of education trained the personality to his taste. Rama had a bramharaksas, i.e., Brahmin demon as his opposer - not enemy - (as he declares he has no enemies); see the 6th lord, Jupiter, in full exaltation aspected by Saturn and Mars-a real formidable opposition: an opposition inevitable due to snatching away of his wife-as the 7th lord Saturn removed his spouse from the scene. Rama has to enter his palace (after the long exile) where his mother and step-mothers remained as widows-location of Saturn in the 4th house. He received the services of monkeys and chiefs like Hanuman, Sugreeva and others-the forest dwellers and fruit-eaters (representing fully 4th lord of the 7th, Saturn), but for whose help and friendship Rama would not have dreamt of getting his missing spouse back. Failure of Rama's wisdom can be shown at several instances as due to the aspect of Saturn on his Moon with Jupiter. He was easily deceived by Māreecha in the form of a golden deer, unheard of and unseen by any in any age, only due to his love towards his spouse whom he wanted to please. Similarly, many a thing can be corroborated from the astrological point of view in horoscopic influence of Saturn. But suffice it to say that when Saturn's vibrations are favourable, the personality tranforms from inside and one can easily recognise such a thing. When his vibrations are adverse,, the personality has to suffer a lot and pay the highest penalty as in the case of Mussolini, who had yogakaraka Saturn with digbala but in debilitation.

Jupiter is a planet of excesses, Mercury of instincts, Venus of voluptuousness, Mars of rashness but Saturn is the planet who imparts to the personality a sense of discipline or niyama, or even-temperment. Jupiter goes beyond his own capacity to help others. Mercury is whimsical. Venus colours the situation by a kind of attraction which concerns with sex. Saturn makes the personality judge properly and help without thinking of taking anything in return, *i.e.,* nishkāmakarma yoga of the *Bhagavad Gīta.* He does it without any haste or fear and he definitely knows that it is justified. He is steady and calm, reserved or just smiling. He does it unknown to any body and he is sure of success for he is the lord of Thrayódashi Tithi.

Complaints of ill health, loss and untoward misery, etc., during Saturn's Dasa or his seven and half years period are all due to the fact that Saturn removes the material one has acquired by way of cheating, greediness or any means which is not due to one's self. Even one's own family increased by way of sophisticated way of life may be cut off by way of the death of children or dear and near persons for it may be unjustified according to nature's law. It is sure that such a planet is dreaded by the unrealised and held responsible for all the ills. No one likes to receive justice as Vibheeshana says to Ravana:

*Sulabhāpurusha rājan satatam priyavādinah*

*Apriyasya ca pathyasya vaktā shrotā ca durlabhah*

meaning that many are persons who always talk pleasantly to the kings but there are only a few, who give their king unpalateable but necessary advice and rarer still are those who listen to such advice.

It is interesting to note that Ashtavākra interpretation answers in a convincing way the Editor's horoscope that is at present subjected to Saturn's major period and Jupiter's minor period (pp. 937, vol. 60, No. 10, *A.M.*). In the public eye, the Editor is experiencing only good and beneficial results as can be seen by the question put by Mr. Jayaraman. Ashtavakra appraises the situation and the loss met by the Editor and mixes up auspicious celebrations, etc. The overall picture is that the Editor has certainly scored above the loss inspite of some situations in which calumny was threatened regarding failure of interpretations about the Prime Minister's election, etc. One can see for oneself how the Dashabhukti of a learned astrologer himself affects his interpretation as I have pointed out in my discussion on *Need for Intuition in Astrology* (pp. 665, Vol. 58, No. 7, *A.M.*). Not that the respected Editor is not endowed with intuition but even the power to think is coloured by Dashābhuktis.

Coming to the mundane aspects of Saturn, Varāhamihira in this *Brihatsamhita* observes that Saturn moving in the arc of Sravana, Swāti, Hasta, Āridra, Bharani or Poorvaphalguni, (as the Editor observes that Saturn is described by scientists as the wonder of the Solar System), assures sufficient rains. If he traverses with good rays in Āslesha, Satabhisha or Jyeshta he causes not excessive rains but makes the earth look beautiful with crops. In Moola, he causes famine, wars and shortage of rains.

In gemnology, Saturn is allotted sapphire or blue diamond. Sapphire is blue corundum oxide of alumina while blue diamond is carbon with some colouring impurity.

In an earlier article, the author has been able to show the significance of Saturn in causing earthquakes (January and April isues of the *A.M.*, Vol. 58, 1969). Although Prof. Raman quotes the results of research work in this field of Dr. Rudolf Tomaschek (former Director, Institute of Physics, Munich) in his book *A Hindu in America* (p. 229), *i.e.*, Uranus is mysteriously near the meridian of the place squaring or trining Jupiter, Saturn or Mars in 70% of the earthquakes numbering 134 or so noted to have occurred from 1900 to 1957, I have endeavoured in my notings that Saturn is the chief cause in bringing about the imbalances of the solar system during very long periods, *i.e.*, geological times. Saturn is the balancing planet of the system as true as he stands for impartial justice in predictive astrology.

The purpose of life, in view of Saturn's philosophy, is not mere enjoyment but it is given to the individual to realise the greatness of the Almighty's creation and fully surrender to and be a tool in His Eternal Plan conforming to the *Gita* statement-Nimitta mātram bhava Savyaachin-meaning, be just a tool in his activities. No one can have royalty all for oneself and no one deserves only poverty, according to Saturn. Saturn makes one see the world with a seriousness of experience and steadiness of activity against the background of Karma and the philosophy of Advaita. Nothing is permanent excepting the Atman. He is aloof from enjoyments and pleasures of life born of voluptuousness, he is singular and of pensive mood. He is the giver of steadiness, serious thinking that scientific research demands.-6.

# 14

# Varahamihira and Viking on Mars

"Orbiters and landers of two NASA spacecraft photograph and examine the red planet as never before, solving some old puzzles levealing new ones." observed the January 1977 issue of *National Geographic* in an absorbing article "Mars as Viking Sees It". Sri Rick Gore of *National Geographic* gives a vivid description of the way NASA is trying to trace life on Mars. Many interesting informations of great significance have been made available for astronomers, geologists, biologists, meteorologists and the general inquirer. NASA projects are of global interest and astrologers need data for confirmation and improvement on mundane affairs.

Viking 1 landed on Mars on July 20, 1976 and Viking 2 on September 3, 1976. The Vikings are said to continue to observe Mars for a full martian year of 687 days. It would be interesting indeed if the observations made by Varahamihira in his *Brihat Samhita* can be verified, so that it would help scientists to consider whether astrology could be a science at all.

In the Chapter "Bhoumachārādhyāyah" Varahamihira gives the five names of Mars based on the retrogression and rise of Mars in certain aros of the Ecliptic as given below:

| *Name of Mars* | *Number of star in which Mars retrogrades* | *Longitudes from rising* |
|---|---|---|
| Ushnamukha | 7th, 8th or 9th | $80^0$-$120^0$ |
| Ashrumukha | 10th, 11th or 12th | $120^0$-$160^0$ |
| Vyālamukha | 13th or 14th | $160^0$-$186^0$ 40' |
| Rudhirānana | 15th or 16th | $186^0$ 40'-$213^0$ 20' |
| Asimusala | 17th or 18th | $213^0$ 20'-$239^0$ 40' |

Ushnamukha Mars is correlated with the general affliction to people who live on thermal-based industries like metallurgists, goldsmiths, fire-arm producers, etc. Ashrumukha Mars is noted to correlate with some kind of facial diseases, poisoning of liquids and rainlessnes. Plenty and prosperity associated with fear of wild animals and reptiles are correlated with Vyālamukha Mars. Rudhirānana is correlated with plenty and prosperity but with the onset of some kind of facial disease. Asimusala Mars is said to indicate shortage of rains and fear of arms.

Fear of arms is very clear now-a-days in modern world. Any imbalance in any part of the world takes no time to spread to the whole world and create fear of war. Such political situations can be easily correlated with the above movements of Mars. Similarly, other observations may be checked by observations based on statistical grounds, for confirmation.

Further it is contended that if Mars rises in the zodiacal are $133^0$ 20' and $160^0$ and retrogrades in the arc $266^0$ 40' and $280^0$ and sets in $40^0$-$53^0$ 20' arc, then the whole world is in the grip of severe affliction. Also affliction to ruling governments is indicated when Mars rises in the 280°-293° 20' arc and retrogrades in the 93° 20'-106° 40' arc and great distress to people governed by the zodiacal arc in which Mars rises, after retreogression. When Mars retrogrades transiting the zodiacal arc of 120°-133° 20' when Mars continues to dissect the arc ranging 200°-213° 20', then famine is noted. Dissecting the arc of the zodiac 40°-53° 20' Mars is said to inflict on humanity deadly diseases.

If Mars transits the southern part of the zodiacal are 40°-53° 20', then inflation and shortage of rains are portended. Mars transiting the zodiacal arcs 40° 00'-53° 20'; 146° 40'-160° 00'; 226° 40'-260° 00'; 240° 00'-253° 20'; 266° 40'-280° 00'; 280° 00'-293° 20'; and 346° 40'-360° 00', specially bordering the North, have been correlated with destruction of clouds (rain-giving).

Some local observations like the death of the person governing Pandya Desha in South India when Mars rises and retrogrades in the zodiacal arc 120°-133° 20' and destruction of people of Pariyatra Desha when Mars is seen with smoke or dark areas in its disc have also been given. However, they are of local importance.

These observations are essentially confined to martian transits of the Ecliptic but have not taken into consideration the influence of other members of the solar family. They can be verified in many of the annual interpretations based on the disposition of Mars at the time of eclipses, its aspects and perturbations with reference to other grahas (planets) of the solar family, specially culled from the Editorials of The Astrological Magazine.

Both Mars and Venus are now known to have much $CO_2$ in their atmosphere. While Mars looks red Venus appears rather bright. This difference may possibly be due to the presence and absence of magnetic field in Mars and Venus respectively.

Martian surface relief is said to be about 19 miles, varying between the heights of Olympus, the volcanic mountain crater, and the Valles Marineris deep, the former 15 mile high and the latter 4 mile deep. Presence of life on Mars is yet debated. Martian atmosphere is reported to contain 95 per cent $CO_2$ and 3 per cent $N_2$. No water is known on Mars but like frost it is noted to change directly from vapour to ice. Mars experiences dusty storms and tidal waves of heat and pressure are said to characterise martian atmosphere.

Scientific intestigations are being carried out with enormous expenditure and space science is the most attractive field in modern times. If the resultas of space science investigations are only of fundamental (?) nature, specially devoid of any application whatsoever to human science directly, it would be of partial use. May be that those investigations will enlarge our mental horizon and also let us know economically important mineral deposits of possible later use, and perhaps another abode of life (!) in the vast universe, but the discipline will be of greater and more fundamental utility, if the foundations of modern science takes into its wider perspective the aspect of 'life' and its relationship to the universe at large than simply search for its presence on other planets. So long modern science deals with life separately with the material universe and does not find a principle which underlies both, until such a time our knowledge will only be partial and unfulfilled. I should like to end this note by the observations of F. Hoyle that "Man's claim to have progressed far beyond his fellow animals must be supported, not by his search for food, warmth and shelter (however ingeniously conducted) but by his penetration into the very fabric of the universe". Further he remarks that "The universe is everything; both living and inanimate things; both atoms and galaxies; and if the spiritual exists as well as the material, of the spiritual things also; and if there is a Heaven and a Hell, Heaven and Hell too; for by the very nature the universe is the totality of all things". He has also made it clear that "there is a general impression abroad that the large-scale aspect of the universe are not very important to us in our daily lives-that if the Earth and the Sun remained all else might be destroyed without causing us any serious inconvenience. Yet this view is very likely to prove wildly wrong. Present-day developments in cosmology are coming to suggest rather insistently that everyday conditions could not persist but for distant parts of the universe, that all our ideas of space and of geometry would become entirely invalid if the distant parts of the universe were taken away. Our everyday experience even down to the smallest details seems to be so closely integrated to the grand scale features of the universe that it is well high impossible to contemplate the two being separated".

These are revelations almost similar to those of ancient sages. Perhaps ignorance, deliberate ignorance, is more powerful than the greatest wisdom! It will be an early deliverance to modern science if its votaries start giving thought to solving problems as the one proposed in the paper.-81.

## References

*Brihatsamhita of Varāhamihira,* Vidyabhavan Samskrita Granthamala 41, Chowkamba Vidyabhavan, Banares 1959.

*Frontiers of Astronomy* by F. Hoyle, Mentor Book, 1957.

*National Geographic,* Vol. 151, No.1, January, 1977.

*Hindu Predictive Astrology,* by Dr. B.V. Raman, 1959.

"Recent discoveries in Astronomy of Solar System" by P.L. Bhatnagar in *Everymians Science,* November, 1976.

# 15

# Is Ayanāmsa Revolutionary?

Professor B.V. Raman should be congratulated for holding a symposium on the "Vexed Question of Ayanāmsa" and publishing thought-provoking papers from leading authorities is astrology in The Astrological Magazine, Volumes 26 and 27 during 1962-63. After going through the many papers one gets into the complex problem but without a way out. Although the symposium is over, now and then papers concerning this problem appear in the magazine. One such paper which is of great interest is "Some Astronomical Blunders" by Prof. Mahata in the November 1973 issue. This paper affirms that Ayanamsa is oscillatory which itself makes known that the Indian Astrology is of great antiquity, for the western school still thinks that Ayanamsa is revolutionary as it is still in experimentation and not systematisation.

On this point alone the problem escalates enormously, for many problems of modern science depend for their explanation on the revolutionary theory of Ayanāmsa (without satisfactory explanation). Since the record of observation by the modern scientists is shorter than that of astrology, they do not have any theory or even provision, for such an alternative oscillatory theory. The problem which required astrologers to fix the nil Ayanāmsa year and find a common value for the present in order to solve the problem of numerous values of Ayanāmsha being used by different authorities has been very interesting and in the course of finding a satisfactory solution to the problem it is proved that Ayanāmsha is oscilltory and not revolutionary, astrology will lead the whole world of modern science and calim the foremost place as was previously the case in Indian universities.

In the west discovery of Precession of equinoxes is traced back to the second century B.C. to the Greek astronomer Hipparchus. If so the west has not even observed one single revolution of Ayanāmsa for it is estimated to complete it in about 26,000 yearș Then it is unscientific to propose the theory that Ayānāmsa is revolutionary...

So far as Hindu almanacs are concerned, they have utilised the amount of Ayanamsa since time immemorial and evidences have been cited that a number of *Siddhāntas* were already current before the Christian Era and the development of astronomy by Greeks. In the absence of clear records which were mostly destroyed during the invasions of Taxila and Nalanda-it is rather difficult to arrive at the beginning of Indian Astrology. A consideration of *Vedānga Jyotisha* would take us beyond 1500 B.C. to an antiquity yet "undefined" in the words of J. Norman Lockyer. Comment by Ginzel has been quoted by Sri Khareat in The Astrological Magazine, September 1963, on the Nakshatra system introduced in the Vedas not only for sacrificial purposes but also for all civil life. The western scholars who came to know about the eastern achievements through the works of Prof. Max Muller may with advantage note that "The language of the *New Testament* is child's play compared to Vedic Sanskrit and Avesta Zend". However, this need not be an evidence in words to prove the antiquity of Indian Astrology. The written evidences communicated by

Prof. Max Muller have been followed by the monumental evidences of Harappa, Mohanjo-Daro and other places in the Indus valley which have proved the existence of a civilisation almost comparable to and as modern as the present-day culture in India, for the development of which it would have taken necessarily several tens of centuries.

In considering these observations, I wish to drive home the point that by the time of *Vedānga Jyotisha* Indian Astrology made a systematic use of the Precession of the Equinoxes, which can easily be deciphered from the notings of Albiruni later. Although his remarks have been quoted to substantiate the sidereal nature of the time-reckoning by Indian astrologers, it should be recognised that it was not characteristic of that period alone but was in vogue much earlier from the Vedic period. The difficulty is only in proper interpretation of the texts. *Siddhāntas* were improving the Ayanāmsa but Ayanāmsa is not a constant but variable. Over a long period of observation the value of 54" year was introduced in *Sūrya Siddhānta.*

With the background of such a long and sustained observational record, the *Sūrya Siddhānta* statement the Ayanāmsa is only oscillatory is under discussion now. The oscillatory nature of Ayanāmsa is the basis of Indian Chronology, which vies with the best of modern chrónologies. The present writer has been able to substantiate this is many of his articles in the earlier issues of The Astrological Magazine.

All the authorities point out to the "Trimshatkrityo...," verse of "Triprasnādhikāra" chapter of *Sūrya Siddhānta* to say that the Bhachakra oscillates, about Nādikrāntivalaya-sampata as at the time of creation, 600 times in a Mahāyuga. Some authorities doubt the clarity of the statement and some believe that the statement is a later insertion. Some authorities state that it is "Trimshat kritwa" and interpret that the Zodiac turns 30 times in a Mahāyuga. This is also believed to have been supported by Bhaskara in adducing that there are "Ayutatraya" Bhaganas in a Kalpa.

The explanation of Bhaskara in considering 30 Bhaganas in a Mahāyuga is not clear but the available texts give an explanation of "Ayanāmsa sādhana" by considering 600 oscillations/Mahāyuga deriving 54"/year. Considering a fixed number of oscillations per yugas *i.e.*, Mahāyuga, it is clear that in this Swetavaraha Kalpa 255,600 number of oscillations have taken place to the end of the sixth (of the fourteen), *i.e.*, Chākshusha Manvantara, and 16,200 oscillations to the beginning of this 28th Mahāyuga in the current Vaivaswata Manvantara. In this 28th Mahayuga 540 oscillations have taken place to the commencement of the present Kaliyuga on 17/18 February 3102 B.C. Hence a total of 273,340 oscillations have been completed from Kalpādi*.

From the current Kaliyugādi the third part of oscillation is current as follows:

17/18-02-3102 B.C. nil Ayanāmsa year

1800first part of the oscilation

...... from nil ayanāmsha position to 27° forword

17/18-02-1302 B.C.

...... 1800 second part of the oscillation from 27° east back to nil ayanāmsha point.

17/18-02-498 A.D.

*(The number may vary if interkalpa, interyuga period is also considered)

From 498 A.D. to 1974 A.D. Ayanāmsa at the rate of 54"/ year will amount to 22° 25'12' in the third part of the oscillation, *i.e.*, backwards to nil Ayanamsa point. Whether the nil Ayanāmsa point on 17/18 February 498 A.D. was exactly coinciding with First Point of Aries or not it is matter of controversy.

But the verses from Brihatsamhita given below are interesting-

*Asleshārdhāt dakshinamuttaramayanam raverdhanishtādyam*
*Noonamkadāchit āseet yenokatam poorvashastreshu*
*Sampratamayanam savithuh karkatādym mrigāditachānyat*
*Uktābahāvo vikritihi pretyaksha pareeksha nairvaktam*

and

*Aprāpyamakaramarko vinivrito hanti sāpārām yāmyām*
*Karkatakamasamprāpto vinivrittasheottaram indreem*

meaning that according to the earlier authorities the Sun used to commence Dakshinayāna from the middle part of Āslesha and Uttarāyana from the beginning of Dhanista, but now Dakshināyana commences from the Sun's entry into Karkataka (Cancer) and Uttarayana from his entry into Makara (Capricorn). The third verse is a rare observation which means that the Sun does not enter Makara but turns back, there will be danger to people living in the west and south. If the Sun does not enter Kataka and he turns back similar effects are to be expected for people living in the east and north. This observation had been confirmed by Garga and Pārāsara.

These may be considered as the implications of the reversal of the movement of the earth on its orbit. The problem is of geodynamic interest and needs thorough investigation, for it may get us some clue as to the confirmation of the oscillatory nature of the Precession of Equinoxes. In the context of the above, the modern observations that the land masses or the continents were drifting from some original place to their present position since about 200 million years of geological age may receive support and the theory of oscillation of Ayanāmsa may provide a suitable explanation.

[illegible]

[illegible] words [illegible] But [illegible] below [illegible]

[illegible]

[illegible]

[illegible]

[illegible] only [illegible] used [illegible] from the middle [illegible] the beginning of [illegible] from the [illegible] and [illegible] from [illegible] is a rare [illegible] not [illegible] to people [illegible] people [illegible] and metal. This observation had been confirmed by [illegible]

[illegible] may be considered as the [illegible] of the [illegible] of the movement of the [illegible] The [illegible] and [illegible] of the [illegible] [illegible] the [illegible]

# 16
# Astrology and National Crisis

There may be very few matters which require express attention than the many national crises that we face today. Energy crisis, environmental pollution, population explosion, food crisis, conditions of excess and little rainfall, natural and artificial hazards, etc., appear to be more at the present juncture of the human civilisation, than in any early period known to history. It is also true that science has witnessed unprecedented advancement and parts of human community have, as a consequence, witnessed a high living standard unknown to history. In spite of the great advancement in science, human suffering has not been suppressed and the path to healthy, cheerful community is becoming narrowed fast. Can our ancient science of astrology come to the rescue and make its observations, so that the scientific community can be able to realise the way?

What is the cause of these crises and how can they be averted? Has it any astrological bearing and what does the astrologer say? Or the crisis is only psychological or is it true? If it is true what remedy can there be? Can the human civilisation get back to the good old days or what is there in store for the millions in the future? These are some of the important points to be considered in order to evaluate the problem. The problem has been very serious, for, the industrially advanced societies have almost forgotten to live with the nature. A shortage in the supply of energy, gas, fuel, electrical, atomic, etc., will throw the modern cities out of gear and supply of food and other consumer goods will come to a halt with consequent results. Urbanisation of human population has a limit and if exceeded will turn out to be a hell. Increased smoke, heat of industries, epidemics, etc., have been raging the urbs. The rate of increase in the poisoning of the human ecological system is so much alarming that it is almost on the vege of threatening destruction. It has not extened the state of panic, but it could be very hard to visualise the consequences.

Astrologically, the heat and smoke of the industries come under the control of Rahu and Ketu, the two Nodes of the moon, the agreeable disposition of whom is more than a necessity for any urb to grow in sound surroundings. Water supply is controlled by the Moon and the aspect that the Moon receives will decide the condition and nature of water. Aspect of Venus is noted in the vegetation the urb commands, and dwelling conditions are ruled by Mercury. While the breadth and expanse of the urb is to be learnt from Jupiter, Saturn indicates cleanliness, sewerage, etc. The Sun, of course, indicates the political seat of the urb while Mars is a measure of industrialisation.

Jupiterian and Venusian aspects suggest about the population. A balanced population is extremely necessary for any urb to be crisis-free. The adverse influences of industry is indicated by Mars/Rahu combination in the chart of the urb. Air pollution by smoke is indicated by adverse Saturn/Ketu set-up, while water pollution is noted by the Moon/Saturn combination with adverse vibrations. Solid waste disposal is suggested by Saturn and industrial hazards are caused by Rahu or Ketu in combination with Mars in inimical positions.

In an urban chart one should see for the graceful and brighter disposition of the Moon powerfully aspected by Jupiter or Venus for a continuous healthy water supply. An agreeable aspect of Saturn on Jupiter or Venus will make for balanced population. Similarly, the favourable Moon/ Saturn combination results in the perfect clearing system of the city wastes and ensures healthy climate. For parks, roadside trees, and greenery, Venus should grace the chart of the habitation. Favourable Mars would give the city a capable and healthy industrial force. The Moon with Mercury has a say about communication system.

From these natural governing forces, it can be seen that any adverse relationship will cause a crisis for the community, whether it be a city, metropolis or the world at large. Presently the life is infested with many crisis, a general feature the world over. The effect of saturnover the natural house of the moon i.e. Cancer in these years as it is under seven and half period has created a crisis mentality. The countries ruled by Gemini are facing crisis and depression. The crisis, although is due to shortage of necessary commodities under conditions of war and decision to cut short production and supply as in the case of oil.

Recently experts felt that crisis, of food, energy, etc. are rather due to the crisis of money i.e. actual work on the part of the public. The main aim of the planned economy for India was to induce the government and the people to work for doubling the country's income in ten years. Perhaps this has been only proved when we consider the improvement in our national income which was something like Rs. one lakh millions in 1950 and multiplied three times by 1970 to something like three lakh millions The per capita income is about a rupee and half per day at present, but the population is also increasing at an alarming rate and the necessary output of the work is not forthcoming. Employment of machinery is resented, deployment of human labour force to various fields of work necessary for increased production is resented, investment over unproductive has drained the public energy; as such the figures of statistics speak of unrealistic standards. Perhaps the demand that public is not putting their full efforts may be partly true, but sudden demands on their efforts by plans is an unnatural bargain. Plans should have been programmed to gear them up slowly and steadily, so that the national plans could gain momentum in the long run.

The effect of saturn coming to the position he occupied at the time of Independence of India warrants some some observations. Since about June 1973 the National Independence chart has the seven and half years saturn period, which will last till about 1980. Although this saturn period is not generally spoken of in national charts, it stands to reason that it cannot be ignored. Price......hikes, artificial scarcity of essential commodities, helplessness of public, tremendous tax doses, etc., speak about the influence of Saturn on the national chart. Since Saturn is the balance wheel of the planetary system, he will set right the situation by the time he completes the seven-and-half year period sojourn over the natal Moon. Conversion of black money, check on wastage of funds, regulated national economy, fair share to one and all, general improvement, etc., are to be effected by Saturn alone. Control of the business community over the supply position is affected by hoarding etc., which will slowly and steadily be rectified. But the moral degradation and corruption in every vein of national development will have to be met squarely, for which, a favourable Saturn-Mars combination aspected by powerful Jupiter is essential. These changes will be inevitable during the coming years. Many of the crises, some of them deep rooted, will be removed.

# 17

# Planets and Self-Generating Economy

The slogan, 'Industrialise or perish' for most developing countries of the world was welcome and there was no other way out even for relatively poorer countries rather than perish. In modern times economic planning heavily depands upon the mineral resources of a country more than any other natural resource. As such a fast developing nation has but to utilise its mineral wealth for raising the living standards of its people. It is clear from statistics (The Astrological Magazine, p. 653, July 1972) that to reach the standard of living comparable to the U.S.A. it requires something like 2.3 acres of arable land per person. On these lines the arable lands of the world (estimated at about 10% of the land surface of 197 million square miles) would be just sufficient to support the 3,500 million human population at the U.S.A. standard of living.

Though considerations of statistics would allow American standard of living for all inhabitants of the earth, is it any wonder that there is such a glaring disparity in the conditions of living in America and developing countries of the world? The U.N. Charter envisages for each member country a necessary minimum standard of living though such a step has perhaps been accomplished by socialist countries. The difference between socialist and democratic countries (also called capitalist countries) is in the degree of removing the disparity that exists between the rich and the poor. In any case there is bound to be, and it is but natural, some kind of dissimilarity and differences in the living conditions. Then what causes such differences? Can living be made just mechanical? Do people wish to exist or live? What makes people happy and contented? What is meant by prosperity? Is prosperity happiness? When will be a group of people or country called peace loving? Do peace and mechanical way of living go hand in hand? These are some of the most important points of discussion before the nature of a self-generating economy which is the most natural way of living can be understood.

It must be realised that the world population needs what can be referred to as minimum standards of living irrespective of the way, socialistic or capitalistic, they decide to adopt. It is the bounden duty of man as a member of human society to see this end realised. Excepting this provision, it is hard to think in terms of uniformity.

The other point for consideration is to find out whether the natural resources of the world can sustain the drain of development. If earlier civilisations are examined, the various metal ages have paved the way for the present age. The present age, however, has drained the non-renewable resources to such an extent that at the present rate the civilisation may not last even for a century hence. The population explosion coupled with lack of education and a sort of unwillingness to work will cause the problem of living more and more difficult in the decades to follow unless good education and a desciplined way of life is enforced on larger sections of the world population, including the economically advanced countries.

It appears that the earth can support certain human population with natural ease. If the human population is less, then a kind of plentifulness prevails. On the other hand if the population is more, then the struggle for survival may lead to undesirable ways of life. Hence, an optimum population that the earth can support will have to be ascertained. For science is making headway in lessening the rate of mortality. Otherwise the fate of Jurassic dinosaurs will repeat.

Since the nonrenewable resources of a country or the world as a whole are limited, those parts of the surface of the earth which they have been exhausted due to industrial advancement face complex difficulties. Strict economy in the utilisation of these non-renewable resources is extremely necessary for long and sustained prosperity. Hence, any planning should consider to lay stress on extreme conservation of non-renewable resources.

It is a general observation that countries have prospered during favourable planetary periods. In the period of Rajayogakaraka, the countries have been extremely powerful and prosperous Soon after that period they either lose their territories which supplied the raw materials for the maintanance of high living or they exhaust their non-renewable resources leading to industrial break. Hence a cool and calculated planning to bring the country to develop a self-generating economy is very much needed The rate of discovery of new deposits of non-renewable resources should guide the rate of utilisation of such materials.

# 18

# Relativity Theory and Judicial Astrology

Pears Cyclopaedia defines astrology as a pseudo-science and that it bears the same relation to astronomy as alchemy did to chemistry. Its branches, *viz.*, natural and judicial as existed earlier, were responsible for the development of modern astronomy and the present day astrology respectively. Thus judicial astrology is supposed to comprise 'sheer superstition' based on 'alleged influence of the stars and planets on human life and fate' (72nd edn. pp. J-5).

It is further stated that astrology owes most to the early Babylonians, who were nomadic and who readily accepted the idea of divine energy as manifested in the planets. The concept was enlarged to govern the connection of events to the motion of the planets in certain positions, the recurrence of which spoke about the event to recur. It was also enlarged to govern parts of the body and emotions and thus astrology played a dominent part in medicine during medieval times. It is also stated that in addition to planetary positions was considered the rising sign (given as 'house of heaven') at the time of birth based on which it was believed possible to foretell the destiny of the individual. It appears that astrology was popular amongst the Egyptians and the Romans also. The Romans are supposed to have expelled the Chaldean astrologers taking them to be a nuisance. Lastly, it is mentioned that the astrologers exploit ignorance because of people's innate desire to see into the future!!!

In the light of the above definition, Judicial Astrology acquires in the mind of the reader of the Cyclopeadia-especially ignorant of the subject-a questionable status. However, the Hindu system of astrology is not included and the reason is not known whether it did have any claim! or it was not worth mentioning. It is also not known what else other than finding a recurrence of once observed positions of planets-the influences of such being given a mathematical expression of a graph-is carried out in predicting the observed event to recur, especially in the modern meteorology or for that matter in any branches of the natural science! Now geo-cosmologists are waiting for confirmation (for both the fields have only one single specimen to study and to stand and observe) of the introduction or otherwise of the Cosmological Constant to give the Universe (observable only a certain shape, mathematically feasible (athough it is teasing) to account for the radio active age determined on the oldest rocks of the crust of the earth through the most modern observations in 'radio astronomy', let alone conjecturing the mountain building activity of the earth, which is almost cyclic.

Especially in the branches of natural science particularly in geology, one knows that "the Nature never duplicates its work". It is well known from the philosophy of geological sciences that we are dealing with things which have "no traces of beginning and no prospects of end". Thus, an event can never be duplicated in the dictionary of Nature, which is having ample proof in the geological record running for over a couple of thousands of millions of years, unlike that of the punny figure the man. This is equally true of the vast heavens. Then can there be any compromise between the earth and the heavens in bringing out events?

Nobody can study the Universe in its entirety. The help of science is sought for mastering principles which govern the whole of the Universe. Generalisations and sets of properties are obvious in the study, depending upon the magnitude of the subject, thought singularly they are characterised. In the non-living manifestation itself there are hundreds of things to be mastered but for the short span of the life. Over and above all, events and the things are connected by Time and that factor is given an equal footing with other dimensions to deal with the universe, of course non-living. Even then, whether the universe is spherical, cylindrical or otherwise, is not definitely known. Whether it is expanding or in a steady state, not finalised. The proposed C-field or the creation field is stated in accordance with the laws of conservation of matter and energy to support the steady-state existence of the universe with out any end or beginning (let alone of absolute condition) altering the time. One hydrogen atom per litre in every billion years is supposed to get manufactured by an unknown principle or possibly later describable as a self-generating system due to imbalance of certain sections of universe that follow the explosive supernovae etc. This field concept owes its origin to Einstein in order to do away with the idea of space being dealt separately from matter Thus the field pervades everything and everywhere in which space and matter or energy are regarded as different aspects of one and the same field. But this field of universe did not include the aspects of life which remains not examined to fulfil the definition of universe i.e. everything in existence, manifest and unmanifest, living and non-living alike. So the concept of the field of universe restricts itself to the non-living manifest and unmanifest, hence is partical truth.

In defending the concept of this field and compromising science and religion, Einstein observed that one should do away with the belief of personal god of the religion to be replaced by faith in the aim of science to establish general rules which determine the reciprocal connection of objects and events in time and space. For such rules or laws of nature he attached an obsolute general validity which may not be proven. He expressed fair satisfaction on the scientific probe in appreciating the systematic order that persists in human heridity in the realm of living things but is less satisfied about the grasp of connections of profound generality. He is not much interested in the knowledge of order itself. The doctrine of personal god belongs, accordingly, to the domain of ignorance.

The above argument advocated by the learned professor appears to be so true as to uphold the value of Judicial Astrology, rather than the repeatedly trodden path of either science or religion Judicial astrology comprises well established general rules which determine the reciprocal connection of objects and events in time. The discipline has prepared rules with absolute general validity, difficult of proof, save personal and mass experience. This knowledge is capable of showing the path of the good, the true and the beautiful (Satyam, Shivam, Sundaram) as suggested by the learned professor, and correct the course of onés life just based on a look of the heavens at the time of birth.

J. Robert Oppenheimer, the great atomic scientist is mentioned to have remarked that 'General relativity is such a beautiful theory! It is a shame that there are no experiment' (p. 60, Advancing Frontiers of Geology and Geophysics, Hyderabad, India 1964). When such is the case, the subtlest of the sciences astrology can be expected to have hardly any experiment for its proof than being certified by personal experience and knowledge alone.

The application of energy-momentum-tensors to elucidate the properties of matter such as density, stress, velocity, etc., is well known from the exposition of the theory of relativity. It can be possible to explain mathematically if energy-thought-tensors can be applied to elucidate the behaviour pattern of the human mind using well-defined properties of the human conduct considering the aspect of life in the field concept. Such an elucidation may reveal the relationship that prevails between the space and thouht aspects of the field.

Hindu astrology deals with individuals as a single crystal with life. The rationale of individual personality can be read threadwise by the application of the astrological principles as also its modifications, drawbacks, etc., in isolated and composite forms. Thus, the formulators of the astrological principles studied the universe in its entirety from the thought angle. They knew by yoga-siddhi, one can get things from the space but limited to one's capacity. It was the same principle on which Professor Hoyle and Narlikar wished to bank upon for the origin of matter from space expounding the C-field. The new matter in the continuous creation idea is noted to come from nothing! Wherefrom this comes is sheathed in the answer for the question wherefrom gravitation comes or why electromagnetic forces exist.

The theory of astrology accepts the life aspect of the universal field, governed by the unquestionable absolute principle and describes the behaviour pattern of the life in the context of the changes in the field realising the relationship underlying life-matter. Can this be 'sheer superstition'? The learned will reply.

Spin of the earth dictates our daily programmes. Revolution of the other celestial bodies considered along with that of the earth dictates programmes of our life. An individual may stick to the programmes in which case he feels a relief of harmony and satisfaction. If one's person does not accept this rule of nature in the form the programme fixed for oneself, he finds only suffering and realises the spirit of command. Unravelling of this supreme truth helps the knowledge of judicial astrology.

The concept that things which have a logical proof should alone get into the fold of sciences or otherwise remain 'sheer superstition' was blown off once and for all times by Srinivasan Ramanujan. It is mentioned of him by no less a person than Professor G.H. Hardy: "The limitations of his knowledge were as startling as its profundity. ... His ideas as to what constituted a mathematical proof were of the most shadowy description. All his results, new or old, right or wrong, had been arrived at by a proccss of mingled argument, intuition, and induction, of which he was unable to give any coherent account." It is also said of Ramanajan that "he believed that his patron god Namagiri, inspired him with formulae in his dreams". Profesor Hardy's remarks that "Though obviously I learnt from him much more than he learnt from me" might be sheer modesty; however, there stand published by the TIFR, Bombay, the notebooks of Ramanujan in two volumes; possibly many a problem awaiting 'logical' or 'simply coherent' proofs as they call, by scientists and mathematicians are likely to be declared great!

It does not presume in any way that the mathematical prodigy had any connection with the argument under discussion. It will be described in another article how his unsullied devotion to mathematics was inborn and the forces responsible for such a life could be clearly made out from the time of his birth. The inborn power of intuition the fuller description of which he himself could not give save the inspiration he is said to have received from his patron goddess Namagiri will be described, for, such is the power of intuition which illumines any field of knowledge that comes under its rays. Person blind to heaven and nature only can claim Judicial Astrology to be comprising of superstition.-189.

# 19

# The Hindu Calendar

The Hindu calendar is essentially based on the astronomical record. The calendar is as follows:

| | |
|---|---|
| Kritayuga ... | 17,28,000 Solar years |
| Tretayuga ... | 12,96,000 Solar years |
| Dwaparayuga | 8,64,000 Solar years |
| Kaliyuga ... | 4,32,000 Solar years |
| Mahayuga ... | 43,20,000 Solar years |

71 Mahayugas make one Manvantara and 14 Manvantaras equal one Kalpa. This gives for one Kalpa 4,294,080,000 solar years. Hubbles constant for the life of the galaxies could find a conclusive number and then possibly the Hindu calendar will stand the storm of the modern scientific scorn.

Further, the Hindu calendar recognises seven Kalpas of the above type in all. The total of the digital numbers of the years of one Mahayuga (9) is possibly, the maximum of the evolution of the numbers from 0, which is the only perfect one. The present wave of creation is noted to be the fifth one. The cycle of creation and destruction is eternal, therefore, they attribute the word Anadyanta, possibly the idea of Steady-State cosmological theory.

Within the present creation, the fifth one called the Sweta Varaha is noted to have completed six Manvantaras and 28 Mahayugas in the 7th Manvantara called the Vyvasvat and in the 29th Mahayuga after completing the first three yugas we are supposed to be running the 4th, *i.e.* Kaliyuga and are in the first quarter having completed 5067 years in the Gregorian 1967. This gives us a total value of 1985, 885, 067 years since the beginning of the present wave of creation. Almost equivalent to the geological age of the Earth mentioned earlier, based on the astronomical calculations and the scale of evolution of life from the geological record! Radioactive dating has doubled this time-factor!

In case the radioactive dating of the Earth stands for its origin, the date of the Hindu calendar is very likely to be that of the Moon, for reasons to be presented later. Suffice here to mention that the sedimentary cycle and life later were consequences of the separation of the Moon from the Earth. Since that time the geochronology fills the record of the Hindu Puranas, as a little mental exercise might show.

The earlier Manvantaras completed so far in this wave of creation are Swāyambhuva, Swārochisha, Uttama, Tāmasa, Raivata, and Chākshusha. These are not to be considered as intervals of Manu literally. Since the man is the crown creation and from the birth onwards he repeats till he stands on his feet all the stages of human evolution, the word Manu should only indicate the life in general. For every 306, 720,000 solar years it may be found from the geological record the beautiful storied facts mentioned in the Puranas. All the ten avataras or incarnations of mythological value, therefore, of religious importance to a Hindu, namely, the Matsya(fish), Kūrma (Tortoise under reptiles), Varāha (wild bore), Nārasimha (a syathesis of lion and man), Vāmana, Parasurama Dasaratharama, Balabhadra Rama, Buddha and Kalki (all of Homosapien class), fit into the chain of evolution wonderfully. Some of the hard facts no doubt remain to be explained satisfactorily. More than one incarnation appear in the Manvantaras Raivata onwards, particularly the later Raivata Manvantara coinciding with the incarnations from Nārasimha onwards, they indicating that the appearance of man on the Earth was as early as Plio-Pleistocene. The synthetic life of lion and man appears to be as old as Cretaceous, for, reptiles become extinct and also mammals possibly on the stage of evolution. This permits the date of origin of man-like forms some 150,000,000 years. It appears that present Manvantara is 145, 265,067 years to date, which possibly supports the above idea.

Since 451,985,067 years to 145,265,067 years, the Chākshusha period includes all the geological periods from Ordovician onwards, with the earlier types of evolutions, right from the eyed animals.

From the Huronian period, *i.e.*, about 760 million years prior to the Ordovician, *i.e.*, the commencement of Chākshusha period, is the Raivata period. From an earlier thousand and odd million years, *i.e.*, of Laurentian time to that of Huronian is the interval of Tāmasa period. About 1,350 million years to that the Huronian, indicated as post-Archean age (Pp. 330, De Sitter 1956), would be the period Swārochisha. The earlier period upto Swārochisha is called Swāyambhuva, meaning thereby self-formed, stretching into the middle Archaean period. The lower Archaean possibly might not have witnessed any river and rain system, and possibly accounts for the appearance of the Moon.

# 20

# Astrological Basis of Economic Planning

The toal area of the earth is some 197 million square miles, of which some 140 million square miles is covered by the continuous and discontinuous water sheet. Of the rest of the area, some 10 million square miles is not habitable for want of better geographical environment, while half of the rest of the area enjoys sub-humid or semi-arid climate, thus leaving some three billion and over human population confirned to some 23 million square miles. Population density increases from the polar regions to the equator and from zero in the desert areas to over 2,500 in arable areas in the equatorial belt itself. The uneven density of population is controlled by natural conditions of geographical environment, in spite of the advanced civilisation effecting sophisticated communication.

It is estimated that the U.S.A. with some 3.6 million square miles area and 190 million human population requires something like 2.3 acres of arable land per peson to maintain the present standards of living. The Soviet Union has an area of about 8.6 million square miles with some 220 million persons. Although these are statistics pertaining to the mid-sixties, they may be taken for general discussion of economic planning, development and other factors depend on the natural forces generally beyond the ken of modern observations.

The standard of living or the status of a country depends upon what we can call the collective forces of immediate and long-standing effect. Although such a collective force is the main theme, it forms for easy comprehension from the combination of various forces like education, food, industry, communication, national and international relationship, stability of a particular ideology, etc. These things are to be traced to the soil and climate of a particular region and the temperament and outlook of individual persons as well as a community of persons, native to that land and climate.

Economic planning is the most important and primary problem of a free country irrespective of any region on the earth. To achieve this, indicating a standard of living befitting to the land and its people, the free community should plan and implement such a plan in a way to achieve the maximum limit of living standard that a region can provide within a short and competitive time to be exemplary. Is it possible to do so and if possible, which are the least resistant avenues of activity and how best it can be implemented and what time interval in the history of such a country the plan implementation requires, etc., are matters of extreme importance and needs extensive study on short and long range effects and detailed and clear observations which are not possible to learn and produce the blue print from any amount of acquaintance of world history or modern scientific knowledge.

Such a fundamental problem can be tackled from the science of Evolution of Time. The seeds of planning sown in time can be found out what type of harvest it will reap. The horoscope of a free land should be subjected to critical examination and found out which is the best Dasa Bhukti for implementing the plan. No amount of effort put in during an adverse period will ever make the plan successful and will go waste keeping the people debtors. The nativity of a country shows what are its natural resources and on which the burden of planning can be put. The recurring assets and the wasting assets of a nation are to be clearly ascertained and the geographical control exerted in that region understood scrupulously. The wasting assets are to be planned for long-range exploitation giving much weight to the principle of conservatism. The strength of a nation much depends on the wasting assets in the modern technological world and far outweighs the recurring assets. However, the recurring assets are not to be neglected and industrialisation and commercialisation of a nation should have its feet both in the recurring and wasting assets balanced otherwise the planned development will be in geopardy.

We may digress on the Independecne chart of India:

| | | | |
|---|---|---|---|
| | | Ascdt, Rahu | Mars Sun |
| | RASI | | Moon Sat Ven Sun Merc. |
| | | | |
| | Kethu | Japiter | |

| | | | |
|---|---|---|---|
| Ascdt, | | | Jupiter |
| Venus Rahu | NAVAMSA | | |
| Saturn | | | Kethu Moon |
| Mars | Merc.. | | |

The sub-continent is noted to have 3,268,090 sq. km. area with some 550 million people (as in mid-1970). It's the seventh country in the world in area and the second in population, with all the great four races of the mankind, *viz.*, Australoid, Mangoloid, Europoid and Negroid represented. India is rich in power and mineral resources. It leads the world in its iron, mica and atomic minerals. She has exportable surpluses of bauxite, corundum, manganese ore, magnesite, natural abrasives and soap stone. She is self-sufficient in most of the minerals. However, graphite, asphalt, platinum, bismuth, cadmum, mercury, tin and few others are short in her mineral resources. The average flow of water is estimated at 1,67,500 million cubic meters through her rivers, of which some 55,500 million cubic meters of water is capable of irrigation use, out of which some 36% is utilised. She has an output of nearly a hundred million tonnes of foodgrains annually and her industrial growth has reached an index of 172.2 in 1969. Her 80 per cent and little over live in rural areas. All these and many more points go to show the inherent strength of the horoscope and befit the present Dasa of Mercury and the sub-period of the Moon. Her Ascendant gains strength through its lord Venus in Association with the Moon, Mercury, Saturn. In the Amsa, the Ascendant is aspected by both Mars and Saturn. Her Navamsa Mercury, is in the 9th from the Ascendant. Her Moon is strong in association with the Sun. Mercury, Venus and Saturn. The major lord Mercury is in an angle from the Amsa Moon. Mercury is the lord of the 2nd and the 5th house. Second house indicating state revenue, wealth of the people, state imports, commercial transactions and the 5th indicating children and growth of population, students condition, morality, etc., are to improve during the major period of Mercury. During the Moon's minor period since he is the lord of the 3rd house, improvement regarding communication systems, shipping, transport, etc., will be seen above ordinary appraisal. Other aspects also improve since they are associated with the Moon.

During the year 1972 Jupiter is the king of the planetary cabinet and also the Prime Minister. Minister for trade, rainfall and commander of the forces is Mercury. Metals and crops come under Saturn. Minister for grains is Venus. This would suggest that trade, rainfall and the activities of the forces will be good and favourable. The natural king, the Sun, is out of the cabinet and is reflected in the disadvantages of that section. Metals and crops will be produced to the better satisfaction of the community. The national exchequer will have no financial troubles.

The above is subjected to the time of commencement of the new year at the capital, which has been discussed by Prof. B.V. Raman on page 6 of the 1972 Annual Number of The Astrological Magazine. He observed that the lord of the 2nd, mercury is debilitated in the new year chart in the 8th in his own constellation but there is Neechabhanga also. Consequently, the tenor of the economic changes will not be drastic and the hard job of facing upto difficult problems of the economy will make our rulers to come to terms with pragmatic considerations. This would indicate a kind of exercise as a slow break upon the national planning. A sound system of taxation necessary for the proper and specific development for regular return and consequent improvement of the general standards of the public is not forthcoming. The lord of revenue, is the Dasa lord suggesting that there is no derth for the raising of required revenue. But his debility in the annual chart is suggestive of created slump which is not real as the Mercury has Neechabhanga.

Which section of the national planning should be emphasised is to be determined in relation to the annual chart. The annual Ascendant of the capital is in the 4th house of the national chart. Its lord is in the 8th from the annual Ascendant, but in the 11th from the national chart. The planning can be effected with full swing in all its aspects and especially in those lines connected with the 4th house, as for example, in the improvement of educational and research organisations, students welfare, national estates, reforms, agriculture, trade, propagation of peace, etc. The annual Ascendant is aspected by Jupiter and the lord of the Ascendant and Jupiter are of compatible vibration as such proper advice will be readily forthcoming. The annual Ascendant is Vargottama and is having Jupiter in he Amsa Lagna; hence much strong and without any kind of difficulties the seeds of planning sown and those contemplated for expansion will be encouraged by natural forces. It is, therefore, to be contended that this year would be able to take up any amount of burden thrown on the activities of the 4th house of the national chart and significant advance can be expected even if small efforts by insignificant section of the public put forth.

The 10th is afflicted by the association of Saturn and Mars in the annual chart of the nation for 1972, the significance of which have already been enumerated by Prof. B.V. Raman. However, it is noted that Mars is exalted in Amsa and associated with Mercury in the 6th, from Amsa Lagna. This would indicate the availability of state loans to strengthen hands of national revenue. The Ascendant lord in the Independence chart. Venus is in the 9th with aspects of Jupiter in the annual Rasi chart but under papakarthari. He is also debilitated in the Amsa chart. This is suggestive of the nation held under serious tension but relieved of the situation on good advice as Jupiter aspects. His debilitation is indicative of general overall development on a low ebb excepting for the section of metals and crops which fare above satisfaction due to the Saturnine aspect from the 7th house with digbala from the debilitated Venus.

Jupiter's disposition in the annual chart is salutary. He is, however, maraka for the Independence Ascendant but religated to the 6th in the Independence chart, aspecting full the 12th or the house of expenditure. He is situated in the 4th house from the Chandra Lagna in the Independence chart. As lord of the Independence Amsa Lagna disposed in the 4th from Lagna and 11th from Chandra Lagna (Amsa), he is the most powerful force to reckon with. He is also the Chandra Lagna lord during 1972 and is disposed in the 10th from Chandra Lagna (Rasi). His disposition in the 2nd from the annual Amsa Chandra with the Annual Lagna Lord, the Sun is extremely beneficial. A strong and wise authority at the head of the state as Jupiter is the king and Prime Minister of the year 1972 is indicated at the expense of certain fundamental values (he is also maraka for the Independence Lagna). However, peace, prosperity and strength will be the rule of the year, with some minor troubles which will, in the larger interest, be ignored.

Turning to the planning, we have recognised that the utilisation of the wasting assets is an index of mineral-based industrial progress, while the utilisation of recurring assets would indicate the general and sustained progress of the nation. The industries based on the recurring assets should have a sound basis as these are based on wasting assets. The various crops, forests and the hydel projects, etc., will be directly affected if there is any imbalance in the natural environment.

Mineral-based industries will not be affected much but may even prove above normal as has already been indicated. The year's cloud called 'Kala' ruled by Mercury, is suggestive of widespread but uneven rains. The north-east monsoon will be heavy but disturbed by high-winds and storms, according to Prof. B.V. Raman. Minister for crops is Saturn, as such, those crops indicated by Saturn will be plenty like oil seeds, sesamem, etc. Other crops may be of average production but some distruction is also indicated as Mars is associated with Saturn in the annual Rasi chart.

A resource-based planning should be undertaken rather than a target-based planning. Although some kind of an orbitary target has to be aimed, it should invariably be the exploitation of a small portion in the case of wasting assets and the major portion in the case of recurring assets. Such a plan conforms to the natural limitations and is very much desirable. Major exploitation of wasting assets to the neglect of the proper and healthy utilisation of recurring assets throws the planning out of balance within short periods of the history of a nation and renders poor for such for ever, resulting in the weakness of such a nation. Minerals are, in other words, the strength of a nation the complete exhaustion of which renders it weak in modern times. This would pose a very difficult but very effective problem for the planners. How little of the wasting assets are to be utilised and how much of the recurring assets are to be exploited and for what period of time is a matter of extreme concern to the students of conservation. The estimates of deposits of wasting assets is a changing data which may be faourable in the virgin lands while unfavourable in many parts of the world where advanced standards of living is in existence for longer times, causing the maximum exploitation of such materials. However, that is controlled again by the history of that nation.

An ill-conceived target-based planning ignoring the natural control of supplies indicates want of clear understanding on the part of the planners. Such a planning would be a great detriment to the progress of the nation. Half-way, the exhaustion of wasting assets will be a deadly break to the industrial advancement. Hence, a balanced and healthy development plan is a character of experienced planning, for which far-sighted outlook and critical study of the limiting control and nature of times is very essential. Here lies the role of a scientist who knows the nature of times and who can advise effective planning, yielding maximum benefit.

Heavy investiments on industries unwarranted for greater returns should be checked, and given a normal flow. Planning for crude petroleum, minerals and metals especially of ferrous is to be encouraged.

Should this note be of some importance of suggestion to the general public and the planners, the discussion is worth its deliberation. Detailed and specific forms of the discussion cannot be taken up for many reasons.

In general, the history of a nation is the history of its people during a section of the history of the world at large. A land which has a major Mercurian period with control over its revenues, education and population will have progress in these directions when he is the planet of conformable vibrations to the lord of the land. A generalisation of such long-range progress can be ascertained as the years pass over and the curve of progress is sure to conform to the natural laws of the science of evolution in time. A science of time has yet to be conceived by the modern scientist to judge about these invisible developments. One need not surprise if such a science is practised by a people whose history of observations extend over several thousands of years and it would be no mean achievement to own such a fund of observational materials gathered by hundreds of alert minds over millennia. Thanks to the sages who have shown the path of progress.-77.

# 21

# Planets and Environment

The materially advanced countries in the modern world are stressing the importance of environmental sciences. The world over, a fear phychosis obtains due to the land, water and air pollution which the industrialised countries have caused. The countries using atomic energy in plenty have not been able to find a dustbin for the atomic waste. The cities have been over populated and the green belts of the world are reducing, causing slow but steady climatic changes to the detriment of habitation. Quick industrialisation or to raise the standard of living as they call it, has affected most of the human values. The slogan *Industrialise or Perish* has been turned into *Industrialise and Perish.*

The great planners are planning for human ends and have planned for economic development of nations based on their natural resources. If the present and next one or two generations enjoy the highest standard of culture (material) that the earth can provide, it appears to have satisfied them. They perhaps think that if the coming generations suffer for shortage of natural produce, it is not their botheration. They would believe that the coming generations should develop yet more advanced science and technology to suit their living conditions. Then once the mineral resources are exploited, which are wasting assets, they are only to be recycled. In any case there is an end, discoverable within the planners' sight of vision. Even if the non-renewable materials could be recycled or any kind of other substances could be found to replace them, the population explosion of the world is going unabated. They are not realising the crux of the problem. The guilt is within human conduct and the good offices of science and technology of the 20th century have been used for improving their guilt. Man is ready to destroy his own clan through the power of the boons of the science and technology, the result of his great penance, over centuries.

If science does not improve the moral fibre of human conduct, it is nothing of a boon but only a curse. Perhaps to improve the moral fibre, one has to resort to religion, one may think. But what is religion and what is the relationship between science and religion? Says Professor Albert Einstein: "Science without religion is lame, religion without science is blind." He continued: "To be sure, when the number of factors coming into play in a phenomenological complex is too large, scientific method in most cases fail us. One need only think of weather, in which case prediction even for a few days ahead is impossible." He also stated: "We have penetrated far less deep into the regularities obtaining within the realm of living things... " He emphasised that "the more a man is imbued with the ordered regularity of all events the firmer becomes his conviction that there is no room left by the side of this ordered regularity for causes of a different nature. For him neither the rule of human nor the rule of divine will exist as an independent cause of natural events". The Professor further advanced the faculty of cultivating a sense of humility by all as members of the religious school beholding the universal order.

What is the universal order? Is it the same as Rta of Vedic bard? Or something different? Is it the prerogative of scientsits to have access to this universal order or can all recognise it? It can only be observed that the universal order is the same as Rta. The true scientist can have an easy access while the ordinary will only admire. While the ordinary admirer is dubbed as ignorant, the learned thinks that he is above superstitions. Being arrogant, even though learned, he is irreligious in the true sense. This is where humanity has erred and in order to be scientific and technological without the realisation of such fundamental order of the universe, they have practised a school of egotism and developed a non-religious attitude. This has led the world actually to the present crisis of humanity.

What is the order and how has it been expresed? The manifest universe with its starry sky and the movements of planets through it is the clear expression of that fundamental order. All events, small or big, are abridged in it. The smallest of the small and the biggest of the big obey this order. This obedience is the school of religion.

In the above context a set of environmental conditions obtain for a particular place due to its geographical position. The climate, rainfall, vegetation, landscape, nature of the country all get set during the sojourn of the earth on its orbit around the Sun and in relation to the influences of other planets on their move. The environment of a place is thus a complex and is directly related to the planetary movements. The environ is incessantly changing and is true of a certain picture for a specific period of time. Small changes effected by man interacting with the environ may get corrected by the nature in its activity. But deep changes involving environmental conditions of a place by scientifically calculated effort may not get corrected by nature and may remain permanent in which case the environment of a place becomes uninviting to human welfare.

It is not that man should not undertake any planning at all. Only healthy planning is recommended. This is a matter of serious concern. Some people, under the title of town planning with a school of scientists called environmentalists, have attempted several exercises of statistics inviting incalculable calamities. Since this takes place over long periods the people actually suffering will hardly be able to get to the root cause. Thus the problem itself has escaped attention.

The people, who care for the cosmic layout and plan accordingly, consider the totality of environment in terms of the long range observations on the movements of the extra-terrestrial celestial bodies whose more than direct influence is invisible. Whether the plan is in cosmic order is one thing; its implementation is another. Consider for a moment the five-year plans of our nation. Three five-year plans were implemented during the major period of Sturn since the time of Independence. Since about September 1965, the national horoscope has come under the saway of Mercury's major period. This period also closed by September 1982, since when the major period of Ketu is current, which will last until September 1989, to be followed by the major period of Venus, Lagna lord.

During the major period of Saturn, the slogan-*Industrialise or Perish*-was *in toto* translated into fact. Heavy industries and irrigation and agriculture were given prime importance. The mojor period of Mercury witnessed unabated inflation. The inflation is explained by leading economists as a factor which is inevitable in the process of development and equitable distribution of the products. The fact that in a country where 95 per cent are non-tax-payers and the burden of tax being borne by the 5 per cent who actually put in lot of effort, the products are said to be equi-distributed by the wonderful principle of statutary laws through inflation! The per capita involvement is not necessarily to be equi-distributed; but it is only in the distribution of products the laws are more effective. In a rule of majority, whether one desires or not by way of justice one has to bow to the laws, which are again conditioned by history.

We may now dwell upon the Independence Chart of India.* How will the major period of Ketu work in the context and what is the developmental scope? Has the ensuing development the approval of the planetary cabinet and nature's seal of protecting its environment? The chart indicates that Ketu is disposed in the 7th, house of foreign relations. It is a house of Mars. Mars is disposed in the 8th house from the position of Ketu. Mars is also in the 12th from the Moon, who is in conjunction with the Sun, Venus, Mercury and Saturn. The ascendant has Rahu separated by an arc of about $8^0$. The divine counsellor is of no avail, being in the 6th from Lagna.

In Navamsa, Dasa lord Ketu is in the quarters of buddhikāraka Mercury, aspected by gnanakaraka Jupiter. He also receives the aspect of the Sun-Ātmakaraka, of course coloured by the association with Rahu. Ketu is disposed in the 2nd Navāmsa from that of the Moon, perhaps indicative of a neutral temperament.

The check on Mars, in Rasi, is effected, however, by Jupiter, but Jupiter himself is in the 6th from Lagna, though in an angle from the Moon. Jupiter is disposed in the 12th from the Dasa lord Ketu, which signifies perhaps the effective death-blow to the mischief created by Ketu and his house lord Mars.

The eternal trouble due to Rahu being with the Ascendant cannot be eradicated. The other planets in association with the Moon arc, however, in the 2nd Bhāva from the Chandra Lagna (the natal Moon) as they are away by more than $15^0$ of arc. Mars, however, is in the 12th Bhava from Chandra Lagna. The disposition of the Moon between Mars and Saturn (and the Sun), is not at all conducive to the healthy mental disposition of the nation as a whole. The foreign policy of neutrality and nation's steadfast value for peace-jupiter in the 4th from the Moon-clearly suggest the national mind. The current Ketu's period will put this policy to test.

The national foreign policy should be backed and supported by the internal policy. The internal policy will have clear bearing on the national environmental conditions. As has already been cited, the industrialising policy is very evident as the manas-kāraka of the nation, the Moon is closed by Mars and Saturn. Mercury, Venus and the Sun are all separated from this cornering of the Moon by Saturn and Mars. Though the nation is hailed to be the third biggest reservoir of scientific talents in the world, education, business, export, administration, etc., have suffered. Jupiter, though in the angle of home-peace-education, etc., is not himself congenial, hence incapable of effecting the same. Royalty, pomp, etc., of national high offices have all been realised because both the royal planets are put up in a good place. But, the association of Saturn in the combination undermines the reality of things.

Though the Ascendant is strong in Navāmsa being vargottama and with Jupiter, disposition of Ketu in the 5th from Navāmsa Lagna does not auger good. Since it is on the solar plane, the Rahu-Ketu axis will naturally undermine the foreign policy of the administration. This is again neutral to the national mind, though firm in its attitude, since the Navāmsa Moon is in a fixed and friendly Rāsi.

These and other more subtle analyses of the horoscope reveal that there is a test period of our national foreign policy during the major peiod of Ketu. Though Saturn's association with the national mind-the Moon in the Rāsi chart is indicative of a crucial nature, the policy formulated on the basis, if examined in depth, is more humane and the world should welcome it. But, the foreign policy of other nations treat neutrality as a weakness. Also, politically, the association of Saturn and the Sun within an arc of about $9^0$ is always indicative of conflict, some kind of an internal dissatisfaction. It is necessary to point out that in the national horoscope, the position of Saturn is very important as he is the only yogakāraka for the Independence Ascendant. He cannot undermine the interests of the nation.

In the case of test of our foreign policy perhaps, the national mind, the Moon will gain strength as he is with many planets and will pull up the situation. The USSR, governed by Saturn, will always help the nation in perils. Mercury, the governing planet of USA, is also a close alley of the Ascendant lord Venus and Saturn, the yogakāraka. It can be substantiated in the brief period that we have witnessed, that the USSR is always happy to strengthen India. Though Mercury also desires to help, it is a planet of double standard-a great diplomat and in conditions of peril, he may suddenly swing into action, and get the nation out of peril. These two are assured, and the policy will survive, as the ideal one for humanity as a whole.

The internal effect of the policy is not so healthy. There is great impact on the natural resources of the nation caused by the mirage of economic planning for development. Until the period of Venus ushers in, the internal policy will create havoc and perhaps bring the economy to a drastic pass. Ketu-who is Kujavat, *i.e.,* similar to Mars in effect-specially being disposed in the house of Mars, does not portend to this Lagna a favourable future-and in the garb of industrialisation will destroy all natural resources turning them to machines and finally ending without the raw materials due to shortsightedness in the planning. Many industries have already become sick and the list of such may grow during this period. Mars is a death inflicting planet of the Ascendant. He is also in the 2nd and in the 8th from Dasa lord, Ketu. These situations drive the country to the brink of economic disaster and only warrant us to make drastic changes in the internal development policy. In this matter one may comment that to support the necessities of the growing population of the land, it is obligatory to pursue the present policy, for otherwise, it creates difficulties. The right direction, perhaps, is to stop and reverse the population growth, otherwise the nation will become bankrupt leading to complex situations.

Jupiter's aspect on Mars will not allow the nation to embark on population control. This is a national bane. Here, it is nothing surprising to the students of the divine science that Jupiter is a bādhaka for the Ascendant. In creating excess, more when he is disposed adversely Jupiter causes difficulties. This is the situation in our country. The people of authority must realise the situation. No land on the surface of the earth can for ever supply the demands of an eternally expanding population. There is a limit. This is the truth of any environmental science. Unless the local environ has the approval of the cosmic signature, it is futile to plan. Students of science must behold the truth of the divine science. This is the universal secular message of the Vedic injunctions.-5.82.

**References**

**Rasi*: Taurus–Ascendant 16° and Rahu 7°; Gemini–Mars8°; Cancer–the Moon 4°, Saturn 21°, Mercury 22°, Venus 23°, and the Sun 29°; Libra–Jupiter 26°; Scorpio–Ketu 7°.

*Navamsa*: Taurus–Ascendant, and Jupiter; Leo–the Moon; Virgo–Ketu; Sagittarius–Mars; Capricorn–Venus, Saturn and Mercury; Pisces–the Sun and Rahu.

*Balance of Saturn's Major period*: 18 years, 0 months and 18 days approximately.

# 22

# Geological Aspects of the "Brihatsamhita"

Brihatsamhita of Varāhamihira is one of the very important texts in Sanskrit dealing with several aspects of geology. Many interesting observations in meteorology, architecture, sculpture, etc., have also been recorded. There are some eight chapters concerning various aspects of hydrology and one chapter under the title 'Dakārgalādhyāya' deals entirely with a few aspects of ground water. One chapter has been devoted to observations in seismology. There are four chapters concerning gemmology. Of the total 108 chapters, most of them deal with the meteorological observations while chapters on symbolism, omens, medicines, etc., show the profundity of the author's knowledge in various branches of science.

The nature and formation of clouds capable of giving rains, the nature and effects of annual rains, the time of formation and the time of expectation of the specific rains, the influence of atmospheric depression on the specific clouds, etc., have been treated in a superb way. The clouds, of pearly or silvery white colour and these with dark colour comparable to that of blue lotus are supposed to give heavy rains. The clouds formed due to the intense heat of the Sun and associated with little air, are also hailed as dropping heavy rains. If the clouds are formed at a time when there is thunder, dust storms, earthquake, auroras, lightning, eclipses, etc., the clouds undergo destruction. Rohini Yoga, Swati Yoga and Āshādi Yoga have been dealt in greater detail, since the clouds formed under those special conditions are supposed to give more advantageous rains.

During the period when the Sun will be with Cancer, the east, north-east, north and north-westerly winds on the full-moon day are supposed to ensure heavy pourdown. The winds from the rest of the directions will be devoid of rains.

Although observations before and after earthquakes are accurate regarding the climatic changes, the prediction part of it is wanting and the data are not sufficient. The effects of rainbow, auroras, thunder, dust storm, etc., demand confirmation after a number of observations over long periods.

In the Dakārgalādhyāya, ground-water inventory based upon the distribution and occurrence of certain types of vegetation has been treated in detail. Occurrences of anthills are supposed to indicate underground water in the areas where surface water conditions are poor. Water below the ground level is assured between a depth of five to twenty metres in the vicinity of the following vegetation in the area where there is surface water scarcity, Vetasa, Jambuka, Audumbara, Arjuna, Sindhuvāra, Badari, Palāsh, Bilwa, Phalgu, Kapila, Shonaka, Saptaparni, Karanajak, Madhūk, Tilak and Kadamba etc. trees indicate the presence of water at shallow depths, particularly if associated with anthills.

Alan M. Bateman states that under the many non-geological features indicating the presence of hidden water the plants whose roots thrive only in ground water may provide valuable information in semi-arid and arid regions. The observations by Varahamihira in this regard particularly in times so remote is commendable when the science of geology was not at all developed. Since the vegetation is controlled by the specific climatic conditions, the tree mentioned above may help indicating ground water.

Varāhamihira appears to have recognised the flow of ground water in various directions and named them after the directions of flow including the one flowing upwards as 'Mahasira'. However, the description of the soilcover noted during the well excavations are but local and have less regional significance in the light of modern geological studies.

The measurement of rainfall has been well developed over the 'Drona' system, but rainful studies in the recent and prevailing draught areas of Bihar for the last sixty years indicates periodicity of dry spells during June, only to confirm the earlier observations instituted by the sixty year cycle of the Hindu calendar. The forecast on such periods made by utilising the modern data may yield a few more advantageors interpretations, but the prediction based on the earlier observations are certainly commendable for their accuracy and ingeniousness.

The Ratnapareekshādhyāya, Muktālakshanādhyāya, Padmarāgalakshanādhyāya and Markatalakshanādhyāya fall under the present day study of gemmology. Origin and distribution of the gems mentioned by Varāhamihira are far from the present data. But the varities, based on colour, like the colourless, red, yellow and dark and the imperfections observed in the diamonds are very modern. The pearl has been mentioned to originate from elephants, snake, sea shells, clouds, bamboo, fish and wild bores. Specific characters of each variety has been described. The origin of padmarāga is attributed to the minerals named as Saugandhika, Kuruvinda and Sphatika. Its characteristics and imperfections have been dealt with. Details regarding Marakata is wanting. By the time of Varāhamihira it appears that vajra, indraneela, marakata, karketara, padmaraga, rudhira, vaidūrya, pulaka, rājāmani, sphatika, chandrakānta, saugandhika, gomedha, shankha, mahāneela, pushyarāga, brahmamani, jyotirasa, sasyaka, mukta, and pravala, were in vogue. Their natural value and the method of evaluation in the then currency has been enumerated.

In a nutshell the *Brihatsamhita* of Varāhamihira is a treasure-house of many scientific observations which vie with those of the modern science.-267.

# 23

# Some Astrological Aspects of Vāstu

Dr. B.V. Raman has devoted one chapter on 'House Building' in his text *Muhurtha.* The rationale for fixing time of house or any civil construction has been discussed by him at length in the chapter and the writer intends to bring in here some salient points noted from important Sanskrit texts.

Kamalākarabhatta in his text *Nirnayesindhu* observes that earlier authorities on "Grihārambha" varied in their opinion. According to Bādarāyana's *Jyotirnibandha:*

*Vaishākhe phālgune poushe srāvane margashīrshake*

*Sutrārambhah shilānyāsaha stambhārambhahprashsyate*

meaning that foundation and/or pillars for house buildings should be commenced during vaishākha Phālguna, Pushya, Sravaṇa, Margashira lunar months. However, Nārada is given to have observed that:

*Soumya phālguna vaishākha māgha sravaṇa Kārtikah*

*Masah syurgthanirmane putrārogyadhanapradah*

by which Soumya, Māgha and Kārtika months are included but Pushya and Mārgashira are excluded.

In *Vāstushāstra* it is mentioned that:

*margashīrshe tatha poushe vaishākhe srāvaṇe tatha*

*Phālgune ca kritam veshma sarvasampatpradam bhavet*

*Kārtike māghamāse ca chaitre jyeshtte tathāswine*

*Māsyashādhe bhādrapade sa kuryāt sarvatha griham*

meaning that no house construction should be undertaken during Kārtika, Māgha, Chaitra, Jyeshta, Āswayuja, Āshadha and Bhādrapada. According to Daivagnyavallabha's text:

***Shokam dhānyam panchatam nishpashutwam***

***Swāptim naiswam sangaram bhrityanasham***

***Swastrīprāptim vahni bhītim ca lakshmīm***

***Kuryāt Chaitrādyāh grihārmabha kāle***

suggesting that sadness, corns, death, cattlelessness, gains, losses, war, death of servants, prosperity, fire and fear are the results of commencing construction of house during the months Chaitra to Phālguna respectively.

However, in Kālāmrita text Venkatesha observed that:

***Chaitrādyāhkramashaha shubham bahudhanam mrityum cagonāshanam***

***Golābham sutanāshanam twanashanam sampūrnasoukhyamsadā***

***Dhānyam vanhibhayam jayam bahusukham stambhapratisthagamam***

***Kuryustadgrihṇīshubhosya shbhakrit maso amalkhyo yadā.***

meaning that auspeciousness, wealth, death, destruction of cattle, increase in cattle, death of children, scarcity of food, all-round happiness, corns, fear of fire, laurels, increased happiness result from Chaitra to Phalguna when the house construction is undertaken.

Dr. Raman has observed in Muhurta that "No house building be commenced in the lunar months of Jyestha,

Āshādha, Bhādrapada, Āswayuja, Mārgsshira, Pushya and Phālguna as they connote respectively death, destruction, diseases, quarrels and misunderstandings, loss of wealth, incediarism and physical danger. This observation is in agreement with the views of Kālāmrita while differs from Daivgnya Vallabh's. This difference in observation is a problem worthy of research by astrologers.

Further, it is observed in Kālāmrita that if the Sun is in dual signs at the time of sthambhapratishthā it portends death to the owner. Also stambhapratishthā on Tuesday and Sunday result in the house being destroyed by fire, while the waning moon without any kalā imparts unhappiness. The owner will be put to lot of difficulties and the house will also be destroyed by fire if at the time of commencing the foundation or stambhapratishtā the Sun is in Krittika, latter half of Bharani or first quarter of Rohini and the Moon in Kritttika and Mars in Krittika, Makha, Revati, Uttaraphalguni, Hasta, Moola, or Pushya constellation.

Further it is said that the house constructed during the transit of Saturn through Anūrādha, Jyeshta, Swāti, Poorvabhādra, Uttarabhādra and Bharani will be an abode of pishachis and brahma rakshasas.

The house constructed commencing from a Lagna with the 10th house occupied by a planet in its enemy's house will be occupied by others, and become their property.

If Mercury is transiting Chitta, Aswini, Uttaraphalguni, Hasta, Mrigasira or Rohini during the foundation of a house, such a house will give the owner wealth. Similarly if Jupiter is disposed in Rohini, Pushya, Mrigasira, Āslesha, Sravana, Uttaraphalguni, Uttarāshādha and Uttarābhādra, such a house will give the owner progeny. If Venus is disposed in Āridra, Punarvasu, Dhanishta, Visākha, Sravaṇa and Chitta, he will give the owner Dhānyalakshmi.-271.75.





# 24

# Importance of Vāstu in Mundane Astrology

The Indian science of civil engineering goes under the name of Vāstu. Before the manuscript in Sanskrit of the text *Mānasāra* was published by Ramaraj in 1934, there was a misunderstanding that there were no texts written in the eastern cultures on the science of civil engineering. In the west, however, the text presented by the Roman architect Vitruvious some 25 years before Christ, was actually published in 1486 A.D. concerned mostly with similar literature. The sections of the text of *Mānasāra* which were about the civil engineering constructions was brought out by K.P. Acharya in 1943. It appears this is not the only text on the subject of civil engineering in Sanskrit. *Mayamatam, Manasollāsa, Abhilashitārtha Chintāmani, Sanatkumāravāstusāstra, Vishnu-dharmottara* and others reveal the extensive treasures of Indian Vāstu. We have to give unrestricted margin for the materials which were lost from the libraries of Taxila and Nalanda. The Harappa kingdom in Punjab and Sindh alone is estimated to have spread over a triangular area with the lines of the triangle extending for 950, 700 and 550 miles. Similar type of base extension is also seen in Mohenjo-Daro and it is also believed that a culture almost similar to the present existed in those times of 3000 B.C. or so. Even the cultures dated still earlier are available in Ranaghundai, Nal, Nandal, Amri and Kulli and other places. Thus it is childish to say that texts concerning Indian Civil Engineering construction did nto exist prior to 1834, for large cities of the dimensions of Harappa and Mohenjo-Daro could not have come overnight and the science of civil engineering was sufficiently well known to the Indus culture, much earlier to the Romans and Greeks.

J. Norman Lockyer, the founder of the Nature magazine, observed in his book. The Dawn of Astronomy (published by the ṂI.Ṭ, 1964) the ancient monuments similar to those of Egypt did not exist in India (at about... the last decade of the 19th century, he wrote the text). But he remarked that "Not so early as these (*i.e.*, the Nile Valey Civilisation), but of an antiquity which is still undefined, are two other civilisations with which we became familiar before the treasure house of Egypt and Babylonia were open to inquiries. These civilisations occupied the regions now called India and China". Further he remarked that "The circumstances of these two groups are vastly dissimilar so far as the actual sources of information are concerned; for in relation to China and India we have paper records, but, alas! no monuments of undoubtedly high antiquity. It is true that there are many temples in India, but, on the authority of Prof. Max Muller, they are relatively modern". These observations need total modification in the light of the discovery of Harappa and Mohanjo-Daro.

The science of Vāstu includes both architecture and sculpture. Broad divisions like Nāgara, Drāvida and Vésara are recognised in Vāstu shāstra. They have different characteristics. Although this is a broad classification, the vāstus of Harappa culture, of the Mouryans, of Mahāyāna Bouddhas and of Guptas, claim individuality of their own. While the Harappa sculpture surpassed that of the Greeks, many comparisons have been drawn between that of the Mouryans and that of the Iranian.

Vāstu is a closely compatible science with astrology. Any civil engineering construction, be it for individual or for the community or the state, underlies critical appraisal of astrological significance. In the construction of a dwelling house, flow of water to the east or north is insisted upon to ensure prosperity. The main door of the house to be fixed in the direction indicated according to the constellation of the head of the house, as

| | |
|---|---|
| Mesha trikona | = eastern door |
| Vrishabha trikona | = southern door |
| Mithuna trikona | = western door and |
| Kataka trikona | = northern door. |

Similarly the location of the wells is supposed to give the below-mentioned results according to *Vāstu Shāstra:*

*Bhootim pushtim putrahānim*
*Purandhreenāsham mrityum sampadam satrubādhām.*
*Kinchitsoukhyam sambhukonadi kuryāt*
*Koopo madhye gehamarthakshayamcha*

meaning that the location of a well in the northest indicates prosperity, in the east health, in the southeast danger to the son, in the south destruction of the house existress, in the southwest death, in the west wealth, in the northwest troubles from enemies, in the north little happiness and in the centre destruction of wealth and the house.

The observations are true to a village, a town, a city or a capital. So far as the national or political interests are concerned more observations have been made, on the basis of Āaya. The length of the construction multiplied by the width and by 8 and divided by 9 is called Āaya. Reminder one is called Dhwajaya, two Dhūmāya, three Simhāya, four Shwānāya, five Vrishāya, six Khurāya, seven Gajāya, eight

Vāyasāya, of which the odd Āayas are good. For the state buildings Simhāya is very good.

Although morphologically the location of a city, a port, a dam, an air field, a military base, etc., are according to the rules, they may lack the most important intrinsic value for which they are constructed thus defeating the purpose. This factor has to be ensured from a detailed astrological examination.

For example the House of Parliament building is circular indicative of no loss and no gain, and the capital drains southeast by the Yamuna, which is not conducive to the prosperity of the nation. Note that the capital cities of prosperous nations drain north, northeast or eastwards. If for strategic purposes the capital is to be located about the central part, it should be compatible with other factors. For some reason, from the times of Bhāskara and Varāha perhaps, the capital of India was suggested to be located at Ujjain, (N. 23° X E. 76°), about 550 m. above the M.S.L. But the central part of the area of the country is located approximately lying between N. 8° and 38° and E. 68° and 98° will be N. 23° and E. 83°-somewhere about Ambikapur in Madhya Pradesh, with elevation about 1075m. From the point of climate and drainage the locations are not satisfactory. Sometime ago a distinguished geohydrologist suggested Betul in M.P. (N. 22° X E. 78°) with elevation about 656 m. for the location of the capital. This also suffers from the same defect.

Our first 'Home Minister Sardar Patel held the view that Delhi was quite unsuitable as the national capital. After that nobody seems to have thought on these lines. When the British changed the capital from Calcutta to Delhi, they appear not to have thought of anything excepting the strategic value, even by which the location is not unvulnerable. By history it was known that Indraprastha or Hastinavati or Gajapuri, etc., was the site of war of

Kurukshetra and of no peace. In the context of these observations, there appears to be no single location for the capital, at least for the country. Netarhat in the East, Simla in the North, Mt. Abu in the West and Ooty in the South could be better places, with a central hold near about Nagpur.

The Himalayan areas like Darjeeling, Naini, etc., are to be excluded, as also Simla for the location of a capital city for obvious reasons. At the same time the hill resorts mentioned may not be suitable from the point of location itself. Strategic and central, with communication to all the parts of the country, a point of location like Nagpur could alone be possible. An underground city of administrative centre is of great necessity from many points of observation. This also would be ideal for the onset of the Aquarian age.

Much has been said in literature on Vāstu about the construction of state buildings, because, such buildings herald the prosperity or destruction of the country for which they are erected. Important decisions affecting the whole of population are taken in such places and for that matter they are to be constructed with utmost care if the country has to prosper. An example may be given. The Vidhana Soudha at Bangalore with a given dimension of 700' X 350' attaining Gajāya, faces south. It heralded the formation of Karnataka. The Mysore Palace occupies a built up area of 245' X 156' with Vrishāya, facing east. An easterly face is not conducive to a building of Vrishaya. Though in the history of Mysore, the period of its influence lasted from 1902 A.D. to 1947 A.D., it could not bring under one roof the whole of Karnataka, the dream of millions. However, it obtained the small state the coveted name of a Model State.

In the context of these observations, it is to be noted that during the Aquarian age underground cities will become important. During this age, a city, constructed with harmonious relationship to Saturnine vibrations, will be extremely influential. An underground city constructed during Saturn's transit of Tula (Libra) or Kumbha (Aquarius) will get the nation all-round prosperity and great influence.-34.

# 25

# Astrological Indications for Ground Water

A lot of research is being conducted with regard to ground water conditions at the regional, national and international levels in order to evolve natural principles applicable to ground water inventory all over the world. The ground water conditions of a region depend upon the nature of the country, the rock formations, their capacity to hold water and retain for long and sustained periods, conditions favourable for the formation of large acquifers etc., notwithstanding the rate of intake and the rainfall the region has been allotted by nature. When we speak finally about the control that is exerted by nature in controlling the ground water conditions of a particular region the subject-matter transfers itself into astro-geological sciences. In other words, the very existence of natural conditions are determined by the disposition of the globe with reference to other bodies in the solar system.

The elevation from the level of the mean sea, the distance from the sea, the co-ordinates of a region, are all geologic/ geographic situations and the climate of a particular region is determined with reference to the above factors as well as the rain-water conditions vegetative capacity etc. Thickly forested mountainous regions are naturés expression of the strong Sun's vibrations. Seas are the natural representatives of moon. Drylands, shrubby areas and hot regions come under the celestial vibrations of mars. Pastoral and cultivated lands, livley tracks, greenary, plain country, deltaic regions, seaports etc. are governed by Venuș Regions of large cities great civilised establishments, banks of large rivers, water, rich lands, large and extensive tracts of cultivation, are generally the expressions of jupiter. Meadows, grassy plains, surface conditions of the oceans, natural parks, shady haunts, graneries etc. are the natural expressions of mercury. Marshy places, inferior grains, vineyards, deserted lands, windy regions, glaciers and icēcapped areas, areas of oil ground etc. are governed by saturṇ Rahu governs deserts and uninhabited regions, deadly caves and natural dangerous places while kethu can be said to exercise control over unknown regions.

The relation between the sea and the land is always one of change according to geological variations and areas once under sea may have been supporting large cities or mining operations now. Similarly, the areas once supported thick and luxuriant forests may have formed large and extensive coal fields. The very distribution of land and sea in one geological period is totally different from the other. Hence, the face of the earth is always changing especially when disposed differently to various members of the solar system during her long and lively history. Thus the belt of the Sun on the earth in the form of luxuriant forests and mountains in one period of her history may change during the other period. Similarly with others.

With the above background, it is easy to appreciate the distribution of water on the earth as well as the underground potential in particular areas. The level of subsurface water is generally referred to as the water-table. It is relatively high in the elevated regions and shallow in the regions nearer to sea, with a balanced level based on the characteristics of the land in mid-regions and plaines. Its fluctuation with regard to seasons is well known and the daily fluctuations can be determined with regard to the disposition of the Moon.

It is generally noted that a major part of the large land mass invariably of hard rock areas and the banks and terraces of large rivers as well as the deltaic regions and the sea coasts are covered by a layer of soil. It is comparatively easier to find fresh water in the soil-covered areas. In the hard rock areas, it is rather difficult and the old and dried-up river valleys are generallyu taken as guide apart from deep cracks and crevices that prevail in the rocks holding ground water. From the surface it is difficult to recognise, especially when thick soil cover obstructs proper location. Much of these can easily be attacked form the astrological point of view, for large human establishments in the form of cities have come to existence only in such areas and scarcity of water is also felt in those parts.

Hints for the location of ground water based on certain indirect evidence coming from vegetative field and natural mounds have been given in an earlier issue of The Astrological Magazine (April 1968, p. 386). Here the importance of time and the disposition of the Moon and Jupiter, as well as Mars and Venus in indicating fresh, sweet and perennial supply of water under ground will be pointed out.

Whenever the Moon in strength joins Jupiter it may safely be assumed that the water-table becomes very shallow, especially when Jupiter and the Moon are in watery signs, *i.e.,* in Cancer, Scorpio and Pisces. A bore-hole or well opened during those Lagnas or their navamsas in other Lagnas is sure to supply fresh water of perennial nature. The soil and/or rock cover punctured during these times will catch the flow of the ground water and ensure constant supply. The chances will be altered during other times. Although Mars owns one of the two signs, *i.e.,* Scorpio, his aspect or conjunction during such times speaks of dryness. Venus equally favourable as Jupiter. Mercury's aspect may affect the continuity at quick intervals, while that of Saturn may give no water, Rahu and Kethu should invariably be avoided and unsullied Jupiter in Pisces with the strong Moon in Lagna during jala thathwa will ensure fresh and sweet water supply.

Drawing more water in the coastal regions beyond the capacity of the flow or the store will result in the supply of salt-water. Based on the Herzberg formula $h=t\ (g-1)$, where $h$ denotes the depth of fresh water beneath the sea-level, to the specific gravity of the sea-water and 1 the specific gravity of fresh water, fresh water floats on the sea-water in the coastal tracts when the density of the sea-water is generally more than that of the fresh water. The contact of the layers fluctuate. Should the supply exceed the limit of fluctation, the salt-water spoils the wells once and for all. Such a thing may happen when the Moon is very strong compared to the weakened powers of all other vibrations, especially in the absence of Jupiter's and venusian rays.

Prof. B.V. Raman mentions that "Ṝevati, Uttarabhādra, Hasta, Anūrādha, Makha, Sravaṇa, Rohini and Pushyami are favourable for digging wells". Although it is the sign of pitcher, Aquarius is not supposed to give good supply of water, as well as Taurus. He further mentions that Venus should be in kendras to the Moon. However, Venus does not own any watery signs. "An abundant supply of sweet water is indicated when the Moon or Venus is in a quadrant identical with a full watery sign" continues Prof. Raman (*Muhurtha,* pp. 137, 138). Venus is exalted at 27° Pisces, *i.e.,* Revati 4th quarter, although ruled by Mercury. Uttarabhādra, Ānūrādha and Pushyami are ruled by Saturn but the last forms an arc of the Moon's house, and the second that of Mars in Scorpio which are watery signs. Hasta and Sravaṇa are stars of the Moon, as well as Rohini his best friend. Makha does not appear to be in any way connected, ruled by as it is Kethu and forming an arc of the Sun's house, the aspects of which for the puncture of the water-table gets obstructed by rocks.

Pisces represents the oceans. Association of the lord of Pisces should be given due importance in selecting the puncture Ascendant. If this Acendant is coloured by Saturn the water may be a hard one containing Ca and Mg salts. Rocks rich in these are governed by Saturn. Specially the cotton-soil rocks are difficult for a proper water diving. Although they are well jointed, they have a very low water-table during summer. Provinces of Maharashtra and Gujarat, northern parts of Mysore, western parts of Andhra Pradesh and other regions have this drawback.

The desert of Rajasthan comes under the control of Rahu. The places of oasis appear to be due to a very strong Moon supported by Venus and Jupiter, although governed by Rahu. Even in the oilshows which are invariably sandy rock formations, the layer of oil floats on a layer of water. A strong Moon with Venus or Jupiter appears to be sheathed by Saturn and Raha, Saturn, an airy planet, can easily be comprehended to keep the oil under pressure. Possibly it is for this reason, people with Saturn related to karma shine in these fields and Aquarian age has the richest of oil-kings.

Jupiter is of ākāsha tatwa. He is stated to give corpulence. He owns the watery sign of Pisces which represents tanks, rivers, all oceans, fountains, pumps, cisterns, fish ponds, and excessive watery tracts (p. 221, *Hindu Predictive Astrology*).

Watery places, tanks, rivers, seas, wet lands, canals, reservoirs are signified by Cancer. The Moon herself indicates water, springs, water, journeys, etc.

But Mars as well as the signs of Scorpio has not been taken to indicate any of the above other than stagnant pool. Venus and his signs Taurus and Libra do not say anything about water except to indicate lively places, etc.

Hence, it appears and is supported by experience that the strong Moon and Jupiter should occupy watery signs for puncturing the surface for a perrennial sweet water supply. Faulted aquifers, deep dislocations, trend of master joints, buried valleys, subsurface flow connected to pernnial streams, the direction of ground-water flow as could be determined by the sophisticated isotopic methods, advantages and limitations of the local water-table fluctuations, help make water divining easy.

The pure rain-water imbibes the taste of the ground it flows in. Under the sunny ground it may be having no taste or get the radioactive materials dissolved. Under the martian ground it may get heated up to form hot-springs and dissolve ordinary earthly materials. Under the Moon ground it may get many salts dissolved. Under mercurian ground, the water may get the light and alkaline elements dissolved. Under jupiterian ground it may be sweet and of a pleasing taste. Venus is likely to give water hardness but may render it crystal clear. Saturn imparts a dirty and iron-rich taste.

Uncontaminated water is an asset, a source of life. A community of people should not depend totally on the annual quota of rain-water alone. Water is the most strategic mineral and its conservation is as important as life itself. Excessive or shortage of rain brings famine, in most parts, which are normally rainfed. Ordinarily as well as under conditions of distress the above principles help tapping the ground water.-190.

# 26

# Astrology and Gems

The modern science or the study of gems, a fascinating subject as it is, is of special appeal to India for it happens to be the home of world-famous diamonds long before the rest of the world came to realise its importance. India was the singular producer of diamonds till the discovery of Brazilian and South African mines. Her name is amplified in describing the history of the famous stones like the Koh-i-nur, Pitt-or Regent, Orlov, Sancy, Shah, Akbar Shah, Nassak, Taj-e-mah, Piggot, Eugenie, Hope, Tuscany or Florentine, Star of Este, Polar Star, Nizam, Dresden White, Dresden Yellow, Dresden Green. Paul I, Cumberland, Pasha of Egypt and various others. For her treasure, she was sought by the foreigners and it is no surprise that in search of her land the Americas were discovered.

The use of gems in India is of very ancient date. Lapis, turquois, jade, agate, rock crystal, chalcedony, serpentine, and fine haematite are known to have been used in the civilisation of Harappa-Mohenjadaro of 3000 B.C. or earlier (Dr. Srikanta Sastry, *Bharatiya Samskriti Darshana,* Bangalore, 1962, p. 18). Indian lapidary of Harappa-Mohenjadaro times excelled even the most modern. The Syamanthaka of *Mahābhārata,* the Kaustubha of the *Bhāgavata* readily stand outstanding from the ancient texts of the Bharata land and references to Vajra, *i.e.*, diamond in the Vedic literature go beyond the comprehension of the modern observers that diamond came to be used about 480 B.C. (Valentine Ball and S.H. Ball in their papers and books). Treatises like *Ratna Sāstra* and *Agastya Matam* by Agastya, *Rasa Jalanidhi*, the text of Hindu Chemistry. *Yuktikalpataru* of Bhoja, raja, etc. indicate the impact of gems on the then civilisation.

Since the dawn of human civilisation, man has been able to appreciate the gems, specially for the purposes of personal decoration. But the Hindus appreciated the gems for their extra-ordinary powers of influencing the personality. Based specially on their colour, they were able to assign therapeutial value for the various gems. Systematic gemmological studies were undertaken and *Rupa-ratna-Parīkshaṇa* was a recognised field of special study. They did not lag behind in the preparation of artificial or imitation stones and the branch was known under Sampādya-Karma. As the branches increased, the study of distinguishing the natural from the imitation was also developed. More than all, their value in Āyurveda, the Vedic science of medicine, was much appreciated and preparation of ratna-kalpas and ratna-bhasmas were prevalent.

Astro-Gemmology is a specialised field of study, the singular object of which has been the investigation of the relation that exist between the gems and the heavenly bodies. It is no more abstract than a crystal-set, using which we can perceive the things which are generally beyond the perception under normal circumstances. The idea that certain crystals can allow specific vibrations, either electrical or electromagnetic as those of ordinary light, is known to crystallographers. The colour of the crystal being a reflection of its internal structure revealed by X-ray, it was no unscientific conjecture that men of thought used it as a basis for effecting certain specific vibrations.

The gravity waves produced by the heavenly bodies during their motion influence the organic systems according to the laws of applied hydrodynamics. The influence is imperceptible, unless the instruments to decipher them are extremely sophisticated. The universal medium of mind characterised by the organic system governing it reacts to these planetary vibrations. Sympathetic vibrations have salutary effect. But adverse effects due to asymathetic vibrations on the organic systems demand remedy for normalisation. Here is the utility of the special field of study of astro-gemmology.

Several important articles by learned authors have appeared on the use of gems as remedial measures to human ailments (specially of mental, *i.e.*, psychological abnormalities) in thc earlier issues of The Astrological Magazine. The gems include rock-forming minerals of special quality and additional characteristic properties; organic materials like shells, bones, horns, teeth, etc.; and of carbon like jet as well as certain gums and resins like amber, etc. They are generally rare being of special quality, and rarity itself may be a factor in determining the cost-value of the gem, notwithstanding its exceptional properties, like brilliancy, shape, colour, size, resistance to weathering and hardness, etc. Due to these factors, they are highly valued and are treated as concentrated wealth, which are easy to handle during economic upheavals. It is stated that ambitions of Napoleon might have received a setback but for the funds raised on the security of the famous Pitt diamond. It is also well known that kingship and costly gems are akin true to the saying *Ratnahāri ca pārthivaha-* (gems should adorn the king's treasury). In Sanskrit, the word *ratna* is not only used for the gems but also to describe the soverign qualities and striratna, gajaratna, nagaratna, etc., do mean the exceptional in certain classes. To protect them may cost life, hence the statement *veerabhogyā vasundharā* meaning that the earth described as ratnagarbhā is enjoyed only by the mighty.

The astrological control bearing on light has been described in the 1969 November issue. Ordinary light with its seven components, described as the seven horses of the Sun, show varying wavelengths. Violet, indigo, blue, green, yellow, orange and red rays react with the gravity waves of the planets in a significant way. Between the wavelengths of ultraviolet and infra-red rays, the colour schemes is noted to vibrate sympathetic with the gravity of waves of specific bodies. Thus, the gravity waves produced by Saturn are in conformity with those of blue, Jupiter's with yellow, Mercury's with green, the Sun and Mars' with red, the Moon and Venus with white, the full composite colour. To add to these sympathetic vibrations, if wanted in a cast of planetary disposition, the horoscopee is advised to utilise the specific gems. Elaborate processes prevail for the purification, cutting, weight to be added, etc., and not all gems of various nature and characters are to be worn for this reason and if worn despite, may work out adversely.

The following is the list of gems to be worn in case the planets mentioned are against them and the list has received many modifications by various authors in recent times based on their experiences:

| *Gems* | *Planets, Stars, the Moon and the Nodes* |
|---|---|
| Ruby | The Sun |
| Pearl | The Moon |
| Coral | Mars |
| Emerald | Mercury |
| Topaz | Jupiter |
| Diamond | Venus |
| Sapphire | Saturn |
| Garnet | Rahu |
| Cat's eye | Kethu |

The list of birthstones recommended by the National Association of Goldsmiths of Great Britain, chiefly based on colour originally but consequently varied from time to time, is:

| | |
|---|---|
| January | Garnet |
| February | Amethyst |
| March | Aquamarine (or Bloodstone) |
| April | Diamond (or Rock-crystal) |
| May | Emerald (or Chrysoberyl) |
| June | Pearl (or Moonstone) |
| July | Ruby (or Cornelian) |
| August | Periodot (or Sardonyx) |
| September | Sapphire (or Lapis-lazuli) |
| October | Opal |
| November | Topaz |
| December | Turquoise |

A comparative study would reveal that although the Sun is the most important in the study of horoscope based on which the second list given above is formulated, the disposition of the Moon, the basic indicator of mind, which controls the organic system is stronger and the first list would decide the relation on which the gems are to be prescribed. However, the strongest of the Ascendant, the Sun and the Moon is to be considered and the lists may be consulted with better advantage.

It is common practice in medicine either to strengthen the system as to withstand the decay or to remove the decay if it has not gone beyond the level of curative control. The same principle may be followed in the acquisition or prescription of the gems also. The weight of the gem is to be decided based on the strength required for the specific planet as could be ascertained by the grahabala (planetary strength).

Gemmology has advanced much in recent time. Minute grains of artificial diamonds are known to have been prepared by the General Electric Company. The famous chemist Moissan prepared artificial diamond in the laboratory. But such are known to be of minute size and grains of large size are difficult to prepare artificially. However, irradiation of colourless diamonds has rendered coloured diamonds. Studies regarding the fine inclusions of other minerals in diamond crystals being carried out in the Carnegie Institution has thrown varied concepts of its formation.

The belief by the ancients that the diamond is formed due to thunderbolt possibly indicating the high speed of the reaction of conversion of pure carbon into diamond crystals may prove a fact. Jet and diamond both are gems. Diamond with its structure is in common vibration with that of Venus while jet is of very inferior quality in all respects. The composition of both is carbon but under different structural modes.

Both ruby and sapphire are varieties of corundum, an aluminium oxide. Pearl is a shell, especially of calcium carbonate, and with other impurities. The phosphatic compounds give rise to organic gems like the ivory, tortois shell, various bones, horns, etc., the hard parts of the organic world. Topaz is a fluosilicate of aluminium. Coral also is made up of calcium and magnesium carbonates. Garnet is an orthosilicate of calcium, magnesium, iron and manganese in varied proportion. The true cat's eye is a chrysoberyl, a beryllium-aluminium oxide, Emerald is the grass-green variety of beryl, while aquamarine is the bluish-green variety. Amethyst, chalcedony, rock-crystal all are generally oxides of silica in various forms. Amber is the gum on exudation of the extinct pine trees, and varies in composition although it generally conforms to $C_{16}H_{10}O$. Lac, dammar, copal, etc., are varieties of organic compounds.

Thus gems include a host of compounds with special properties.

The gems form the simplest remedies prescribed by the astro-gemmological studies, especially for curative purposes in case of ailments of various kinds and for improving of health. The medicinal properties of gems are of very effective nature. The burnt ashes of the gems cure even highly incurable diseases. The remedial means can be ascertained by the strength of the horoscope. A minimum of 3-1/2 rattis weight of the gem is recommended and this weight may vary for various planets and the loss of strength they suffer in the system. Thus the study of astro-gemmology is of great practical importance of extreme utility.-277.

# 27

# Planets and Sound Vibrations

The rationale of sound-planet relationship is clear in Indian Philosophy which expounds that the visible Universe is just an expression of space which is characterised by sound. The chain of evolution from space to material manifestations is linked by air, fire and water successively, characterised by touch, form and taste while matter responds to smell. One of the ten important Upanishads states that

*Omiti brahma prasouti*

meaning that creation proceeds with 'Om'. 'Om' is composite word of A, U and Ma and it expresses the whole of the alphabets, the *beejaksharas.*

According to the following verse the utterance of these *beejaksharas* produces vibrations sympathetic to respective planetary vibrations:

*Kavarga pūrvān kujasukrachāndri*
*Jeevārkajānām pravadanti santah*
*Yakārapūrvāh sashino niruktāh*
*Vārnāstwakāraprabhavah ravesyuhu.*

Thus it is understood that *beejaksharas* of Kavarga belong to Mars; Chavarga to Venus; Tavarga to Mercury; Thavarga to Jupiter; Pavarga to Saturn; Ya to Ha to Moon; and A to Ahah to the Sun. Just the utterance of the letters amounts to invoking of the planets of the specific varga and careful and clear pronunciation of groups of letters in the form of words with certain meaning serves as a vehicle for the mind or *chit* to proceed along these vibrations and repetition or *purascharana* of each meaningful statements will produce on the nervous system a sort of vibration which may be harmful to the native. Helpful pronounciation lead to even the removal of defects in the body and give the system (body and mind) an unusual power and natural strength. The body gains a certain radiation and the mind super-strength by the repetition of a favourable system of words.

The Vedas or Srutis are *Shabda Pramāṇa.* Since they have sound as evidence and the sound is characteristic of space, they are spread in space. The *upāsaka* (votary) has to try to get revelations and the mantras of the Vedas were such revelations to the Maharshis who tried to know the reality underlying the Universe. On this basis the Vedas do not have origin but the present texts are just revelations percieved by the interested and put in the form of mantras. Each word and statement with meaning if repeated gives the student the kind of knowledge of the specific material/ space relation.

It is said that one should recite the mantra of the lord of the 5th house in one's horoscope. But, for the world in general, the Gayatri has been a boon as it is the mantra of the Sun, the 5th lord of the zodiac. Gayatri means that which is sung by three, *i.e.,* the Vedas (*Striyāmrksāma yajusha iti vedah traystrayee-Amarakosha*)-the Rigveda, the Yajurveda and the Samaveda; and that is the Sun, who is also called Trayee mūrti.

Not only the letters are thus recognised by the sounds, but the undercurrents of certain planetary vibrations can also be known by surveying certain literature of easy comprehension. Take for example *Rāmāyaṇa* and *Mahābhārata,* the great epics of India. The former has an undercurrent all through the 24,000 verses of vibrations of Jupiter while *Mahabharata* composed of over a lakh of verses (the longest poem in any literature known) has the undercurrent of Saturn. This does not exclude certain sections of the above expressing the general thought vibrations of other planets, like the Sundara Kānda in *Vālmīki Rāmāyaṇa* which has a clear undercurrent of Saturn, for it is said that:

*Chandrabimba samākāram vanchitārtha pradāyakam*
*Hanūmatsahitam dhyāyét soundarekānda uttame.*

and the whole of Sundara Kānda is a praise to Hanuman and Siddhi.

While the literature of Purusha Sookta expounds the actions and evolution of the Virāt Purusha, the absolute principle of the Universe, Sri Sookta expounds the nature and actions of Prakriti; thus they are counterpart of calling vibrations of the Sun and the Moon. While Rudra mantras are recited to invite the favourable vibrations of Saturn, the Vishnu mantras are recited to invite the favours of Mercury. Similarly Kartikeya mantras for Mars, Dakshinamurti mantras for Jupiter and Shakti mantras for Venus are expounded.

Similarly in music the sapta swaras (seven notes) are given specific expositions to call the natlural forces. The ragas like Sandhya, Udaya, Megh Malhar, etc., are known for their significance. The effect of music on the mind is salutary. Even snakes are caught due to their weakness to Punnāgavarali. The peacocks are said to pronounce Shadja dhwani, the cattle Rishabha, the goat and others Gāndhāra,

Krouncha birds Madhyama, the horse Dhaivata, the elephants Nishāda, the cuckoo Panchama, etc. They have their respective planetary influences and help the upasakas of Nāda-Brahma.

To rouse Kundalini through the nerve (solar) plexus certain mantras can be pronounced and its way through the plexus to the Sahsrāra is controlled by the proper set-up of vibrations with respect to planets ruling various plexes. Nerve centres are easily excited by the action of sound, and unfavourable sound is the greatest harm. The present-day sound therapy will be much benefited if the material-sound relation is taken into consideration and the ruling planet of the person and his peace of mind understood with reference to his horoscope for certain vibrations.

Thus the sound-planet relationship cannot be over-exaggerated, than observing that it is the only vehicle (save chit-shakti) to convey one's thoughts.-142.

# 28

# Operation Hiroshima

The atom bomb was dropped at 9-15 a.m. on 6th August 1945 on the city of Hiroshima located at 133°E. and 35°N. The approximate geocentric longitudes of the planets are given below:

Saturn 2s 25° 06'; Jupiter 5s 03° 11'; Mars 1s16° 07'; the Sun 3s 19° 59'; Venus 2 08° 38'; (R) Mercury 4 11° 36'; Rahu 2 15° 38'; Kethu 8s 15° 38'; the Moon 2s 27° 16'; and Ascendant 4s 21°.

| | | Mars | Moon<br>Saturn<br>Rahu<br>Venus |
|---|---|---|---|
| | RASI | | Sun |
| | | | Mercury<br>Ascendant |
| Kethu | | | Jupiter |

| | | Saturn | Moon |
|---|---|---|---|
| Rahu | NAVAMSA | | Mercury |
| Jupiter | | | Mars<br>Kethu |
| Sun<br>Venus | | Ascen-<br>dant | |

Balance of Jupiter's Dasa: 7 years, 6 months and 6 days.

This explosion was preceded by another one on the 16th July and succeeded by the third one on the 9th of August the same year. The previous one was a test explosion while the later one destroyed Nagasaki. The test explosion made Oppenheimer, the architect of the Mannhatten project, remember the statement from *Bhagavad Gita*:

Kālosmi lokakshayakrit pravriddhah

when they cabled the President who was at Berlin that the birth of the baby was safe!-the birth of the baby which appeared on the world scene to destroy humanity, the peace of mind of millions.

A look at the heavens at the time of bombing Hiroshima clearly reveals the powerful destructive tendency. The Ascendant lord the Sun is in the constellation of Mercury who is in turn governed by the constellation of Kethu. Kethu is in the Venusian star while Rahu is in the incendiary star Āridra owned by himself.

The Moon is in close association with Saturn in Jupiter's star, but is subjected to strong Papakartari Dosha. Jupiter is in the constellation ruled by the Sun who has been under the serpent star effect. Venus is out of Kālasarpa Dosha but is in the constellation of Rahu and is subject to Papakartari Dosha. Mars is in Rohini star governed by the Moon whose disposition has been given above.

The Lagna being in Simha (Leo) it is evident that the move was political, coloured by vicious intention. Mars in the meridian house is with Digbala. The Moon and the Sun are weak. However, the Ascendant is in Thulāmsa, the destructive sign of the world. Jupiter is weak being in debility in Navāmsa. The world at large was in the midst of darkness. The Sun being under the complete darkness of Āslesha star, the lord of which was governed by the star of Kethu. The event had on its back the best of the scientific knowledge of the day, the solar vibration supported by Mercury. The Moon with Saturn is clear that it was absolutely secret and destructive for, the arc between Saturn and Rahu is only about $10^0$. The heavenly pattern has got more *doshas* than good combinations. Pāpakartari, Kālasarpa etc., are prevalent while the Gajakesari which is weak due to Jupiter being in debilitation amsa could not withstand the bad effects. Over and above the opinion of many of the greatest scientists and other authorities, the event proved to be destructive at last.

It was a Monday; the ruling constellation was of Jupiter's. It is noted that in spite of the bombing Japan was not thinking of surrendering, thanks to the strength of the Gajakesari Yoga. But the Ascendant appeared to be stronger, another bomb fell on Nagasaki, the situation demanding their unconditional surrender. The strength of Simha lagna, especially with Mars, Yogakaraka in the meridian and others in the 11th house proved stronger in spite of the Lagna lord being weak. It is said that the constellations get purified after the transit of the Sun through the arc. It must be accepted that the Sun is strongest and stands for truth.

The event carried in its bosom all the things mentioned above. The move was ingeneously manoeuvred and was most subtle, for Mercury was associated with the Lagna. It was equally secretive and sharp as it was aspected by Saturn from the house of Mercury. It was said that the making of the bomb was delayed but steady; see the aspect of Saturn. Jupiter aspected Mars in the merijdian. The Sun, Mercury, Jupiter and Mars have thus conjoined, especially to the detriment of the other party Venus and Saturn.

In the context of the then world, Hitler born in Thula (Libra) Lagna with Mars, Venus, Mercury and the Sun in the 7th house, *i.e.,* in Mesha (Aries) and Saturn in the 10th was to be uplifted to the level of the planetary combinations demanded and as the 10th Saturn had to give his share his downfall was equally to be brought in. But his (Hitler's) move did not subside. it turned into some complication. Japan entered the arena. Einstein, born in Gemini Lagna with the Sun, Mercury, Venus and Saturn in the 10th, was the supreme intelligence to put an end to the power hungry wars by his scientific acumen. (Both the horoscopes are available in Prof. B.V. Raman's book *Notable Horoscopes*). Their Moon is in Dwirwadasa relation, indicating that the Moon in Hitler's haroscope was equally responsible for the exit of Einstein from Germany and the Moon in the horoscope of Einstein was the death blow to power mad Hitler. Horoscopes of the other personalities in the then world scene will stand akin to one of these, some with full co-operation and some with adverse vibrations.-210.

# 29

# The Vedic River Saraswati

## Introduction

The Vedic sage Gritsamada in Rig Veda mantra 16 of Sookta 41 of Second Mandala makes a prayer to river Saraswati thus:

*Ambitame nadeetame devitame saraswati*
*Aprashastaaiva smasi prashastimamba naskridhi*

meaning that Oh! the best of mothers, the best of rivers, the best of goddesses Saraswati, we are left impure (in mind, wealth and strength) and we pray you to bless us with purity (of thought, wealth and strength) and make us worthy of respect. Probably not even the river Ganga is so respected in any hymn of the Rig Veda, neither Yamuna nor Sindhu has received such admiration from the Vedic sages. Sages like Medhatithi, Deerghatamaa Ouchitya, Agastya Maitrāvaruṇi, Gritsamada, Gaadhina Vishwaamitra, Devashravaa Yaamayaana, Vasushruta Aatreya, Barhaspatya Bhaaradwaaja and others have praised the river Saraswati in such superlative terms which is unpralleled in the history of mankind describing any river on the earth. Ila, Bhaarati (or Mahee) and river Saraswati have been treated as Goddesses Trinity (Tisro Devyaha) and have in their mantras been elevated to such respect as attributable to gods. One sage prays to Saraswati for getting prosperity; another requests for linguistic superiority; yet another prays to get him intelligence and many for blessing them with winning in wars. Bharadwaaja has a full sookta addressed to Saraswati (No. 61 of 14 mantras in Mandala VI). His praise to Saraswati is something superb; he prays to her for relieving him from debts, for keeping the land with lush cool climate, for bestowing good progeny, for eternal youth, for strength of speech, etc., etc. Thus many sages have sung the glory that was Saraswati and it is difficult to bring all of them in detail here. The climax of such praises is that of the hymn of Gritsamada quoted at the beginning and it is nearly impossible to estimate the reverence implied in it.

To get such respect from the Vedic sages in such unparalleled songs what greatness was there of the river called Saraswati? Was there a river called Saraswati at all? People of the recent generations doubt the very existence of the river Saraswati and many believe theat it is a river flowing subsurface joining the revers Ganga and Yamuna at Prayag to make it sacred for pilgrims as 'Triveni'. At present the geographical maps of India do not show any such mighty river by the name Saraswati. Then is it really a subsurface river (Supta Nadi) as claimed. Why did such a famous river become a sub-surface flow? When did it become so? These are some of the questions which normally make problems for students of Indology, and in general to one and all.

The story of the river Saraswati is really very fascinating and there lies the root of the Vedic culture. It is not only a problem for historians, archaeologists but an interesting one for geologists too. The students of the earth with the help of students of sister disciplines must strive for solving the problem so that the rewriting of the early chapters of Indian history is made more authentic and real.

In tackling this problem many have made their attempt worthy of mention. Early students of the Vedas including Winternitz, Griffith, Macdonald, Blumfield, Maxmuller and others have tried to delve deep into the Vedic problem of its origin, its linguistics, its historicity. etc., but they have not been able to make out the region in which the Vedas presented to the world were percieved. Had it been attempted, possibly they could not have instituted the theory of Aryan migration into India from else where. Probably they left it for convenience of their pet theory! More probably, geological basis of such problem was less appreciated.

According to Dr. M.S. Krishnan, 1968, "The Saraswati has been described in the Vedic literature (probably 5000 B.C. or earlier) as a great river-greater even than the Indus and the Ganges. Between that and the time of Manu and *Mahabharata* its upper course had dried up, probably because of the easterly diversion of the waters of the Yamuna. The lower course in Bikaner, Bahawalpur and Sind continued to be well watered, for during the invasion of Alexander of Macedon in the fourth century B.C. and of the Arabs in the ninth century A.D. the Rann of Kutch was a fairly deep gulf and ships moved up the river into Sind. In Todd's-*Annals of Rajasthan* it is stated that the Hakra (identified with the extinct Saraswati) in Bikaner became dry for the first time about the year 1044 A.D.".

He further observed that "The river Saraswati appears to have been originated in the Siwalik hills of Sirmur on the borders of the Ambala district between the talus fans of the rivers of Yamuna in the east and of Sutlej in the west and was flowing in a general southwesterly direction finally debouching into the Rann of Kutch. The dry bed of Hakra, which is as wide as 3 to 5 miles in the territory of Bikaner, has been recognised as the course of the now extinct river

Saraswati. On both the banks of Hakra it is stated that several mounds containing remnants of prehistoric and historic settlements have been identified which revealed ruins of temples, dwellings, pot shreds, etc., of the Mohanjo-Daro type".

He continues stating hat "The withdrawal of the waters from the Sutlej, and possibly from the Jamuna, dried up the Saraswati". This is an interesting observation from the point of study of geomorphological changes due to headward erosin of a river resulting in river piracy. The silting up of the Rann of Kutch and the landward march of the desert conditions probably hastened the drying up of Sarsswati. It was finalised by the 1819 earthquake which resulted in considerable upliftment of the Rann of the Kutch".

The dried up course of the river Saraswati can be traced by a detailed study of aerial photos and land-sat imageries. The *satellite* photo studies have, viewing an area of several thousand sq. km. from space, been able to present the data so coherently which would not be possible by land survey, though land surveys carried out earlier have been able to bring out all the dried up courses of tributories of the river Saraswati. It is stated by Bhargava (1964) that the Saraswati had three original tributories and later seven and many more making it a system but observed that on the statement by Cunningham that more than geological changes, man-made canal systems during the time of Firoz Shah Tkughluq have introduced complications in an attempt to trace the original course of the river Saraswati. He averred that Drishadvati apparently formed the southern limit of the territories of the Bharatas in the days of Devavrat and probably of Manu.

This land between the rivers Saraswati and Drishadvati was called Brahmāvarta or Divine Land according to Barooah (1971). The implications of such statements can be of great use in assessing the problem. Manu, the originator of mankind according to the Hindu scripts-hence the name Maanusha for man in Sanskrit-probably lived in this part of the land evolved from the homo-sapiens, after evolution from the original primates. According to Prasad *et. al.* (1978) "The earliest record of Hominolds goes back to upper Eocene (Pondaung beds, Burma). Subsequent to the evolution of Lemurold forms, there is a wide gap in our knowledge about the radiation of Hominoids. However, the first Hominoid Ramapithecus has been recognised from Siwalik formations". These studies indicate that evidences of early man are located in the Himalayan region in the Siwalik hills and nearby regions. The river Saraswati also originated from the Siwalik hills. This is no coincidence that Manu the originator of mankind would have represented the advanced early man in this region, hence the word Brahmavarta-the land of creator-is aptly instituted. The chain of kings and law makers originating from Manu is well known from the two national historic records, *Rāmāyana* and *Mahābhārata.*

These studies indicate that the theory of Aryan migration into India from elsewhere is a myth and Manu the originator of mankind was born in the land between Saraswati and Drishadvati rivers. Manu was a sage and many sages who have seen the truth of the Vedic mantras were natives of this land of Brahmāvarta. It is quite clear from scientific data that the early theory of Aryan migration into India from outside the Indian sub-continent is incorrect. The Vedic civilisation originated and was nurtured in the land of Brahmavarta mostly. Similar to the radiation of Hominoids during the Quaternary geological period, the radiation of man after Manu took place. Man's migration to other places in Asia from the Brahmāvarta started even during the period earlier to Manu and evolved in those parts. Parallel to the Vedic culture developing on the banks of the Saraswati and Drishadvati, sages moved out and occupied various places within and outside the Indian sub-continent. According to Barooah (*ibid.*), the following lands of peoples could be recognised:

1. Āryāvarta-land between the Himalayas and the Vindhyas.
2. Madhya desha-land between the present Prayag and Vināshana.
3. Antarvedi or Samsthali-land between Ganga and Yamuna.
4. Kurukshetra/Dharmakshetra-the site of the Mahābhārata war.
5. Dakshinapatha-land south of the Vindhyas.
6. Mleccha mandala-barbaric tribes in lands bordering India.

The evidences from Central Asia and Europe reveal that those lands were peopled from India, mostly with related cultures. The cultures of the Mid-East and Central Asia have mostly originated in India. According to Josyer (1966). "The earliest emigration appears to date sometime after Manu. One of the oldest colonies founded by the Hindus was in Egypt". Count Bjornstjerna is quoted by Josyer (*ibid.*) as stating that "It is there (Āryāvarta) we must seek not only for the cradle of the Brahmin religion, but for the cradle of the high civilisation of the Hindus, which gradually extended itself in the West to Ethiopia, to Egypt, to Phoenicla; in the East to Siam, to China and Japan; in the South to Ceylon, to Java and Sumatra; in the North to Persia to Chaldaea and to Colchis, whence it came to Greece and to Rome, and at length to the remote abode of the Hyperboreans". Josyer (*ibid.*) quotes Colonel Olcott saying that "The modern school of comparative philology traces the migration of Āryan civilisation into Europe by a study of modern languages in comparison with Sanskrit. And we have an equally, if not a still more striking means of showing the outflow of Āryan thought towards the West in the philosophies and religions of Babylonia, Egypt, Greece, Rome and Northern Europe. One has only to put side by side the teachings of Pythagoras, Socrates, Plato, Aristotle, Homer, Zeno, Hesoid, Cicero, Soevola, Varro and Virgil, with those of Veda-Vyāsa, Kapila, Gauthama, Pathanjali, Kanaada, Jaimini, Nārada, Paṇini, Marīchi, and many others were might mention, to be astonished at their identity of conceptions-an identity that upon any other theory than that of a derivation of the younger philosophical schools of the West from the older ones of the East would be simply miraculous... And this again corroborates our convictions that the old Egyptians were emigrants from India; nearly all the famous ancient philosophers had been to Egypt to learn her wisdom, from the Jewish Moses to the Greek Plato".

Josyer gives the following identity of the lands of the world as seven great islands (dweepas):

| | |
|---|---|
| 1. Jamboo | Asia |
| 2. Plaksha | South America |
| 3. Pushkara | North America |
| 4. Krauncha | Africa |
| 5. Shaka | Europe |
| 6. Shaalmali | (Antarctica-Australla) |
| 7. Kusa | Oceania |

Further Josyer (*ibid.*) traces the migration of Hindus to Egypt and Ethiopea, Persia, Turkistan and Northern Asia, Scandinavia, Eastern Asia, China, Japan, Cambodia, Sumatra, Bali and the Americas. The present author (1979) has been able to bring out the details of *Sūryasiddhānta* relating to the four great islands of the world on the equator located at equal distances, probably suggesting the Chaturdweepa Vasumati concept-a concept which was instituted at the beginning of such migrations to four great lands as given below:

1. Bharatavarsha with Lanka as prime city
2. Kethumālavarsha with Rome as prime city
3. Kuruvarsha with Siddhapuri (Maya-Inca Nazka in cities)
4. Bhadrāshwavarsha with Yamakoti (Java Islands).

Later migrations probably supported to develope the concept of Saptadweepa Vasumati theory-a concept which accommodated seven islands of the globe on migration.

Thus the entire world peopled from India had their origin traceable to the banks of the river Saraswati in Brahmāvarta. The river Saraswati supported the Vedic civilisation for many thousands of years before it disappeared in the sands of Vināshana. The antiquity of the Vedic schools is really the antiquity of the river Saraswati which could be established by geological evidences.

**Conclusion**

Existence of the river Saraswati is a geological truth. It originated in the Siwalik Himalayas in the Ambala region and flowed south-west-wards into the Rann of Kutch in the vicinity of Prabhāsakshetra of the well-known Somanātha temple during the Vedic India. It was a system of rivers mightier than the present-day Sindhu, Ganga or Brahmaputra. It supported a vast land of agriculture and the oldest civilisation of Indus Valley and proto Indic. A geological study of the origin and evolution of the river system Saraswati as available in ancient Indian literature of the Vedas and other texts indicate that Āryans are local people who originated with Manu in Brahmāvarta-an area between the rivers of Saraswati and Drishadvati, from where the various world cultures radiated, later evolved in different lands.-1.83.

# 30

# The Solar Control of Mountain Formation

The Science of the Earth declares that mountains are formed of materials accumulated in the oceanic basins by slow and steady uplift and are denuded by various geological agents over long periods of time, hence unstable and the process is incessant and a cyclic one. The principal force behind this phenomenon of mountain formation, *i.e.*, orogeny appears to be due to the solar energy received by the earth, which is of the order of 2 cal per minute per square centimeter. During the long interval of geologial periods, the cumulative solar energy accounts for the enormous heat required for the stupendous phenomenon of giving rise to mountain chains, over and above the heat lost by conduction through the crust of the earth.

It is justified, therefore, to think the cycles of orogeny in terms of solar history. The sacred scriptures of the Hindus, *i.e.*, the Vedas declare that the Sun was born (formed) in Krittika star in Prabhava samvatsara, Māgha māsa, Shukla paksha, Saptami day. Therefore, it can be taken that the Nebula took the shape of the Sun from the hot clouds of the Milky Way within the arc of Krittika star, *i.e.*, approximately between $26^{0}$ 40' and $40^{0}$ 00'. His formation within the galaxy is at abouta distance of some 30,000 light-years from the centre of the galaxy, and he takes about 200 million years to complete a single rotation.

The equatorial plane of the galaxy which includes the Sun is inclined 63° to the celestial equator. The Sun's velocity being 296 km/second, his orbital movement causes the polar motion of the galaxy. Referring to the Equinox of 1950, the north pole of the galaxy was located at R.A. 12th, 49m, and declination + 27°.4'. The Sun is located at 147° .5' from the centre of the galaxy which is located at R.A. 17th, 42m. 4, declination-28° 55' (1950). Presuming that the galactic pole was located at Oh. Om. during the time of the formation of the Solar system, the history of the earth can be correlated with that of the Sun.

Major orogenic cycles have taken place at intervals of roughly about 300 million years on the surface of the earth. In all, six major cycles, three prior to the Cambrian and three post-Cambrian periods of mountain formation have been recognised. In the global scale the following cycles may be mentioned:

6. Alpine-Himalayan
5. Variscan or Hercynian
4. Caledonian

   Cambrian = fossils of advanced life

3. Killarnean
2. Animikian or Keeweenawan
1. Laurentian

Equated against the past Manwantaras of the Hindu Almanac, we arrive at the following:

6. Chākshusha
5. Raivata
4. Tāmasa

3. Uttama
2. Swārochisha
1. Swāymbhuva

Presently, the seventh Vaivaswat Manwantara is running. It appears from the above that galactic pole has traversed arcs of two hours each to the beginning of the current Manwantara. Hence it may be represented in the chart as follows:

<table>
<tr><td>-</td><td>Swayambhuva<br>Laurentian</td><td>Swarochisha<br>Animikian</td><td>Uttama<br>Killarnean</td></tr>
<tr><td>-</td><td colspan="2" rowspan="2">Chart showing the motion<br>of the<br>galaetic Pole</td><td>Tamasa<br>Caledonian</td></tr>
<tr><td>-</td><td>Raivata<br>Variscan</td></tr>
<tr><td>-</td><td>-</td><td>Currently<br>Vaivaswat</td><td>Chakshusha<br>Alpine</td></tr>
</table>

During the current Manvantara the galactic pole appears to have traversed an arc of about 49m. which brings us to the 28th mahayuga. Therefore, a clear understanding of the movement of the galactic pole will possibly enable us to evolve a standard almanac, which will be more scienficic as well as technical.

The standard stratigraphic scale of the geologist requires more perfection and it can have an astronomical scale of relative higher perfection.

The Hindu Almanac has the strong basis of astronomy, and appears to be the best of almances. If the polar movement of the galaxy could be confirmed by critical observations, it will enable readers of the earth's history to refer the pages of the history, *i.e.*, the rock units to this perfect calendar and also correlate without much doubt the existing transition formations of rocks. The 'rock-hour' unit of the galactic pole will come very handy for the modern stratigrapher.

Evolution of the Sun on the H-R diagram (Hertzsprung-Russel) shows a close influence on the crust of the earth. This evolution is chiefly based upon the changes that attend the Sun type of stars in the Universe. The solar movement controlling the motion of the galactic pole appears to be very sensitive while changing from one arc of the 2h. to the other, influencing the earth's crust to balance within itself getting relieved of the stresses which accumulate during the course of the 2h. interval of the pole.

The Sun brings about the growth of the stress field of the earth by way of regulation of the seasons. The decline of the stress field resulting in the orogeny, etc., diastrophic phenomena is brought about at the time of the galactic polar transgress of every 2h. arc. Thus the system gains rejuvenation, hence the solar control of orogeny.-141.

# 31

# Geological Veracity of Cheiro's Earthquake Prediction

World Predictions by Cheiro, first published about 1925 and reprinted in 1967, contain interesting information about the earth-quakes predicted then and to occur in later years. The Editor in the preface to the book observed that he (Cheiro) also told the commencement of series of earthquakes in countries that for hundreds of years have been more or less free from such occurrrences, and nine months in advance indicated clearly the one that occurred in the Channel Islands in July, 1926, and that it "would be followed by another over a large area of England in the autumn of the same year". The Editor also remarked that he (Cheiro) also made a valuable addition to his *Predictions* in Part III, by forecasting `Coming Earthquakes, Subsidences and Upheavals which, even while we are going to press, are being borne out to a remarkable degree'.

Cheiro, writing on the Precession of the Equinoxes recalls that it was calculated by the Chaldeans and the Hindu astronomers ages before our era. He equates the duration of solar years 2150 to the equinox to precess one zodiacal sign-70 years and 9 months for one degree, the latter having been referred to by him to the biblical "three score years and ten". He considers that the Vernal Equinox was in the first degree of Aries in the year 388 B.C. and traversed the sign Pisces upto about 1762 A.D. heralding the Aquarian age. This junction period is significant for, he relates it to the discovery of the new nation United States, birth of Napoleon, etc. He has also observed that we are now in the "Great Year of the Precession" 700 years of its larger Cusp before the precess is fully accomplished. By the year 1982, we will have passed only 220 years in this long period, and 480-year period remains to be passed.

Cheiro observed that "The coming five hundred odd years will be a period of upheaval in every sense of the term, breaking up of Empires, birth of New Nations, Revolutions and Wars, leading upto the Great Armageddon, which will take place about five hundred years from now". He continued and stated that "From another point of view the change that the Axis of the Earth is slowly and steadily undergoing as each `process' of the Equinox makes its effect, has in the past, and must in the future, cause equally important changes in the climatic conditions of each country".

His observations on the cause of earthquakes are very clear. He is convinced that the equilibrium of the centre of the globe is altered causing the earthquakes. He contended that "As the equilibrium of the centre of the globe becomes altered great earthquakes will take place in all parts of the world until the earth-crust will again become settled and normal. From now on, severe earth-tremors and quakes will affect countries which have been more or less immune from such occurrences. Extinct valcanoes all over the world will become active, while tidal waves and cyclones will cause enormous destruction to property". This conviction of Cheiro is more than scientific. It is a major step in realisation of a very important chapter in modern seismology. Even to this day, seismologists have doubts about the exact causes of earthquakes. That Cheiro had such an important vision is really amazing and call it prophesy or anything, his concept of the true cause of earthquakes is something superb.

Cheiro further observed that "During the coming 50 years an earthquake zone will develop in a North-Easterly direction from the Pacific Coast of Peru, passing through Panama and Mexico, through the Northern States and Canada to the Arctic regions". He predicted serious situation to the North American cities like Washington, New York, Buffalo, Boston and Toronto. He also said that a new ridge or belt of land will appear in the North Atlantic due to which the course of the Gulf Stream will be altered causing climatic changes in the eastern States of North America. This change will affect the north European countries which will become uninhabitable, due to the severe cold climate of advancing glaciation.

This change in the course of Gulf Stream will be compensated by the development of a temperate climate in countries like China, India and Africa, he stated. This observation is based on his views about the changes caused by the precession of equinoxes traversing the Aquarian section of the zodiac. He also mentioned that during the next 50 to 100 years (*i.e.*, from 1925 A.D.), a series of devastating earth-quakes will take place and the island of the Azores will rise from the Atlantic with the lost continent of Atlantis. This upheaval is closely connected with the break up of the Isthmus link of Panama, causing the gap between the Americas to increase in due course. Cheiro's vision has a green view to the north African continent removing the great desert of Sahara and turning the major portion of the continent into a land of temperate zone causing them to be the granaries of the world. He also foresaw the prosperity of Palestine. Most interesting is the formation of a World Government at Palestine radiating laws of life and humanity about the end of first quarter of the 24th century. By about the 24th century A.D. Cheiro predicted, the Negro, the Arab, the Hindu, and the Yellow race will be drawn into universal co-partnership whose purpose will be the uplifting of the entire human race.

In the above context one can read with advantage the observations made by Mr. G.R. Josyer in his book *Sanskrit Wisdom* including a chapter on Kaliyuga. Accordingly, it is stated that "During Kali the castes will become indistinguishable, and there will be a general mix-up. As Kali advances men will be artizans, untruthful, fond of wine and meat, and know the wives of their friends. In Kali thieves will fare like kings, and kings will act like thieves, and the servants will enjoy unfixed incomes. In Kali wealth will be spoken of highly, the character of the pious will be despised, and the fallen will not be censured. The widows, divorced from the consciousness of virtue and sin, the ascetics and men of fifteen years of age, will procreate offspring through promiscuous intercourse. In that last cycle, the villagers will sell food, the Brahmins will sell the Vedas and the women will sell their persons. The Sudras, following the tenets of Buddha, will abstain from taking meat. The beasts, with tusks and teeth, will be set to plough and carts. Men will till with the water of ponds, and the clouds will irregularly discharge their contents. Blowing high and downwards, the wind will shower dust in the rainy season. People will feel doubts about the next world. Everyone will be wicked by nature, will villify God, and be agjostic. Fruitless will be a man's joy, and fruitful will be his anger. The wicked and ignorant men, proud of their learning, will be atheists. They will have reverence for the apparent meaning, and be fond of discussions. With the decrease of the duration of life, there will be decay of strength. It will lead to pervrsity of colour, which will produce diseases. This will give, birth to repentence, leading ultimately to consciousness of God, and revival of virtue."

Though the above quotation is slightly out of context, it is pointed here to show that almost all these earlier observations have been realised in our present day world, specially in India, the cradle of human civilisation. This is all the more true in the words of Cheiro who has made similar observations in the topic entitled 'Coming Earthquakes Subsidence and Upheavals'. He stated that "Egypt, Persia, India, China tell of ages so far beyond our dreams that we wake with wonder and beg to get more light, but they themselves have lost their history, and point to silent monuments whose only language is a broken piece of stone".

Cheiro remarked further that "The more pronounced lean-over or tilt of the axis of the earth, itis logical to assume, produces new zones of earthquake activity and the reopening of long closed fissures which affect countries where earthquakes have been considered "things of the past". He has alluded to the return of volcanic activity in Mount McKinley and the eruption of Mt. Sheshadin in the Aleutian Islands. Due to the ressumption of volcanic activity in the latter on 11-11-1925, he has stated that great changes in the climate of Alaska have ·been witnessed. Similar changes in Norway have been attributed by Cheiro to the changes caused by the slowly advancing equinoctial precessiona in the current Aquarian age, perhaps the age of earthquakes!

Cheiro has then referred to many instances of land upheavals which are true of geological evidence. He then observed that "The weakest part of the earth's strata is undoubtedly a zone of belt lying 40 degrees of latitude both above and below the Equator. The northern part of the belt passes through Japan, the middle States of North America, through Spain, Italy, Turkey, Asia Minor, Persia, India and China. It affects all countries from 40 degrees down to the Equator. The southern part passes through Argentina,

South Africa, South Australia and New Zealand, and affects all countries from the $40^0$ latitude to the Equator. This zone has two great centres of activity-one in the East in or about Japan, and the other situated in the West in or about Mexico, Central America and the Isthmus of Panama. Any disturbance in any of these centres is carried by this belt from one side of the globe to the other. This central zone radiates earthquakes, shocks and tremors through fissures or cracks in the earth's crust, extending for thousands of miles in every direction. He further mentioned that "These fissures have a zig-zag formation, like forked lightening, and follow the course of least resistance through the rock outer crust of the earth. Under some circumstances they exhaust or spend their force through vent holes such as volcanoes, which accounts in a large majority of cases for the activity of volcanoes both before or after a seismic disturbance". Then he goes on with the description of some major earthquakes from newspapers of the day, including the one of Assam in 1897.

The statements of Cheiro, though popularly referred to as his prophesy, have some important scientific bearing. He has made a theory of earthquakes which considers that they are essentially to do with the motions of the equinoctial precession. He has recognised two belts of earthquakes one each girdling the earth around $40^0$ latitudes, north and south. He has also noted two centres of activity-one at about Japan and the other at about Mexico. Disturbances in these centres of activity radiate earthquake shocks through the belt.

The cause of disturbance of the centres of earthquake activity is to be traced to the movements of the precession of the equinoxes.

Geologically, the earthquake belts and the belts of volcanoes almost coincide and are recognised to be the Alpine-Himalayan and Circumpacific. The exact causes of earthquakes are yet not understood excepting for the fact that they may be due to motion of earthblocks along well-defined deep-seated faults due to water seapage or isostatic adjustments of subsidence and upheavals of land masses. Though much data have been collected since the theory of propagation of and origin of earthquakes was propounded on modern lines by Oldham on the basis of the 1897 Assam earthquake, no definite cause has been pinpointed for the origin of earthquakes.

Cheiro's theory fixes the cause of earthquakes to the movements of precession of equinoxes. But the prophesy part of the theory can perhaps be substituted by a recognition of the earlier concepts of the earthquakes mentioned by Varāhamihira in his text *Brihatsamhita.* While the terrestrial truths have been presented in a general way by Cheiro, the extraterrestrial truths of the cause of earthquakes could be well culled out from observations made in Bhūkampalakshana-adhyaaya by Varāhamihira.

Much of the information based on these observations have been presented by the author in the following papers published in the earlier isssues of The Astrological Magazine. For easy reference they are mentioned below:

1. Causes of Earthquakes October 1967, p. 934.
2. Forecasting Earthquakes-I, January, 1969, pp. 42-46.
3. Forecasting Earthquakes-II, April 1969, pp. 409-412.
4. Varahamihira on Earthquakes, May 1969, p. 548.
5. Tides and Earthquakes. June 1970, pp. 568-69.
6. Planetary Purturbations and Earthquakes, January 1973. pp. 32-34 and 40.
7. Prognotication of Earthquakes, May 1974, pp. 407-09.

Dr. B.V. Raman, in his address "Astrology and Earthquakes" to the scientists of the National Geophysical

Research Institute, Hyderabad, A.P. on 6.7.1981 observed that "astrological data lent support to the theory of correlation of planetary configuration with natural disasters. The groupings of planets in certain signs (of the zodiac) showed significant correspondence with earthquakes". According to him "earthquakes generally occurred on or two days before or one or two days after eclipses and new moon and full moon days". He predicted the solar eclipse of 31st July 1981 and also indicated the powerful earthquake in Iran and Turkey which came true. He has also predicted occurrence of earthquakes in Turkey, Mexico, Iran, Japan and Western Asia when Jupiter moved into the zodiacal arc of Libra, particularly traversing the arc of Chitta constellation (*A.M.* October 1981).

Though predictions based on Indian Theory are being successful, there is much scope for perfection in it. The exact time and location of earthquakes yet remain matters of much conjecture and need refinement.

It is a matter of great interest and satisfaction that Dr. Raman has appealed to the scientists not to ignore as powerful a tool as astrology in tackling the problem of earthquake prediction. The big gap that exists between the terrestrialists and the celestialists in dealing with the above problem can only be narrowed by each appreciating the others' point of view.

In the context of the above, the author proposes to the authorities concerned in the various Institutions of the States, Government of India and International Seismological Institutions to form a forum with competent astrologers to get into a dialogue and to propose concrete projects of research based on all these observations to tackle the problem of earthquake prediction in right earnest to help mankind to face this monster. The problem, if it could find a satisfactory solution, should be pursued, irrespective of the discipline of knowledge receiving the seal of science or not. With this in mind, the author of the paper earnestly appeals to all those concerned to consider the proposal and advance in research based on Astro-Geological data on modern lines. To start with a meeting of the Committee with members including the following may be called at a suitable place and time to discuss the proposals and advance research projects:

1. The Director General, India Meteorologial Department.
2. The Director General, Geological Survey of India, Calcutta-16.
3. The Director, Earthquake Engineering Research Intitute, Roorkee.
4. The Director, National Geophysical Research Institute, Hyderabad, A.P.
5. Dr. B.V. Raman, Editor, The Astrological Magazine, Bangalore-20.
6. Director, Seismological Observatory, Pasadena, California, USA.
7. Selected Seismologists from USSR, Sweden, Japan, New Zealand, Mexico, Iran, Iraq, and other countries in the sesimic belt.-6.82.

# 32

# Varahamihira on Earthquakes

Of the earliest observational records available to us on the Hindu Astronomy, those of Varāhamihirāchārya of the city of Ujjain merit our attention in the field of predictive science regarding the occurrence of earthjquakes. The book *Brihatsamhita* authored by Varāhamihirāchārya contains a complete summary of the earlier views of various astronomers like Kāshyapa, Parāsara, Garga and Vasishta. According to him the earthquakes occur in the north-west, south-east, east and west, most probably with reference to Ujjain, in the first, second, third and the fourth parts of the day (three hours each) and night, respectively.

I. The earthquakes occur in the north-west direction when the Moon transits the below-given arcs of the zodiac:

146° 40' to 200° 00'; 0° 00' to 13° 20' and 80° 00' to 93° 20'.

A week ahead the sky is rendered dark being filled with smoke in all the directions and tempestuous wind strike the ground removing the trees. Due to the smoke-covered sky the ground recevies a weak Sun's rays.

II. The earthquakes occurring in the south-eastern direction happen when the Moon will be transiting the below-mentioned arcs of the zodiac:

13° 20' to 40° 00'; 93° 20' to 106° 40'; 120° 00' to 146° 40'; 200° 00' to 213° 20' and 320° 00' to 333° 20'.

These are suggested by the fall of large meteores and a sort of burning sky a week ahead.

III. The Moon's transit of the below given sections of the arc of the zodiac bring about the earthquakes in the eastern direction:

40° 00' to 53° 20'; 213° 20' to 240° 00' and 266° 40' to 306° 40'.

Heavy pourdown associated with lightning and thunder will preceed a week of these earthquakes.

IV. Occurrence of the earthquakes in the west will be there during the transit of the Moon in the below given sections of the zodiac:

66° 40' to 80° 00'; 106° 40' to 120° 00'; 240° 00' to 266° 40'; 306° 40' to 320° 00' and 333° 20' to 360° 00'.

A week head there may be heavy rains without any thunder or lightning of appreciable nature.

Varāhamihira observes further that the quakes commenced from the east will die out in the west and the reverse is true. Similarly wih the other pair of directions.

The earthquakes occurring in the first group of arcs vanish during the second part of the day or night. Similarly those earthquakes occurring during the second part of the day or night die out during the Moon's transit of the first group of arcs of the zodiac. This is true for the other groups and the parts of the day and night.

If the earthquakes occasion during the first part of the day or night when the Moon is transiting the first group of arcs, they will be severe.

The four parts of the day and night are considered to be comprising of single time waves of 90 minutes rise and an equal time of fall. This time wave is further divided into the multiples of 6' each as given below:

| | | |
|---|---|---|
| I | ... | 6' |
| II | ... | 12' |
| III | ... | 18' |
| IV | ... | 24' |
| V | ... | 30 |
| | | 90' |

and the earthquakes are found generally confined to the I and the IV sections of the time wave.

But these observations are so empirical that conclusions based on them are not proving successful in forecasting the earthquakes.

Modern geological studies have declared that the Alpine Himalayan belt is a weak zone of the earth and earthquakes of quite high magnitude have visited this belt often. This viewed from the angle of the author of *Brihatsamhita* is true to this day, for, he did recognise the NW-SE and the E-W directions of the earthquakes with references to location Ujjain.

However, they were able to read out the earthquakes against the factor of time and list made out above may possibly be a statistical review of the study of the earthquakes extended over a long stretch of time.

The results of the observations as it stands do not reveal the cause of the earthquakes. Morover, the range of specification is so wide and the hints given for occasioning so simple and common, the forecasting of the earthquakes based on the above have not been supported.-308.

# 33

# Prognostication of Earthquakes

"At present there is no possibility of earthquake prediction in the popular sense; that is, no one can justifiably say that an earthquake of consequence will affect a named locality on a specified future date. It is uncertain whether any such prediction will be possible in the foreseeable future; the conditions of the problem are highly complex. One may compare it to the situation of a man who is bending a board across his knee and attempts to determine in advance just where and when the cracks will appear," remarks a leading authority in seismology, C.F. Richtor, Further writing under the head "Amateurs and Astrologers" he comments that "Some predictors are astrologers and professional soothsayers, who claim to foretell future events of all kinds. Some are astrologers in disguise, who are actually basing predictions on the positions of the planets but justify them by some alleged mysterious radiation or modification of the law of gravitation". He also says that "Predictions based on positions of the Sun and the Moon have to be regarded a trifle more seriously, since there is evidence that tidal forces may occasionally act as triggers for earthquake otherwise on the point of taking place; in this way the dates and hours of occurrence may show a slight statistical correlation with the tides". He also gives a case history of an Italian earthquake predictor.

As Prof. B.V. Raman remarks "people are not frank" and scientists, especially do not like to accept anything outside the otrthodox field of science. They are much more conservatives than the religionists.

Prof. Raman in his book *A Hindu in America* states that "Among the non-astrologers, the contribution of Dr. Rudolf Tomaschek to the seismological aspect of astrology is indeed praisworthy. Dr. Tomaschek... is a former Director of the Institute of Physics, Munich. For the first time in recent times in the West, he sensed that the cause of earthquakes was extra-terrestrial. He arrived at significant conclusions on the correlations between earthquakes and planetary movements. Using 134 severe quakes between 1900 and 1957, Dr. Tomaschek uncovered what Western scientific circles consider an amazing fact concerning the placement of Uranus at the time and epicentre of the disturbance. In nearly 70% of the cases studied, Uranus "was mysteriously near the meridian of the place squaring or trining Jupiter, Saturn or Mars" (p. 230).

A leading scientific journal *Tectonophy* sics issued a special volume *Earthquake Prediction* presenting the papers by leading scientists on the topic at the proceedings of a symposium held during October 1967 at Zurich, which gave an upto-date impression of the present state of earthquake prediction work", but did not ventur any forecasts.

J.F. Simpson of Goddyear Aerospace Corporation, observed in his interesting article "Solar activity as a Triggering Mechanism for Earthquakes" (*Earth and Planetary Science Letter,* Vol. 5, No. 3, February 1968) that "Maximum quake frequency occurs at times of moderatly high and fluctuating solar activity. Terrestrial solar flare effects which are the actual coupling mechanisms which trigger quakes appear to be either abrupt accelerations on the earth's anglar velocity or surges of telluric currents in the earth crust" and has presented graphs to assist probablistic forecasting of earthquakes when used in conjunction with local indicators.

The writer has examined the problem from various points of view and has presented the ideas in earlier articles in The Astrological Magazine (October 1967, January and August 1969, and January 1973).

There are however some scientists who believe that forecasting of earthquakes is no part of seismology at all. If it is not be included in modern seismology, the problem will certainly be included in what can be referred to as celestial dynamics. If the outside or external feature of the earth are to be explained in terms of genic forces, the problem of earthquakes remains to be explained by the same principles or theory. However, in mundane astrology, this branch has received as much attention as possible from astrologers. The simple observation that the eqarthquakes are expected during certain planetary combinations of significance underlies much of the history of geodynamics.

The earth should be deemed to be a ball of matter with movements in space set in geodynamical equilibrium. The endogenic forces of the earth are either due to chemical changes or physical (mechanical/dynamical) forces. Even chemical changes should seek a cause in the final analysis. Hence it boils down to the fact that physical forces producing the stresses and strains in the earth are caused by its movements, which are caused by forces of gravitation. Thus the problem escalates and the ulterior cause for the earthquakes are to be found in the extrāterrestrial field.

A simple theory formulated by the writer was presented in the January and April issues of the Astrological Magazine for

1969, by which the astrological observations for predicting the earthquakes were explained in terms of dynamics. The importance of angular momements of planetary bodies in the theory was realised and taken advantage of to explain the cause of earthquakes. The earthquakes which rocked the Indian Peninsula with considerable effect during the past seventy years were examined in that light and significant conclusions were drawn.

In the present write-up, the writer brings out a relation between the global strain release and the changes in the path of the resultant angular momenta of remote planets From a dynamical fluctuation it is clear that the earth is constrained to its various movement. Hence, there should be clear relationship between the accumulated stress in the earth over periods of geological history, and the changes in the path of resultant angular momenta of remote planets, and the angular velocity of a planet is characterised by the planet in motion. These considerations show some changes in the path of the resultant angular momenta of planets obtained for future ages would indicate possible timing of cumulated stress in the earth. For the given time of stress accumulation, the behaviour of the gravity map of the earth would make it possible to localise the area of release of strain, *i.e.*, quake.

A graph is presented here showing the path of the resultant angular momenta of remote planets during the period 1880 to 2050 A.D. The remote planets, Jupiter, Saturn, Uranus and Neptune have considerable angular momenta. This fact has been taken into consideration and their position aintervals of every ten years has been utilised in arriving at the resultant. The resultant has been obtained by a simple geometric method by taking the proportionate (angular momenta) between two adjacent planets in the planetary trapezia and finding a common point for all the four members.

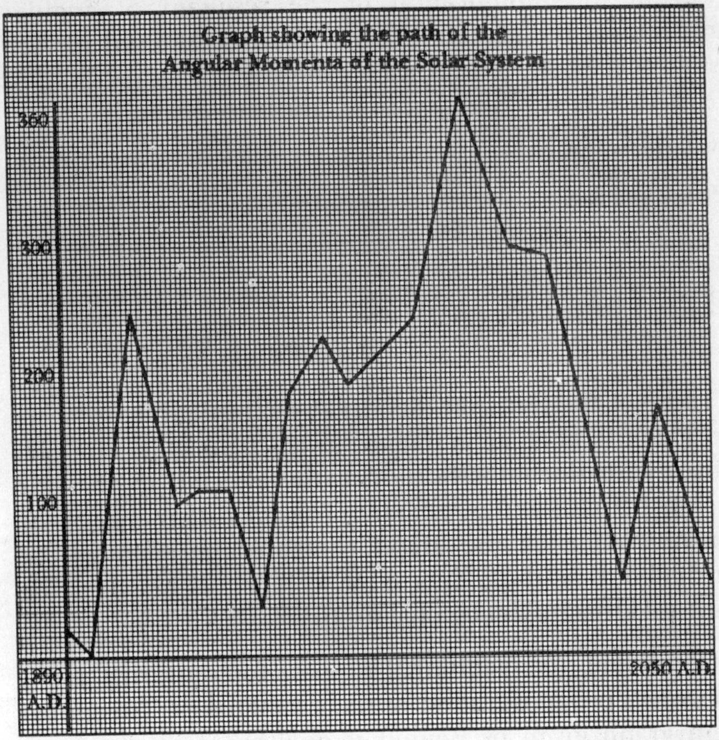


The resultant of angular momenta of remote planets is an extremely sensitive point. Its abrupt change in its otherwise smooth path should indicate some kind of dynamical inequilibrium, the accumulated stresses have to be relieved of the system. The global strain graph has been prepared by Benioff for 1900 to 1955 A.D. (p. 369, *Elementary Seismology*, by C.F. Richtor, 1969). Hence, it is reasonable to make a comparison of the global strain graph with the graph accompanying this paper.

In considering the angular momenta of the planets, the satellite Moon and the star Sun, and those, of inner planets, Mars and Pluto, and of the Moon have been left out for simplicity's sake. However, they are negligible but they have a say in the modification of the resultant of angular momenta of the remote planets when considered for the system accurately. If we consider the angular momentum of the earth as unit X, then those of others are given;

| I | II |
|---|---|
| Mercury 0.03 x X | Jupiter 725 x X |
| Venus 0.69 x X | Saturn 294 x X |
| Mars 0.13 x X | Uranus64 x X |
| Pluto X? | Neptune 95 x X |

Those of the Sun and the Moon are negligible when we consider the angular momenta of the planets in group II above. With due modification to be effected to the line tracing the path of the resultant of angular momenta of the remote planets in the graph presented here, it can be concluded that there is a close comprison between the graph and the graph of global strain release.

This would give additional support for venturing a not too unreal prognostication of the earthquakes. The global strain graph given by Benioff is only based on the large shallow earthquakes. The shallow and deep focus earthquakes, if considered, modify the graph.

Based on the changes of the resultant angular momenta of the remote planets, a first approximation to impending quakes, rather the time of accumulated stress demanding release, can be made out. The graph can be refined further by plotting the resultant for every year, month, day and the moment of release of stress, based on the same method. That would indicate the exact timing of an impending earthquake.

Richtor states that "These bursts of high activity (release of global strain) were during 1896?-1900, 1904-1907, 1917-1924, 1931-1935, 1938-1942, possibly 1945-1948 and 1950."

From the graph presented here, these periods can easily be correlated. Close comparison could be made if the graph showing the resultant is prepared for intervals of day, when the fact will be clear. However, the trend is satisfactory even at intervals of ten years.

From the graph, it can be discerned that there would be much seismic activity during 1990-2000 and 2000-2010 and 2020-2030 and about 2040. The sudden rise and fall in the path of the resultant is a clear indication of the time of stress accumulation and strain release. Since the interval is large, yearly interpretation can only be given after refining the graph. Similarly for the month and the day. Computerisation of the programme would indicate the future dates of earthquake with certainty.-290.

From the graph presented here these periods can easily be understood. Closer comparison could be made if the graph showing the results is reproduced in intervals of days, then the fact will be clear. However, the trend is evident even in intervals of ten years.

From the graph it can be concluded that there would be much seismic activity during 1990-2000 and 2008-2016 and 2026-2030 and about [illegible] The sudden rise and fall in the pace of the resultant [illegible] The seismic disturbances [illegible] and [illegible] large [illegible] periods [illegible] comparison [illegible] and the [illegible] would indicate the future dates of earthquakes with certainty.250

# 34

# Causes of Earthquakes

An analysis of the geophysical phenomena of the annual period of variation like the variation of angular velocity of the Earth's rotation, the oscillation of the poles, the rate of drift of geomagnatic field etc. suggests that they are caused by the annual fluctuation in the Earth's gravitational constant.[1] Variation in the Earth's gravitational constant is generally accompanied by the annual periodic fluctuation in the radius of the Earth.[1] A reduction in the radius of the Earth results in the increase of radial and tangential compression, which causes imbalance in the stress field of the Earth. The two weak belts of the crust of the Earth, *i.e.*, the Alpine-Himalayan and the Circumpacific, being the most vulnerable zones, respond to the stress imbalance occasioning earthquakes.

The greatest increase in the rotation of the Earth about its axis takes place around June-July (maximum on the 5th of June) when the most rapid reduction in the radius of the Earth is possible causing the maximum frequency of the earthquakes during the period. During June-July the constellation of Taurus forms the background to the Sun. There is a powerful radio wave emitter, the Crab nebula (Decl. + 22°03' : R.A. 05h 31.4m), remnant of the supernova exploded in 1054 A.D.[2] The radio waves passing through the Sun's corona have a peculier effect on the geomagnetic field which is responsible for all the geotectonic processes, as a result of the influence of which magnetic storms, volcanos and earthquakes occur with maximum frequency during such periods. The relation between the geomagnetic field and the thermal processes inside the basaltic volcano has been satisfactorily interpreted after detailed studies of the volcano Mihara on Osima island, Japan.[3] Increase in the volcanic activity and recovery after its ceasing, was found due to demagnetization and magnetization of the volcanic mass, resulting in the local anomaly of the geomagnetic field over the volcanic area. The change in magnetization was considered to be due to the heating and cooling of the volcanic mass *i.e.,* the thermo-remnant magnetization, (T.R.M.). In July 1950 the volcano became active and ceased to be so in June 1951. Instead of the interpretation that the demagnetization was a result of increase in the temperature of the volcanic mass, the reverse would stand if it was due to the abnormality caused by the solar effect during the period in question.

Although several attempts were made by earlier workers for detecting geomagnetic variation in cases of earthquakes, it was not possible to bring out any relation between them as a result of the geomagnetic surveys carried out before and after the earthquake in Western Japan in 1946. Since it has been found out that the geomagnetic field influences the Earth's gravitational constant, in turn the stress field of the Earth, variations in geomagnetic field effects the stress field, however, indirectly. The geomagnetic field is influenced by the magnetic field of the Sun and the integalectic and intragalectic magnetic fields. Since high energy cosmic rays influence these magnetic fields, the orign of these rays being still under research it can safely be assumed to have orginated from the exploding supernova. Since supernova happen to be the source of radio waves has to do with the directions of influence of various magnetic fields. However, the distribution of the sources of radio waves being not in any regularity, the major planes of disturbances have to be determined. In general, these planes of disturbances have to do with the planes of weak zones in the crust of the Earth, the zones of catastrophic upheavels.

The following conditions require fulfilment for the earthquakes to occur:

(1) The Earth, the Sun and the exploding supernova should align in one plane so that the magnetic field of the supernova can influence that of the Sun which in turn influence the geomagnetic field, all forming an activēmagnetic-plane.

(2) Since the vertical oscillatory movements of the crust of the Earth will be (maximum) felt in the weak belts of the Earth, the areas including the HimalayāNagāLushai block, *i.e., the Alpine Himalayan belt and the Circumpacific belt should fall within the active-magnetic-plane.*

(3) The direction of the plane of maximum disturbance caused by extra terrestrial bodies will determine the direction of the release of strain at the level of the Earth's crust.

With the above assumption it is also possible to predict eqrthquakes sufficiently in advance, based upon the coincidence of the weak belts of the Earth and the active-magnetic-plane. Timing and location of earthquakes, a function of this coincidence, needs detailed observation before any clear prediction can be ventured.

Although the radio stars have been distributed throughout the sky, the following may be considered for their activity on the crust of the Earth.2 Of the radio stars Cassiopeia-A (+ 58032' * 23 h. 21.2 m.), Taurus-A, i.e., Crab nebula (+ 220 * 5 h. 31.4 m.), Cygnus loop (+ 30048' * 20 h.

49.5 m.) and Auriga (460 * 5 h. 01 m.), are supernova remnants. The Orion nebula (- 5027' * 5 h. 33 m.) and the Trifid nebula (- 23002' * 17 h. 59 m.) are ionised hydrogen regions. Excepting the Virgo-A (12049' * 12 h. 28.2 m.), which is a peculiar galaxy, the other extra galactic radio stars are Cygnus-A (40035' * 19 h. 57.8 m.), Centaurus-A (- 42035' * 13 h. 22.4 m.) and the 3C 295 (52026' * 14 h. 09.5 m.) which are interacting galaxies. The magnetic influences of these stars are under study for considering the phenomenon of earthquakes.

The influence of the high energy cosmic rays upon the magnetic field of the Sun is changed by the pattern of the planets also. The planetary patterns indicative of the earthquakes are just surfacial observations but the scientific basis for the occurrence of earthquakes appears to be due to extra terrestrial causes, particularly the supernova explosion. The planetary dispositions observed so far, at the time of earthquakes, just corroborate the heavenly activity.[8 and 9]

Based on the above discussion, the suggestions put forward for the occurrence of earthquakes may form the basis of what may be referred to as Astro-Seismology, a subject of vast interest developing at the frontiers of two oceanic branches of study. Researches in the above field may give scope to enlarge our understanding about the relation that may exist between cosmic and terrestrial activities.-184.

## References

1. Kropotkin, P.N. and Trapeznikov, Yu.A. (1965) "Variation of the angular velocity of the Earth's rotation, the oscillation of the pole and the rate of drift of geomagnetic field and the possible association with the geomagnetic processes." International Geology Review, vol. 7, no. 11, pp. 1949-1962.

2. Pears Cyclopaedia-1963-64, 72nd Edn.
3. Nagata, T. (1961) Rock Magnetism
4. Hoyle, F. (1957) Frontiers of Astronomy
5. Hazra, P.C. and Ray, D.K. (1962) "A short note on seismic phenomena in India and their relation to tectonics" Indian Minerals. vol. 16, no. 3, pp. 241-246.
6. Voldavets, V.I. (1965) International symposium on forecasting volcanic eruptions and relationship between types of eruptions and corresponding magma typēInternational Geology Review vol. 7, no. 3, pp. 501-503.
7. Irwin, E. (1964) Palaeomagnetism.
8. Ketkar, R.N. (1967) "Prediciting Earthquakes". The Astrological Magazine, vol. O.S. 56, no. 7, pp. 665-668 and 698-699.
9. Varahamihira's Bṛhatsamhita-Vimala interpretation Chokhamba Vidyabhavan Publication, Varanasi, India, 1959.

3. Press, F. [illegible] 2nd Ed.

Stacey, F. [illegible] Rock Magnetism.

4. [illegible] (1959) [illegible] Magnetism.

[illegible] and [illegible] "[illegible] earthquakes" [illegible]

5. [illegible] (1969). In: National Symposium on [illegible] and [illegible] [illegible] Roorkee [illegible]

[illegible]

6. [illegible] "[illegible] earthquakes" [illegible] [illegible] and [illegible]

[illegible] Publication, [illegible], India.

# 35

# Planetary Perturbations and Earthquakes

Despite spectacular advancement in seismology it has been hard to expect an earthquake at a certain place. Even the leading authorities in this specialised field of study amongst the earth sciences make the modest observation that there has been no method so far known for telling an earthquake in advance. It is a fact that the problem of forecasting earthquakes is extremely complex. Reason for not yet propounding a theory for prediction is evident from the fact that the collection of data necessary for a formulation is still continuing and the cause for earthquakes is still in the stage of speculation. Whether earthquakes cause faults or slight creep along the established planes of dislocation in the crust of the earth is the cause for occurrence of earthquakes is uncertain. Sudden release of strain accumulated in certain zones of weakness in the crust of the earth, favoured by many, suggest and speculate that the strain is caused by some extra-terrestrial forces. Some kind of cause is noted by a few authorities in the development of sunspots, through magnetic disturbances. Some authorities think that fluctuation in the gravitational constant may cause earthquakes. As such the cause of earthquakes is not known for certain and a formal theory for predicting earthquakes has not been possible.

"Tidal forces may act as triggers for earthquakes otherwise on the point of taking place," says an authority, but no serious studies seem to have been carried out on these lines, excepting some statistical correlations. If it be so, attempts to solve the problem of earthquake prediction based only on the study of forces acting from within the crust of the earth is partial. May be that unilateral interpretations based on the planetary movements alone are also partial. Hence a co-ordination of the fields of study is essential to prepare the blue print of a theory to predict the earthquakes.

It must be realised that the earth is in dynamic equilibrium with other members of the solar system. Considering about the dynamics of rigid bodies rotating about a fixed axis it is noted according to D'Alembert that the system of effective forces (the forces acting from within) is as a whole statically equivalent to the system of external forces. Subject to the attractions of the other members of the solar system, the simple eliptic motion of the earth departs in a complex manner, generally referred to as purturbation. Study of the purturbations produced in the orbit of one rigid body by the attraction of other rigid bodies is a special problem of Celestial Machanics.

The nature of perturbation of the earth's orbit at the time of certain specific dispositions of other planets forming conjunction, opposition, square, sextile etc. relations must be studied in precise detail. The strain map of the earth should be examined in the light of the purturbations of the earth's orbit and the intensity of purturbations necessary to ascertain before it would be possible to theorise prediction.

The surface features of the earth are but skin depth in proper perspective. The earth as an oblate spheroid for all purposes with about 6400 km. radius, contains three shells and including the crust they are referred to as mantle and the core. Leaving about 40 km. thick crustal material, some 2850 km. mantle material next and the rest (the core) make up the earth The crust is mostly consisting of aluminium silicates; 90% of the mantle is made of magnesium, iron and silica while the core is believed to be consisting of nickel and iron. The shells appear to be separated with clarity and the earth moving on its orbit can cause slight shift in the disposition of the shells with reference to the centre of the earth when purturbed. This shift may also disturb the position of the gravity centre of the earth (which is different from the body centre) and the centre of the earth-moon system Under such disturbed condition it would be natural to expect earthquakes.

It is observed by a superior authority that the earth although rigid like steel when small rocks are examined deforms like a putty under the influence of forces extensive in space and time. It is a great wonder that the earth/is dancing her way in spite of the forces internal and external. But for the dynamical equilibrium the earth would have been resolved into space. An unstable earth may look hard but is literally weak.

The earth in motion is constrained and moves on its orbit under equilibrium conditions. Purturbation produced in the orbit of the earth by the attraction of other planets specially Jupiter and Saturn can be described by considering the effect as due to instantaneous impulses A force which produces a finite change of momentum in a time too short to be appreciated is regarded as infinitely great and the time of action infinitely short. Such an effect is possible when the planets are distributed only in certain patterns, but not always in a system of moving bodies. Due to this instantaneous impulse the velocities are changed in order to keep the total impulse of the two bodies or a system of bodies mutually equal and opposite. The sudden change in the velocity of a body shifts the axis of rotation of the body for the time integral out of the mass centre. To keep the forces in equilibrium the mass centre of a body in motion should not only lie along the axis of rotation but the axis of rotation should be a principal axis. The shift in the mass centre of the body, under the instantaneous impulse, out of the principal axis of rotation tends to wrench the axis. As a result of the shear the crust is disturbed which can be described as an earthquake.

The origin of an earthquake may be a point, a line or an area as a whole. Location of the origin of an impending earthquake by mechanical failure or disequilibrium is possible on a clear understanding of the strain map of the earth but this problem is rendered more complex by other factors. However, based on these concepts, one of the causes of the earthquakes being rationalised, the focus of an earthquake can be predicted and astrological methods of prediction can be brought into effect.

The strength of the planets (rūpas in astrology) for these purposes are to be replaced by their respective specific angular momenta and the instantaneous impulses of the combined planetary forces (from various patterns) calculated affecting the degree of shift of the mass centre of the earth from the position of the principal axis of rotation. The result would indicate on the basis of the direction of wrench the location of the focus within the earth.

A recent study of the extent of sudden ground movements on active fault in 44 world earthquakes revealed that some 24 shocks could be correlated with suspected or established steeply dipping tear faults or wrench faults. This study suggests that more than half the number of major earthquakes are related to wrench or tear faults. The wrench tectonics of the earth as a whole should be deemed to be in some kind of relation to the shifting of mass centre of the earth from the position of principal axis of rotation based on 'geodynamical considerations when the orbit of the earth is under perburation. This would clarify the relation that exists between sudden jerks or concussions the earth suffers due to perturbation and the consequent earthquake.

The cause for the shifting of the mass centre of the earth from its position in the principal axis of rotation of the earth under perturbation can be analysed and the planet or planets responsible for inducing the orbital change can be decided. Consider for illustration the disposition of planets at the time of great Bihar earthquake at about 2.15 p.m. on January 15, 1934. It appears that Saturn. Mars, Venus, Mercury and the Sun are all grouped together within an arc of $35^0$ around one of the nodes of the Moon. Jupiter is disposed almost at a triangle to the grouping and the earthquake occurred about longitudes in trine to the above two groups.

(Approx.) Geocentric longitudes of the various planets at thc time of the earthquake are given below:

| | | |
|---|---|---|
| Saturn | ... | $9^s 23^0$ |
| Jupiter | ... | $5^s 30^0$ |
| Mars | ... | $9^s 21^0$ |
| Sun | ... | $9^s 02^0$ |
| Venus | ... | $10^s 02^0$ |
| Mercury | ... | $8^s 30^0$ |
| Rahu | ... | $9^s 27^0$ |
| Kethu | ... | $3^s 27^0$ |
| Moon | ... | $8^s 28^0$ |
| Ascendant | ... | $2^s 02^0$ |

Epicentral area can be considered as Monghyr in North Bihar about 87°E longitude, and the origin or the focus of the earthquake was calculated to be some 14-15 km. below the surface of the earth between E longitudes 86°-87° at about N. latitudes 25°-26°. The astrological rasi chart is given below:

| | | | |
|---|---|---|---|
| | | | Ascendant |
| Venus | RASI | | Kethu |
| Rahu<br>Saturn<br>Mars<br>Sun | | | |
| | Moon<br>Mercury | | Jupiter |

It may be of interest to note that it was also a day of Uttarāyaṇa, *i.e.,* the day of the Sun's entry into Capricorn. It was also a period when the earth was nearer to the Sun.

It can be seen from the above that the earth is subject to a peculiar set of force of shear or couple under the planetary pattern. Since the inclination of the orbits of Jupiter and Mercury is not much to the Equator, the specific angular momenta of these two can be considered together as also that of the Sun. But the orbits of Saturn, Venus and Mars are considerably inclined to the Equator but nearer to that of the earth, the specific angular mementa of these three can be considered to act in a particular plane. The numerical factor can be resolved resulting in the evolution of shear subjecing the earth to wrench. The forces acting in different planes are given below:

| *Group* | *Planets* | | *Specific Angular Momenta* | | *Inclination of Equator to the Orbit* | |
|---|---|---|---|---|---|---|
| I | Jupiter | ... | 28.28 | = 2.89 | 3° | 7' |
| | Mercury | ... | 0.61 | | 7° | ? |
| II | Saturn | ... | 3.08 | = 5.16 | 26° | 45' |
| | Venus | ... | 0.85 | | 23° | ? |
| | Mars | ... | 1.23 | | 24° | |

That of the Sun being about 20, groups in the I and the plane of inclination of the orbits of the members of the I group is within 7° while the plane of inclination of the orbits of the members of the II group is varying from 23° to 27°. The latter group conforms to that of the earth's orbital inclination of 23° 27' to the Equator and can be thought of in some kind of equilibrium. In the specific pattern of their distribution at the time of the earthquake, the two groups are in trine and the earthquake focus occurred at the third point of the triangle.

A mathematical resolution of the forces acting in the horizontal plane and the plane at an angle to the Equator is beyond the scope of the paper. It turns out to be a difficult geodynamical problem involving wrench tectonics of the earth. Suffice it to say that the astrological observation that the earthquake occurs consequent upon certain patterns of the planetary disposition, is true beyond question. An attempt at precise prediction requires additional extensive research and observations.

A shift in the mass centre of the earth most probably accounts for the abrupt changes in the angular velocity of the earth, variation in the day time, G constant, geomagnetic field, etc. It is also likely that the shift in the mass centre of the earth accounts for readjustment or redistribution of electrical conductivity inside the earth. Almost all the causes speculated till now as possible causes of the earthquakes seem to owe their origin to the shifting of position in the mass centre of the earth consequent upon the planetary perturbations. Hence, formulation of a sound theory based on planetary dynamics would be very necessary to predict the sudden shifting of the mass centre of the earth from its position along the principal axis of rotation due to planetary perturbations. The disposition of the forces in different planes and the occurrence of wrench as a result of specific patterns needs to be calculated. The direction of the release of strain to be ascertained under conditions of wrench suggests the likely position of focus of the impending earthquake.

A planet's entry into a group or to a critical position in the planetary disposition pattern marks significant changes. This can be substantiated in the case under consideration. Although Venus, Saturn and Mars were already moving about the Moon's node with Jupiter in a triangular position from them, it appears that it was the Sun's entry into a closer group which affected the balancing forces. The system of wrench appears to have been critical on the entry of the Sun within an arc of about $20^0$ from the position of Mars. The stability of the earth under the triangular forces seems to have been affected more by the Sun's entry into Capricorn. The Sun was also in the system and his say was not there till this disposition. The balance force changed at an angle of the triangle resulting in the sudden change in the mass centre of the earth due to perturbation. This observation need not be the same for all cases, but stress is laid on the general pattern or the distribution of the planets, which has been recognised by many astrological authorities.

In the above connection an observation made by earlier writers may be of interest.

In the day time and night the first three hours if any earthquake occurs it is reterred to as vāyavya kampa, the second three hours as hauthāśa kampa, the third three hours as māhendra kampa and the fourth three hours as varuṇa kampa. This observation seems to be in conformity with the two groups of orbital planes of the planets mentioned earlier, the equatorial plane and the other plane at an angle to the equatorial plane. Whether the earthquakes referred to above are related to the respective systems of the wrench forces is to be examined.-7.

# 36

# Tides and Earthquakes

The rise and fall of the level of the oceans twice at a place in a little more than a day was ascribed by Newton to the gravitational attraction of the Moon and the Sun (Baker, 1965). The gravitational attraction increases as the celestial bodies come closer; hence, the part of the ocean directly facing the Moon is pulled up to a greater distance than that which faces away from the Moon. The oceans, thus, assume the shape of an ellipsoid of revolution, generally with its major axis directed toward the Moon. Due to the eastward motion of the earth under the tide figure, the high tide occurs at a place of observation at 12 hrs. 25m. intervals and the low tide at times half way between them. Thus the tide crests, occurring in succession, move westward around the earth. Due to the friction caused by the ocean floor the longitude directly under the Moon is ahead of the longitude of the tidal crest causing certain amount of displacement by observation. Harmonic analyses of a year's tidal observations registered by means of automatic tidegauges at standard ports give harmonic constants for tidal predictions.

The New or Full Moon causes spring tides and when disposed square to the Sun, neep tides occur as a result of one set of tides being neutralised by the other. The difference in the level of low and high tides will be specially great when the perigee Moon joins or opposes the Sun.

The earth itself undergoes deformation under the luni-solar tides but to a much smaller extent. Hence, the observed tides give the differences between the earth and the ocean tides.

The luni-solar positions noted at the time of four Indian earthquakes, *i.e.*, Kangra-4-4-1905, Quetta-31-5-1935, Assam-15-8-1950 and Assam. 12-6-1897 are significant in the above context. In the first three cases, it happened to be the New Moon while in the last case the Moon had squared the Sun.

Although the Sun contains the lion's share of the mass of the Solar system, the tide producing force of the Sun is less than half that of the Moon. Even then the implications of such a luni-solar disposition during the earth-quakes is apparent in influencing the crust of the earth pulling it out to a greater distance against the unyielding core, the ride crest of which sweeps the areas of similar lungitude. The forces of attraction sweeping the crust rupture the rocks under stress reaching the limit of elasticity releasing strain through the weak planes already in existence or evoking new planes of weakness.

The density of the material in question varies from 2.5 to 3.0 than that of the liquid surface. Since tides varying in height from 25 feet to 75 feet are caused in the liquid surface, it is just possible that the surface layer of the crust of the earth can also give rise to tides, of course, two and a half to three times or even less than that caused in the liquid surface. More so in the areas of considerable gravitational anomaly where sufficient mass is wanting.

It follows from the observation on the motion of the liquid surface that the crest tide of the surface layer of the crust of the earth, facing directly the Moon, should be more than on the surface lying away from the moon. Also, it is to be expected that a certain amount of time interval exists between the effects and lunisolar transit of a certain longitude of meridian. The difference in time between the luni-solar transit of the meridian and the effects produced thereby is a function of various factors governing the nature and response of the areas in question. This may or may not be constant for a particular meridian, unlike the harmonic constant in the case of tides, and is essencially a geological/ geophysical factor, of course, determinable over a long time-long in the geological sense of time, since the phenomenon is closely connected with the geotectonic processes, especially the orogenic activities.

The interaction between the varying luni-solar forces of attraction and the areas characterised by high negative/ geoptential in certain longitudes of meridian clearly show that some of the earthquakes are due to the tides produced in the crustal layers. The force of luni-solar attraction varies directly as the Moon approaches the Sun and also from tapogee to perigee. The luni-solar effect on the surface of the earth increases directly from the earth's position at aphelion to its position at perihelion. Thus the maximum force of luni-solar attraction is exerted on the surface of the earth when the earth with the New Moon in perigee approaches the perihelion position early in January, and the minimum when the earth with the square Moon in apogee approaches the aphelion position in early July. Although a certain longitude on the surface of the earth characterised by the presence of negative geopotential segments poses to this varying force of attraction, it is obvious that its behaviour is different for every position of motion. Thus its reaction is more towards winter while it decreases towards summer. This explains the annual maximum and minimum observed by Perrey Gunther, Milne and others (Giekie,

1903, p. 364) as the earthquakes occur most frequently in winter and least frequently in summer.

In India the Archaean ranges of the Aravallis, Dharwars, Satpuras and the Assam Plateau are regions of positive gravity anomaly whiel the Cuddapha basin, the Chittishgarh and Gwaliar region containing thick sedimentary beds are zones of negative gravity anomaly (Krishnan, 1956, p. 85). The Gulf of Cambay is a zone of positive gravity anomaly extending outwards to Bombay coast. In the country occupied by the Deccan traps in western and central India, the gravity anomalies are erratic. The Upper Assam valley and the Ganges valley in Bihar regions are regions of negative gravity anomlay studies (Qureshi andothers, 1968, p. 120), and the Chakrata-Cape Camorin gravity profile along E 78° longitude shows a high negative Bouger anomaly corresponding to the IndōGangetic and Himalayan foothills in the north followed by a less negative anomlay zone in the central region, gradually increasing to as much as -70 to -80 mgals south of 17° latitutde.

The modern geotectonic studies especially the Russian school of thought believes in the vertical movement of large segments of the crust of the earth, and recognise rhythmic oscillations in the rising and subsidence causing major structural developments (Belousov, 1962). The vertical displacement during the Assam earthquake of 1897 is recorded to be 12 metres, about half of the maximum crest of tide in the liquid surface! This case resembles the effects of the sweeping forces of attraction of the Moon squaring the sun causing neep tide during June when the earth is approaching the aphelion position, the earthquakes, however, being less frequent. The amplitude of visible displacement appears to be the maximum recorded in the case of violent earthquakes (Belousov, 1962, p. 611), active zone being only about 20 km.

The amplitude of visible displacement of the crust is a function of the gravitational force of attraction exerted by the luni-solar disposition in order to satisfy the condition of isostatic inequilibrium attaining balance. The luni-solar attraction works against the earth's gravitational attraction and the surface layers are kept maintained in balance whenever imbalance sets in due to various geological causes.

Fluctuation in the earth's gravitational constant is ascribed to the shortening in the radius of the earth in the geocynclinal areas and lengthening in the uplifting of continental masses. The Bombay and Madras areas are given to subside 0.2 and 1.2 mm/year respectively (Belousov, 1962, p. 215). Isostatic anomaly approaches zero in the central portion of the Peninsula but departs considerably towards the borders (Qureshi and others, 1967). This anomaly towards the borders of the Peninsula results from the sedimentary, alluvial and beach covers. Such areas show a readiness for adjustment behaving as loci of tectonic changes. Subsidence in the Madras areas is more than in the Bombay area. The Bouger anomaly in Cape Comorin is less than that at Chakrata. This is suggestive of more of lighter material in the form of sedimentary cover in the northern border of the Peninsula, due to the weight of which the tilt may be more to the north than to the east, causing shortening in the radius of the Everest Spheroid which results in the variation of the gravitational constant of the earth. Maximum limit of shortening of the crust is apparent during June-July for the earth approaches the aphelion position experiencing the minimum luni-solar force of attraction. When it approaches the perihelion position during December-January due to the maximum force of luni-solar attraction, the shortened radius of the earth will change in favour of lengthening of the radius for the surface layers particularly the sedimentary cover, being subjected to the extra-terrestrial forces will be pulled out.

Thus results fluctuation in the gravitational constant of the earth. This fluctuation is related to the annual fluctuation of the various geophysical phenomena like the frequency in the earthquakes, Chandler period and the drift of the geomagnetic field, etc. (Kropotkin and Trapeznikov, 1965). During the aphelion period the greatest increase in the rotation of the earth about its axis is noted (specially on 5th June) in consonance with the most rapid reduction in the radius of the earth resulting in the increase of radial and tangential compression and the angular momentum. Thus, it is clear, that the earthquakes are caused when the maximum tideproducing forces sweep the meridians characterised by the maximum negative gravity anomaly segments in the crust of the earth.-360.

## References

Beiousov, V.V., 1962 Basic Problems in Geotectonics.

Baker, R.H., 1965, Astronomy.

Giekie, A., 1903, Text-book of geology.

Krishnan, M.S., 1960, Geology of India and Burma.

Kropotkin, P.N. and Trapeznikov, Yu, A., 1965, Inter. Geol. Rev. No. 11.

Qureshi, M.N. and others, 1967, Sympo. Upper Mantle Project. Hyderbad, A.P.

Smith, J.P., 1968, New Scientist, Vol. 39, No. 609.

# 37

# Forecasting Earthquakes

Planetary patterns noted at the time of high intensity earthquakes signify a type of configurations and the occurrence of earthquakes. Knott observed that the maximum frequency of the earthquakes occurs near the time of the Moon's perigee. Oldham thought that the maximum frequency of earthquakes could be observed at the time of passage of the circle of maximum horizontal tide-producing force. Perry cited that earthquakes are more frequent in the winter than in summer. Cargill Knott attributed the annual periodicity of earthquakes to long continued stresses over large areas caused by brometric pressure and accumulation of snow. Milne has found frequency of deep-seated earthquakes near the times when changes occur in the direction of the polar movements. Milne's *Catalogue of Earthquakes* shows close correspondence between the occurrence of earthquakes and the periodicity of sunspots and of Jupiter's movements. Perry asserts that earthquakes are numerous about the time of the New and Full Moon, particularly when the Moon is nearest to the earth and when it crosses the meridian of observation. Stetson remarked that when the orbit of the Moon is in a particularly close relation of the epicentre of the earthquake source, the strain on the earth at that point is at its maximum and therefore likely to produce an earthquake.

Although the disposition of the Moon at the time of earthquakes has been given prime importance, the disposition of other planets especially Jupiter and Saturn appears to be no less important in causing earthquakes, when we examine the planetary patterns significant of earthquakes.

The origin of deep-seated earthquakes is attributed to the elastic rebound of the earth, which is purely an internal effect. The elastic rebound of the earth is the tendency of the earth to return to normal after it had been slowly strained over long period of time as a consequence of the growing stress field of the earth. Gibbs mentions that the energy which is released in an earthquake takes a long time to accumulate and the exact instant of release depends upon the slipping of the fault. Due to many incalculable factors, he says, it difficult to predict earthquakes.

It is veident that the law of gravitation has a direct control over the growth of stress field of the earth by way of regulating the season. The growth is very slow and is not perceptible but becomes very clear when the geochronology is read in the context of astronomical background. The diurnal changes and the changes of seasons are clear from the spin and revolution of the earth around the sun, respectively. Changes caused from the motion of the moon on the liquid face of the earth is also clear on the new and full moon days Similarly parallel approach to the terrestrial changes caused by the motion of other planetws is fairely clear from the earlier observations of periodicity of the earthquakes etc. and a look at the heavens to solve the terrestrial problems justified.

Eiby is of the opinion that planetary attractions are so smaller than other variable forces at work that they can have no appreciable effect. Atthe surface of the earth one does not feel the spin of the earth except by way of sunset and sunrise. Even though the earth is moving at a speed of 29.8

km. per second it is hardly ever possible for any one on the earth to realise it and as also that the solar system is revolving around the centre of the galaxy at about 296 km. per second. In fact that the effect of planetary attraction is not appreciable is only relative and it becomes clear when read over long stretches of time common to the earth and the heavens.

Conjunction, trine, square, opposition, sextile positioning of the planets exert relatively greater forces of attraction evolving long directions of release of strain especially characterised by negative gravity anomlay. Many of the negative gravity anomaly zones are also zones in which rocks are held under long and continued stress approaching in particular the maximum limit of elasticity. Such actions release the strain being attracted by the extensive forces exerted by the combined attraction of the remote planets, for, a large amount of angular momentum is invested in them.

Table 1 gives the planetary position and the time of seven high intensity earthquakes which occurred in the border of the Indian Peninsula.... spread over etc.

**Table 1: showing the geocentric longitudes of the planets at the time of the earthquakes**

| | *Assam* | *Kangra* | *Bihar* | *Quetta* | *Assam* | *Bhuj* | *Koyna* |
|---|---|---|---|---|---|---|---|
| Sun | 106 | 14 | 142 | 70 | 141 | 55 | 258 |
| Moon | 228 | 10 | 200 | 72 | 158 | 349 | 12' |
| Mars | 165 | 235 | 110 | 186 | 212 | 84 | 306 |
| Jupiter | 156 | 35 | 209 | 225 | 334 | 115 | 155 |
| Satwon | 226 | 329 | 326 | 339 | 168 | 227 | 5 |
| Uranus | 236 | 273 | 23 | 33 | 97 | 115 | 157 |
| Neptune | 80 | 95 | 162 | 160 | 195 | 207 | 215 |
| Venus | 40 | 46 | 114 | 113 | 115 | 27 | 214 |
| Mercury | 60 | 35 | 125 | 92 | 165 | 77 | 248 |
| | 12-6-1897 | 4-4-1905 | 15-1-1934 | 31-5-1935 | 13-8-1950 | 18-5-1955 | 11-12-1967 |

spread over a period of about 70 years. A study of the disposition of the planetary positions during the earthquakes reveals the following:

In case of the Koyna earthquake, the Moon was with Saturn trine the Sun and Mercury, the latter group being set in a square to the combination of Jupiter and Uranus. Mars was in sextile relation to the Moon-Saturn combination and is squared by the combination of Neptune and Venus.

The Moon was with Jupiter in case of the Bihar earthquake, opposed by Uranus, squared by the combination of Mars and Venus, trined by Saturn in opposition to the joint effect of the Sun, Neptune and Mercury, the latter group sextile to the Moon-Jupiter combination. Uranus trines the Sun group.

It was a New Moon in the case of the Kangra earthquake, sextiled by Saturn and trined by Neptune with the latter two in opposition. Neptune squared Mars, the latter in opposition to the group of Jupiter, Mercury and Venus, in trine to Uranus and squared by Saturn.

It was also a New Moon in the case of the Quetta earthquake, squared by Saturn and in trine to Neptune-Mars combination. Jupiter trined Saturn on one side and Venus-Mercury on the other. Venus-Mercury combination squared the combination of Mercury-Mars the latter in sextile to Uranus, opposed by Jupiter and sextiled by Saturn.

In the case of the Bhuj earthquake the Moon was in sextile to the Sun, the latter in sextile to Uranus-Jupiter, in trine to Saturn on the other side which is in opposition to Mars-Mercury. The latter combination sextiled by Venus which was opposing Neptune. Neptune was sextile Saturn, squared by Uranus-jJupiter and disposed in trine to Mercury-Mars.

In the two cases of the Assam earthquake, on 12th June 1897, the Moon-Uranus-Saturn combination trined the Sun and opposed Venus-Mercury. The Sun was sextile to Mars, Jupiter which in turn sextiled the Moon group. Venus-Mercury also sextiled the Sun. Mercury-Venus combination trined Mars-Jupiter group, the latter squared by Neptune. On the Indiependence day of 1950, the earthquake of Assam followed the New Moon and the Moon with Saturn and Mercury opposed Jupiter which was disposed in trine to Uranus-Venus combination on one side and to Mars on the other. Mars squared the Sun, the Sun sextiling Neptune. Neptune was squared by Uranus-Venus combination which was disposed sextile to the Moon group.

The above planetary patterns signify that the earthquakes occur:

(1) Near the time of the New Moon days, especially when associated with eclipses,

(2) the planets tend to dispose invariably in conjunction, square, trine, opposition and sextile position; and

(3) the relation of the Moon with Saturn and Jupiter is critical, although the influence of other planets are not negligible.

**Gravitation**

If one km. thickness of rock of average density of 2.5 per sq.cm. produces an increase in gravity by 100 milligals, certain areas bordering the Indian Peninsula, *e.g.*, the Himalayan belt and parts of the Deccan trap country show about-80 milligals of gravity anomaly indicating a shortage of nearly a km. thick rocks of average density of about 2.5 per sq.cm. Although this is less than skin thickness compared to the radius of the earth, the shortage in material influences the geopotential in a very significant manner.

Considering the geopotential at the surface of the earth to be 978 gals near the Equator, the centrifugal force at the Equator divided by the gravity gives a value 1/288.4, which is the resultant of lifting and sliding effects, Since the gravity is less by nearly 0.1 gal in the areas mentioned above, it will increase the value of the centrifugal force, consequently in the component of the lifting and the sliding effects. This increase in the components of the centrifugal force gives way for adjustments due to disparity in density to take place at the Moho's level. The rigidity of the crust of the earth being about $5X10^{11}$ dynes per $cm.^2$ rocks in the zones of anomaly having attained the limit of elasticity subjected to long continued stresses responds quickly to any small force of attraction exerted from without any yields to the joint influences of the increased lifting component of the centrifugal force and the resultant of the combined angular momenta the of the remote planets.

Based on the similarity of the fluctuations in the gravitational constant to the frequency of earthquakes, Dick proposed a hypothesis explaining the cause of variation in the gravitational constant. His proposition of the gravitational constant in the equation has a substitution for v the velocity of the earth relative to the whole Universe.

$$G = G_0 [1 + 2(v/c)^2]$$

With uniform motion of the earth in a circular orbit (R) with velocity V and uniform motion of the solar system relative to the metagalactic with a velocity V, a change in the resultant vector of velocity is found and attributed to that of G which shows annual periodiodicity due to the complications in V and $V^1$. The magnitude of G being 6-673 X $10^3 cm.^2$ dynes/$g^2$ is supposed to reach a value of $1.3X10^8$ during the orbital motion of the earth.

In the text of the theory of relativity gravitation is characterstic of particular framework of reference.

Therefore, the G constant restricts the variation of G to the solar system alone. Since the solar system appears to have been subjected to no external forces which could have augmented its angular momentum (mvR) during its existence over a couple of thousands of million years, it is believed to be an isolated system. Since the problem of forecasting the earthquakes related to a member of this isolated system a consideration of the velocity of the earth relative to the universe possibly needs correction, for, the system behaves independent of the forces acting from outside.

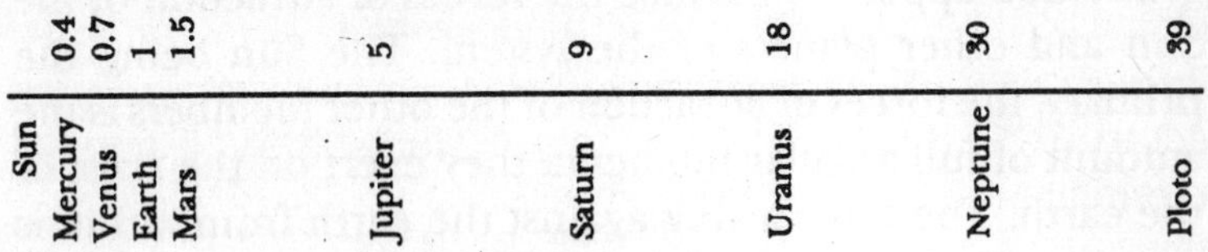


**Graph I**

***Relative mean distance of planets from the Sun : Astronomical Unit— Mean distance from the Sun to the earth—149.5 x*** $10^6$ ***Km***

Isolated negative gravity anomaly are susceptible to earthquake (e. g. part of West coast of the Indian Peninsula) do occur within the relatively earthquake-proof shields. Within the Deccan Trap country they may sometime be due to the voids that are created by the removal of intra and intertrappean beds by the action of ground water. The Koyna earthquake, with its 80km. long NNW-SSE dislocation at the surface and its focus at some 13 km. down below in the region of the Deccan Trap country abutting the Western coast is a puzzle to the geologists since they are clear about the oscillations of the Peninsula based on structural map of the country. The dislocation, it is very significant, is parallel to the West coast The Peninsula acts as a single unit, for, the shocks at the time of the Bihar quake were felt at Quilon. Hence the direct bearing of the structural patterns of the coastal units on gravity.

Forces acting On the Crust of the Earth

The crust of the earth is subjected to various kinds of forces acting from within and from without, which are normally balanced. Any imbalance causes diastrophic activities.

Rigidity and strength of the crust associated by the hydrostatic pressure acting in favour of the earth's gravitation appear to balance the forces of attraction of the Sun and other planets of the system. The Sun being the primary, the forces of attraction of the other members is the amount of full angular momenta they exert on the crust of the earth. The force acting against the earth from within is the centrifugal force of the earth. The negative gravity anomaly zones increasc thc centrifueal force. A decrease in the strength of the crust due to a corresponding increase in the hydrostatic pressure also favours the gravity anomaly but its negative trend indirectly effecting thė forces acting against the crust of the earth Thus sets an imbalance in the forces acting on the earth's crust over a long period of time.

Based on the above assumption the forces acting on the crust of the earth can be resolved as follows:

Acting from within are:

(1) The gravitational force of the earth

(2) rigidity of the crust

(3) strength of the crust, and

(4) the normal hydrostatic pressure,

Acting from without are:

(1) The force of attraction due to the Sun,

(2) the angular momenta of the planets, favoured by

(3) the centrifugal force of the earth in addition to

(4) negative gravity anomaly belts; the last two aspects acting from within the crust favour the forces acting from without.

The forces have been grouped as above for the simplicity of the discussion to follow. However, they are interrelated.

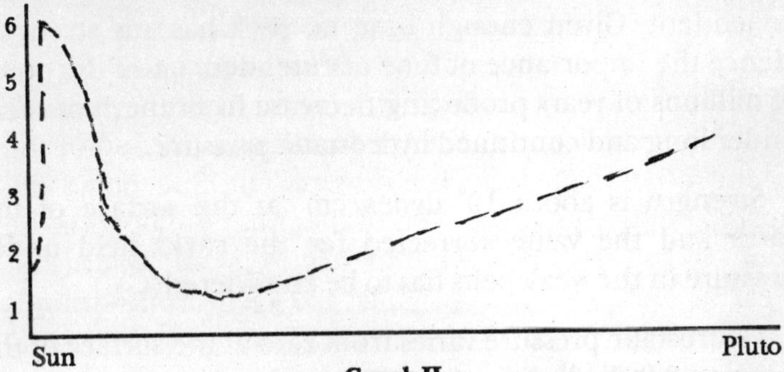


**Graph II**

***Density of the planets (Water - 1)***

The earth's gravitational pull at the equator is 978.049 gals and varies towards the poleș This value in the zone of the negative anomaly is to be considered.-A

Rigidity of the earth is of the order of 3 x $10^{11}$ dynes Rigidity $cm^2$ in the crust reaching 4 x $10^{11}$ dynes/$cm^2$ at the core. The value corrected to the negative gravity anomaly zones is to be taken into consideration.-B

Strength of the crust is different from the rigidity. The elastic properties of a perfectly homogenous body are determined by two moduli,

(a) Bulk modulus-controlling the changes in volume under pure compression and

(b) Co-efficient of rigidity - controlling the change of form under pure shear.

Therefore, coefficient of rigidity is proportional to tangential stresses that are necessary to produce distortion(shear). It indicates the effect of creep.

Strength is the maximum stress that a substance can withstand without undergoing flow or fracture. In other words, the bearing strength of materials is their resistance against plastic flow. Strength, internal friction, creep, etc., arrive at the coefficient of viscosity, and are purely time-dependent. Given enough time no rock has any strength. Hence the importance of time of extended, *i.e,* of the order of millions of years producing decrease in strength of rocks under long and continued hydrostatic pressure.

Strength is about $10^9$ dynes/$cm^2$ at the surface of the earth and the value corrected for the rocks held under pressure in the weak belts has to be considered(C).

Hydrostatic pressure varies from zero at the surface of the earth to $3.92X10^6$ dynes/$cm^2$ at the core, *i.e.,* at a depth of 6371 km. The value of the hydrostatic pressure at a depth of maximum gravity anomaly is to be noted (D).

Regarding the forces acting from without the force of attraction of the Sun on the surface of the earth will be that of the earth multiplied by the mass of the Sun varying inversely as the square of the mean distance from the Sun to the earth. (corrections to the mean distance to be effected).

$$\frac{(5.975X10^{27}) \text{ X } 333420 \text{ X } 978.049}{\sqrt{1.495=10^{15}}} \quad \ldots \text{(A-1)}$$

The force of angular momentum of the various members of the solar system is shown in the Graph III.

Angular momentum of the earth is = *mvR*

$(5.975X10^{27}) \text{ X } (29.8 \text{ X } 10^5) \text{ X } (1.495 \text{ X } 10^{13}) = \text{X (unit)}$

that of

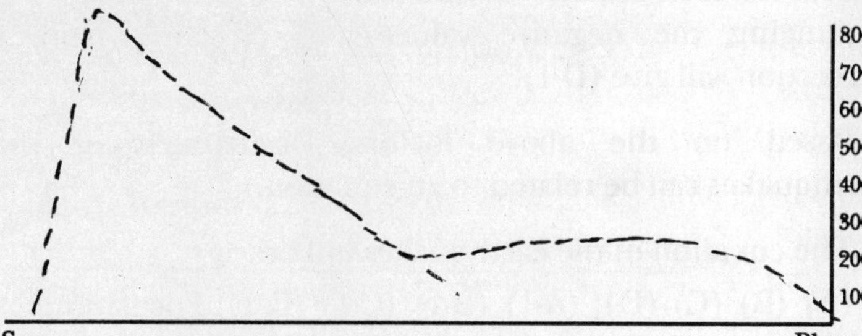


**Graph III**

*Full Angular momentum of the planets (Times that of the earth)*

Mercury = 0.03 X

Venus = 0.69 X

Mars = 0.13 X

Jupiter = 725 X
Saturn = 294 X
Uranus = 64 X
Neptune = 95 X

= 1178X = Z

Pluto = X

The value of the trapezoidal resultant of the full angular monenta of the remote planets (excepting Pluto) which is about 1178 times strenger than that of the earth creaters imbalance coinoiding with the 'active zone'. The force exerted by the Z on the surface of the earth is the distance between the edarth and Z.

$$\frac{Z}{\sqrt{\text{the distance between the earth and Z}}} \quad \ldots \text{(B-1)}$$

Increase in the lifting and sliding effect of the centrifugal force varies with the negative gravity value, hence a correction to the value 1/288.4 (C-1).

The corrected value of the earth's gravitational force expunging the negative values and effecting latitude correction will give (D-1).

Based on the above factors, occurrence of the earthquakes can be related to an equation.

The equation of the earthquakes will be

(A) (B) (C) (D); (A-1) (B-1) (C-1) (D-1); Focus: Energy released.

Since the energy of the seismic waves of the earthquakes with hypocentres shallower than 60 km. is noted to be of the order of $0.1 \times 10^{27}$ ergs/year varying by as much as $10 \times 10^{27}$ ergs/year during mountain formation. Based on the intensity of the earthquakes the probable energy likely to be released for a given focus can be determined.

The three values in the equation of the earthquakes being determined, the focus of the earthquake for a given energy release can be arrived at and the duration of time for the strength in the equation gives the timing of earthquake.

It is necessary to emphasize here that the elliptical motion of the planets is largely responsible for the fluctuations of the gravitational constant, although other aspects like the variation in the composition of planets and the distribution of material in them do account for the same. This variation in gravity induces changes in the stress field of the earth, which controls the geotectonic activities. Variation in the gravitation appears to be responsible for the change varying from the diurnal scale, *e.g.*, variation in the length of day to that of the formation of mountains. Gravitational variation read in the context of these changes reveals that high intensity earthquakes occur at a particular variation for a given duration of time for particular depth of focus subject to alteration by other factors like the gravity anomaly, the strength of the rocks, hydrostatic pressure, etc.

Based on these observations, earthquake cannot be viewed as due to an unknown trigger action. When the variation in gravity sunpasses the limit of elasticity of the rocks in question automatic rupture takes place resulting in an earthquake, and will not cease till the balance is attained, hence the minor shock follow over considerable period. Similarly the minor shocks precede the high intensity shocks, the latter being demanded by the variation in gravity for the zone.

Variation in the gravitational constant surpassing the limit of elasticity of the rocks is evident from the motion of the planets as the resultant angular momenta of the remote planets decide the issue of earth-quakes. Rutpuring of a body is due to two factors, the bearing strength of the body and the degree of imbalance of the applied foreces from within and without. Since the attraction from external sources amounts to negative application the line of imbalance will be the direction of rupture. Therefore, any interpretation of the earth-quake based only on the forces acting from within will be untenable and will not lead to any reliable prediction. Similar is the unilateral interpretation based on the movements of the planets alone and will not give proper results. Therefore, a zone in the crust of the earth wherein the rocks have attained the limit of elasticity should be referred to the resultant of the angular momenta of the remote planets for timing the earthquakes.

# 38

# Astrological Evaluation of Personality

How far a person differs from the ideal person that the community or the humanity is striving to achieve or to evolve can be evaluated from theoretical astrology. One may be a king, a saint, a teacher of religion, a popular minister, a man with high principles in public service, a yogi, president of a nation or organisation but how much one differs from the true way of life, how much he has to strive to realise the ideal path of life can be ascertained with mathematical precision utilising astrological knowledge.

In theoretical astrology it is understood that the planets form into two groups of antivibrations. The Sun, Jupiter and Mars form one group, Saturn, venus and Mercury form another group, the Moon joins the group in such a way that the mind of a person is moulded by the vibrations of the planets of the particular group to which his Moon at birth belongs.

In identity, a personality with natural vibrations of the group to which he belongs will be faourable to the personality alone. But he may be a good deal away from the ideal. The question then is what is the ideal personality?

Theoretically we may define that a personality will be ideal in whose horoscope the vibrations of the two groups of planets are harmoniously blended and carve out a strong median path of life. That such a personality can only be theoretical and no person of history or epics has qualifications to be an ideal person can be shown clearly by astrological analysis.

One of the best methods to find out the difference between a real person and the ideal person is by plotting the total amount of shadvarga balas of planets belonging to the two groups. The Shadbalas like Sthana, Dik, Kala, Chesta, Naisargika and Drik of individual planets should be ascertained and added as given below:

| *Shadbalas* | *Planets of group 1* | *Planets of group 11* |
|---|---|---|
| Sthana | | |
| Dik | Sun | Saturn |
| Kala | Jupiter | Venus |
| Chesta | Mars | Mercury |
| Naisargika | | |
| Drik | | |
| Total rupas = | a | b |

These Shadbalas can be calculated as enumerated in *Graha and Bhava Balas* by Prof. B.V. Raman. They are calculated in rūpas and the rūpas of various types of strength given by different planets should be added up as shown above.

If the strengths of the planets of the group I are plotted against those of the planets of the group II a spread of points can be seen in the graph (Fig. 1). The accompanying graph has been prepared on the data given in the book referred to above by Prof. B.V. Raman for the standard horoscope given therein. The lesser the width of the spread of the points in a band the smoother the life of the person without much variation of spectacular nature. The wider the spread of the band and the greater the distance between the points so will the life of the person be riddled with complications. The points must be closer to the arrow line to carve out a life of the ideal person.

In the graph given the number of points show the strength of the shadvargas arrived for the two groups of planets.

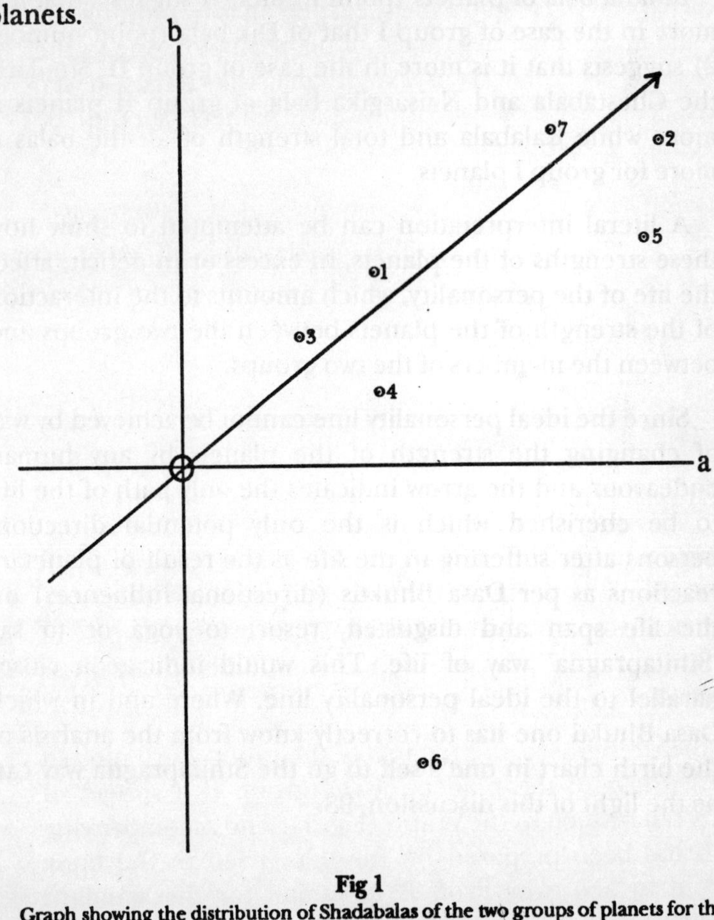


**Fig 1**

**Graph showing the distribution of Shadabalas of the two groups of planets for the standard horoscope given by Prof. B.V. Raman in the book '*Graha and Bhava Balas.*' Arrow line is the theoretical way of the ideal person or 'Sthitapragna'.**

Points numbered 1 to 6 give the Shad varga strength of planets enumerated above respectively. Point number 7 is the total Shadbala strength of group I and group II planets. If the strength of the planets is harmoniously mixed the points fall on the arrow line of the ideal personality. Since they are not falling on the arrow line it should be contended that the various strenghs of the planets differ from the ideal personality line and that there is scope for improvement.

Sthana bala of planets (point number 1 suggests that it is more in the case of group I that of Dik bala (point number 2) suggests that it is more in the case of group II. Similarly the Chestabala and Naisargika bala of group II planets is more while Kalabala and total strength of all the balas is more for group I planets.

A literal interpretation can be attempted to show how these strengths of the planets, in excess or in deficit, affect the life of the personality, which amounts to the interaction of the strength of the planets between the two groups and between the members of the two groups.

Since the ideal personality line cannot be achieved by way of changing the strength of the planets by any human endeavour and the arrow indicates the only path of the life to be cherished which is the only potential direction, persons after suffering in the life as the result of planetary reactions as per Dasa Bhuktis (directional influences) on the life span and disgusted, resort to yoga or to say 'Sthitapragna' way of life. This would indicate a closer parallel to the ideal personality line. Where and in which Dasa Bhukti one has to correctly know from the analysis of the birth chart in one's self to go the Sthitapragna way can be the light of this discussion,-98.

# 39

# Rationale of the Ashtakavarga

In his elegant and beautiful elucidation of the *Ashtakavarga System of Prediction*, Prof. B.V. Raman refers to the famous work *Horāmakaranda* which almost defines Ashtakavarga as the collective factor which sets in as a result of the progression of seven planets from their respective radical places and from Lagna. He further states that Ashtakavarga also takes into cognisance the actions and interactions of the transiting planets with regard to their radical situations and by a certain manipulation of the benefic and malefic influences given rise to by such movements and measured numerically by certain units based on which specific events can be determined.

Prof. Raman's remarks that the sages seem to have devised a numerical scheme of interpretation and timing of the events, which is unique and capable of further development is fully substantiated when the problem is viewed from the angle of celestial mechanics. From the point of view of modern dynamics the object of which is to investigate the motion of bodies as affected by the forces which act upon them, by application of the laws of Boscovich's hypothesis concerning the angular momentum of rigid bodies, by considering the rigid bodies as a system of particles, it is possible to resolve the forces in terms of the events. In reverse, given the velocities of motion of individual bodies in a system, it is possible to arrive at the time of events in advance.

The laws of dynamics become complicated in dealing with the motion of bodies with epicyclic, bearing elliptical motions like the planets in the solar system when we consider the perturbations although for simplicity they are governed by Cartesian equations. Lamb observes that if the system is subject to frictionless constraints a geometric relation could be evolved by which the unknown in the reaction can be determined. But the complete solution of such problems is generally difficult like the 'problem of three bodies' the solution of which demands elaborate methods of approximation.

In evolving the system of Ashtakavarga the Hindu exponents have reduced the complex processes of mathematical reasoning into simple laws. According to Prof. Raman, by the Sun's Ashtakavarga we mean the collective forces due to the projection of positive beams with reference to himself and the other six planets and the Lagna. The benefic places of the Sun can be arrived at by manipulating the equations of the surface and others. Bhinnāshtakavargas can be prepared for individual planets and Sarvāshtakavargas by a process of interference and elimination/reduction to get the composite picture.

In the composite picture read in the light of progressed positions of the planets, events can easily be deciphered with all their peculiarities. Thc observations recorded in the ancient texts are generally statistical. The Nadis may be outstanding in their true exposition. But all these observations necessarily lack in considering the motion of the Sun around the centre of the galaxy with the changing background of stars in long ages which is geologically and astronomically true. The Sun's motion must also necessarily be epicyclic, thus robbing the statistical truth by the degree of epicyclic advancement. However, they may not differ much for all the practical purposes to be realised within the short span of human life or, for that matter, for a few generations after which corrections are equally necessary.

The benefic places for planets can be arrived at by the application and extension of Cartesian equations. For determining the benefic positions of the Sun, it would be necessary to visualise and apply the laws of 'n dimensional' geometry for formulating the general principles of the Ashtakavarga system to be realised with all details once and for all times. This would form a separate field of research for strengthening the astrological facts and possibly form the border between the observations of modern science and the principles of astrology. The wide gap that exists between the modern science and the supreme subject of knowledge, astrology will vanish and the latter will form the core of knowledge as it is but little realised, at present.

The maximum number of bindus, *i.e.*, benefic points capable of being contributed by a single planet is 8 and the planet in a house with less than 4 bindus will affect adversely. More than 4 bindus, and more the number of bindus than 4, a planet in a house will cause these factor improve above normal and proportionately. The strength of a bhava is more or less numerically amenable for exposition based on the Ashtakavarga delineation. In other words, the strength of a house is reinforced by the increasing number of points about a planet in the house which is a measure of dynamical force that plans gains at the birth in respect of the Ascendant and is sure to bring about the facts within the periods allowed for by progression based on Vimshottari and possible of contemplation in the relatively short future based on Gochara.

Thus, a rationalistic view of the Ashtaka varga System of Prediction permits one to delve deep into the realms of modern dynamics and feel that the observations are most scientific 313.

# 40

# Using Divisional Charts in Horoscopic Studies

The importance of divisional charts in interpretative astrology is of great significance. The *phalabhāga* or the interpretative section of astrology keeps as its base ·the perfection attained on the section of casting and finding the strength of *graha* (planet) and *bhāva* (significance) of the horoscope. Determination of the strength of a planet and the house in horoscopy has been dealt with in a superb and lucid way by Dr. B.V. Raman in his book *Graha and Bhāva Balas.* He has rightly observed in the preface to the first edition of the book: "It is an admitted fact that without proper calculations it would be difficult to make correct predictions." It is very ddifficult to evaluate the validity and scope of this statement in full. All the blame that the science of astrology has been receiving at the hands of critics possibly points to the lack of strict application of or consideration of clear mathematical basis of horoscopy, specially in determining the strength of planets and houses. Without clearly ascertaining the strength of planets and houses any interpretation is liable to be a mistake of incalculable harm to the astrologer as well as the recipient.

The rank and file of astrologers do not delve deep into the mathematical part of horoscopy. Even serious students of the science do skip the calculation part of a horoscope for want of time and mostly depend upon intuition. Intuition, if supported by a proper base, will be able to get at the true picture of events to come. But, intuition, when not supported by a sound base, will result only in erroneous interpretations which will be a target of ridicule bringing ill-fame to both the science and the student.

Any amount of caution is not sufficient in collecting fundamental data and there should be no dispute between two serious students on the ground of collecting data though there may be differences in interpretation of the data depending upon the experience of each. This is true of any branch of modern disciplines of science, and astrology is no exception. While any student of science can verify the data for its correctness, it may not be the same case with interpretations based on such data. Though skill and intuition are very essential to read the events in their proper perspective, it is not so for collecting the data which is routine and rigorous. To this section belongs the part of mathematical astrology and the section could be easily computerised for easy processing. Though students like to get away with the hard task of the mathematical section of horoscopy, by way of computerisation of data for processing, they should be failing in their duty if they are not aware of the significance of the sole that such fundamental data play in interpretation which could predict events for complete realisation, thus enriching the value of the science.

The importance of divisional charts is considered as one of the many factors in the determination of strength of planets. According to Dr. Raman, it would be necessary to scrutinise the position of planets in the zodiac from various points of view to estimate the exact potency of a planets and a house. The various sources of strength are generally considered under six categories and referred to as Shadbalas. They are:

1. Sthanabalā-positional strength
2. Digbalā-directional strength
3. Kalabalā-temporal strength
4. Cestabala-motional strength
5. Naisargikabalā-permanent or natural strength and
6. Drikbala-aspectual strength.

This system of calculation of planetary potency is on the lines advocated by Parāsara.

In calculating the shadbalas of a planet, the following points are looked into:

1. Occabala,
2. Saptavargajabala,
3. Ojoyugmarasīamsabala,
4. Kendrabala and
5. Drekkanabala.

It is difficult to comment upon the selection of these items only for calculating planetary potency. Each system has its own peculiarity. Out of the above criteria, our attention is drawn for Saptavargajabala in considering the importance of divisional charts. Why only the seven divisions are selected to the exclusion of many others by Parāsara is not very clear. But the theory works.

According to Brhat Parāsara Horasara edited by Sitarama Jha, there is one chapter completely devoted to this discussion. There, Parāsara observes, following Brahma, that there are 16 divisional charts in this system. He lists them as: griha, hora, drkkāna, caturthāmsha, saptāmsha, nvamāmsha, dashāmsha, dwadashāmsha, shodashāmsha, vimshāmsha, caturvimshāmsha, saptvimshāmsha, trimshāmsha, khavedāmsha, akshavedāmsha, and shshtyamsha.

Dr. Raman has given the rules for preparing all these charts, in his book A Manuel of Hindu Astrology.

Consdieration only lagna, or rasi, hora, drekkana, navāmsha, dwadashāmsha, and trimshāmsha has been called Shadvarga system. With saptāmsha, the system is called Saptavarga system With aditional vargas like Dashāmsha, shodashāmsha, and shashtyamsha, the system goes under the name dashavarga.

The planet occupying more than one varga of division is considered to be stronger. If a planet occupies its own varga twice, it denotes its Parijatāmsha strength; thricē Parvatāmsha; four times-Simhāsanāmsha; five times-Swargalokāmsha; six times-Indrāmsha; seven times-Rajapadmāmsha; eight times-Gopurāmsha; nine times-Bhrapadāmsha; ten times-Vaishnavāmsha; eleven times-Shaivāmsha; and twelve times-vaisheshikāmsha.

It is difficult to find planets with Indramsha and more in a horoscope. The people who have been addressed as Daivamsha sambhūta locate some such strength in their horoscopes It would be worthwhile to examine the horoscope of Sri Rama and other incarnations mostly from this background to know how they have influenced the world during their lives.

The significance of the various vargas has been given by Parāsara as follows:

1. Lagna/Rasi-to be read to ascertain information on one's body;
2. Hora-wealth;
3. Drekkana-brothers;
4. Chaturthāmsa-prosperity;
5. Saptamāmsa-children and line of progeny;
6. Navāmsa-wife;
7. Dasāmsa-job or rajya;

8. Dwadasāmsa-parents;
9. Shodasāmsa-sisters;
10. Vimsāmsa-faith in religion and god;
11. Chaturvimsāmsa- learning;
12. Saptavimsāmsa-personal strength;
13. Trimsāmsa-untoward events;
14. Khavedāmsa-good and bad;
15. Akshvedāmsa-all matters and
16. Shashtyamsa-one's fundamental nature.

There are certain differences in considering additional charts. The Panchāmsa is known to be referred to ascertain progeny by some authorities; Shashtyamsa for ascertaining the enemies and diseases; Ashtāmsa for theknowledge of death; Ekadasāmsa for all positive balances. Moreover, the special field of Nādi system considers units of 12 minutes of arc which amount to 150 units, in each Rasi. Dr. Raman observes that "This minute division sets the seal of the destiny of an individual". He also says that "if the correct Nādi Amsa is established, then there is a bird's eye-view of the entire past and future of the person concerned".

Each system of interpretation has its own advantages and drawbacks in astrology as in other disciplines of science. In the system of Parāsara which is perhaps the oldest and widely followed, the determination of planetary and sign potency considering only *saptavargas* and other details, is employed in interpreting the *dasābhukti* (directions) and ascertaining the exact time of an event to come. The Nādi systems, on the other hand, would give directly the age of the person when the events are graduated in his lifetime. Though a numerical method is employed in ascertaining the *saptavargajabala* of planets in Pārāsari system, it may be necessary to make modifications by research considering various other modern data. The method may be employed giving credence to the angular momentum of a planet as it implies almost all the potential qualities of the moving bodies. The system, if modernised, may help better and clarified interpretation.

It is common to find that many astrologers give only Rāsi and Navāmsa charts for a horoscope. Some may include the Drekkana chart. They are supported by the statements like *Praayo navaamsekhilam* meaning that almost all aspects of life can be gleaned through the Navamsa chart. Also, the Drekkana chart is given to indicate the Padavi or status based on the statement-"Drekkane padaveem". If that were the case, there would have been no necessity for all other charts presented by Parasara. Also, normally, for that matter, the general tendency has been to salvage any horoscope of a person, even in educated circles, only at the time of marriage, for which purpose the Navamsa chart would have been given by the astrologer. Until then one normally does not bother about his or her horoscope. These situations have been created amongst the public in recent times. Perhaps this was not the situation that obtained during the early times when they would have given due important to all divisional charts and full interpretations were made in advance to be taken advantage of by the native. This kind of presentation of only Rāsi and Navāmsa charts should be discouraged as it would belittle the respect that is commanded of the divine discipline astrology. A horoscope should be evaluated in all respects. Otherwise one should not venture at all, which only leads to partial interpretations which are more erroneous than thought of.

The importance of divisional charts is more in the case of mundane events than even in interpreting individual horoscope. True, the determination of planetary potency and the strength of various houses is rather time-consuming and laborious. Students of research in this science, though, should insist on personal scrutiny of these mathematical processes for one's satisfaction, and, a routine method of ascertaining the strength may be evolved even at the cost of employing the calculating machines. Or other methods need be instituted based on modern astronomical data and ancient observations, on due verification and confirmation.

The importance of these charts has been emphasised to ascertain the various aspects of human life. If one has to evaluate his property level, he needs to consider the strength of the 4th house of his birth chart, the lord of the 4th house, the aspects it receives and the fructification period. Similarly, if one has to ascertain the job potential, he needs to examine the 10th house lord, his association, aspects etc. However, the jobs under the sun are so numerous that it is rather very difficult to pin point them. This is the general observation by many a student of astrology. Though a broad outline can be made by reading one's chart, the exact disposition is hard to be ascertained by limited data provided with the horoscope. There are several aspects of a job acquirement. Job description, the time of getting a job, the time of leaving one job and getting a different one; agreeable job and disagreeable job; whether one gets job satisfaction if one undertakes the job indicated; whether one is really carrying out the responsibilities of the job he has been assigned by circumstances; any job improvement etc. etc. Much of these things has been accomplished by the Nādi system of reading. The data on Nādi reading can definitely be substantiated, if only one takes the trouble of collecting more details and interprets on the strength of the planets and the Bhava.

For e.g. there will be tremendous deliberations on the topic of Rajayogas alone. Under one type of Raja-yoga, based on the strength of planets and the house, one may be a powerful president of a state, a country, the United Nations now, or a minister, a low ranking officer, a head of village or the leader of a section of people. The exact strength on such a range of dispositions is pointed only by employing the strength of planets and the bhava. This aspect of skillful interpretation is implied in all the later astrological texts. While the textual interpretation literally translated in most of the modern versions, the real purport behind such statements has been conveniently forgotten, deliberately avoided by many practioners of astrology.

# 41

# The Vedic Science of Aeronautics

Developments in the modern science of aeronautics can be traced to the times of Leonardo da Vinci (1452-1519). The invention of the balloon in 1783 was a great step in the advancement of this science. American airman Orville Wright with his brother Wilbur Wright began gliding experiments on the sand dunes of Kitty Hawk, North Carolina, in the latter part of the 19th century and made successful flights by adding a power-driven engine to their glider. On December 17, 1903 they made four flights, the longest being 852 feet. It is stated that "These flights were the first in which a man had been carried from the ground on flight by a power-driven aeroplane". Later developments in this science are simply spectacular.

Although many achievements of the Indians in ancient times have been known especially in some of the positive science-disciplines like mathematics, astronomy, medicine, civil engineering and architecture, botany, mineralogy, etc., etc., as evident from the available texts in Sanskrit, it is not yet known to many that they were at home with the modern science of aeronautics as well. This has been made clear from a book published by the International Academy of

Sanskrit Research, Mysore. The title of the book is *Vymaanika Shaastra* by Maharshi Bharadwaaja, and has been rendered into English by Mr. G.R. Josyer and was first published by the Coronation Press in 1973.

The book is unique in many respects. It is stated that it is part of the greater text in Sanskrit by Bharadwaaja under the title *Yantra Sarvasva* or *All about Machines.* The section treated here is called Vymaanika Prakarana, and contains 21 chapters. Qualifications of a pilot, description of aerial routes, parts of an aeroplane, clothing of pilots, food of pilots, the metals used in the construction of aircrafts, mirrors used in the aircrafts, fuel and power of the aeroplanes, parts of the aero-machines, varieties of aeroplanes including Shakuna, Sundara, Rukma and Tripura varieties have been dealt with at length.

There is also another text attributed to Bharadwaaja on the same subject under the title *Brihadvimaana Shaastra* with a commentary by Brahmamuni published by the Chowkhamba Vidya Bhavan, Varanasi. The text by the International Academy of Sanskrit Research contains the commentary of Bodhaananda. In addition to this commentary, comments from some 64 other Sanskrit texts have been utilised to make the text as complete as possible. These texts are given below:

1. *Agatattwa Laharee,*
2. *Amshubodhinee,*
3. *Ashana Kalpa,*
4. *Bhastrikaa-Nibandhana,*
5. *Brihat Kaandika,*
6. *Chaara Nibandhana,*
7. *Chaayapurusha Shaastra,*
8. *Darpanaprakarna,*
9. *Gopatha Kaarika,*
10. *Khetasamgraha,*
11. *Khetavilasa,*

12. *Ksheera-pata-kalpa*
13. *Khetayaanapradeepika* of Chaakraayoni,
14. *Kriyaasaara,*
15. *Kundanirnaya,*
16. *Lalla-kaarika,*
17. *Lohasarvasva,*
18. *Lohatantra,*
19. *Maniprakarana,*
20. *Maniratnaakara,*
21. *Manikalpapradeepika,*
22. *Maanibhadra Kaarika,*
23. *Moolikaarka Prakaashika,*
24. *Mooshaakalpa,*
25. *Mukura Kalpa of Lalla,*
26. *Naalikanirnaya,*
27. *Naamaarthakalpaka*
28. *Nirnayaadhikaara,*
29. *Niryaasakalpa,*
30. *Patakalpa,*
31. *Patapradeepika,*
32. *Pata-samskaara Ratnaakara,*
33. *Paakasarvasva,*
34. *Paarthiva-paaka Kalpa,*
35. *Paribhaashaa Chondrika,*
36. *Prapanchasaara,*
37. *Rahasyalahari,*
38. *Ritukalpa,*
39. *Sammohanakriyaakaanda*
40. *Shabdamahodadhi,*
41. *Shabdanibandhana,*
42. *Shananirnayachandrika,*
43. *Shaktibeeja,*
44. *Shakti Kousthubha,*
45. *Shakti Sarvasva,*
46. *Shakti Tantra,*
47. *Sandhaana Patala,*

48. *Shownakeeya,*
49. *Shownaka Sootra,*
50. *Soudaminee Kolaa,*
51. *Samskaara Darpana,*
52. *Uttara-Taapaneeya Vimaana Chandrika* of Narayana,
53. *Vasishta Swatassiddha Nyaya,*
54. *Vishwambhara Kaarika,*
55. *Vishanirnayaadhikaara,*
56. *Vyomayaana Arkaprakaasha of Dhundinaatha,*
57. *Vyomayaana Tantra of Shownaka,*
58. *Vaalmiki Ganitha,*
59. *Lohatatwaprakarana,*
60. *Yaanabindu of Vaachaspathi,*
61. *Yantra Kalpa of Garga,*
62. *Yantra Kalpataru,*
63. *Yantra Sarvasva and*
64. *Udbhijya Tatwa Saaraayanee.*

Most of the above texts referred to are not available at present.

The author of the text must have been a first rate engineer. According to him the pilot must have been trained in the science of knowing the seen and unseen, contraction-expansion, etc., special siddhis, secrets of manoeuvring, hearing distant sounds, exercising magnetic pulls, etc.-in all 32 secrets. He then describes many recognised air routes in the various regions of the atmosphere named as Rekhaapathha, Mandala, Kakshya, Shakti and Kendra. He describes the whirlpools in these regions. After enumerating the body of an aeroplane as consisting of some 31 parts, the text deals with the clothing and food of pilots. Then follows a treatment on the metals used in the construction of aeroplanes. The author mentions three numbers of what he calls root metals by name Souma, Soundaal and Mourthwika, by processing of which in certain proportions by accepted procedures, 16 metallic alloys could be prepared which are light metals used in the construction of aeroplanes. He refers to other texts like *Lohukalpa* wherein it is mentioned that there are 3,000 metal bearing layers within the earth of which 1,300 layers contain better quality metals. In the 7th layer 27 types of metals are known of which the third type has five-fold qualities of the root metals. According to *Lohakalpa* the following forces from outside the earth interact with the four other forces active within the earth in the production of these metals. They are: Forces from outside the earth; forces from inside the earth

| *Nature* | *Number/ proportion* | *Nature* |
|---|---|---|
| Koorma | 3 | Vaarunee |
| Kaashyapa | 8 | Shesha |
| Maarthaanda | 11 | Gaja |
| Bhoota | 5 | |
| Bhanaam | 2 | |
| Arka | 6 | |
| Indu | 4 | |
| Badva | 9 | |

Processes for purification of these metals are then mentioned, followed by the proportions of various beeja or root metals to be mixed for making alloys. Some 407 different crucibles and 532 varieties of furnaces are known, the text states. The details of the preparation of these light metals and also the types of bellows are given. The chapter dealing with the preparation of mirrors contains very interesting information. Television type of mirror, powercapturing mirror, appearance changing mirror, terrifying type mirror, etc., have been described as also their preparation. Then the fuel for the aircraft is given. Seven kinds of distinct operating forces have been recognised in the functioning of an aeroplane. They are:

1. Udgama;
2. Panjaraa;
3. Sooryashaktyapakarshinee;
4. Paraashaktyaakarshinee;
5. Kuntinee;
6. Moolashakti; and
7. A set of 12 other forces.

These powers are produced by seven engines or yantras called Tundila, Panjara, Amshupa, Apakarshaka, Saandhaanika, Daarpanika and Shaktiprasvaka. A detailed account has been presented on the mechanical contrivances numbering 32 required for the various functions of the aeroplane. Some of them are very interesting like the anti-lightning machine and the machine to overcome the various destructive forces produced in the upper stretches of the atmosphere, etc. Preparation of anti-lightning glass for the anti-lightning machine has been described. Also Dambhola loha or thunderbolt metal and its preparation is given. According to *Khetasamgraha* it is stated that Kritttika, Satabhisha, Makha, Mrigasira, Chitta, Sravana, Pushya and Aswini are said to be luminous stars. The planets during their course approach the fields of these stars and generate eight kinds of forces which are destructive of the aeroplane. Such forces are nullified or neutralised by the shaktyudgama yantra, it is mentioned.

Then follows a description of a variety of aeroplanes. They have divided the aeroplanes as Mantrika, *i.e.,* based on spells and Tantrika, *i.e.,* based on techniques. The former are 32 in number and are not possible now and include aeroplanes like the Pushpaka described in *Rāmāyaṇa.* The latter are of 56 kinds and their names have been given. The text ends with the description of the following four kinds of aeroplanes:

1. Shakuna Vimaana;
2. Sundara Vimaana,
3. Rukma Vimaana and
4. Tripura Vimaana.

It is extremely difficult to comment on the text. First of all many at the present juncture of civilisation tend to question the scientific development of the Vedic times. Though they accept the marvellous advancement made by the Vedic seers on the fronts of medicine, mathematics, astronomy, linguistics, etc., etc., many hesitate to comment on the advance in science and technology of the Vedic civilisation. But the description given in the aeroplanes in this partially available text is simply amazing. The preparation of different kinds of mirrors, the energy-producing machines, construction of aircrafts, etc., etc., appear to be something novel and difficult to accept. Secondly, assuming that such advanced technology was in existence, what happened to it and how it got-completely lost in later history-is difficult to make out in spite of a consideration that the internal industry met with external threats. Thirdly, one must think, if at this phase of history, whether ancient technology can be revived with a modern touch.

One can see the number of texts that this partial book on the construction of aeroplanes has made reference to in an earlier section. It is evident that most of them are not available at present. A search for similar texts must be made in all the oriental research institutes the world over for an inventory. If any of them could be made available then it is evident that such an advanced technological civilisation existed in the Vedic times, otherwise it would not have been possible to make such clear-cut observations. Also, experiments, details of which have been so nicely described, should be conducted for their truth of information. We have now bullet-proof glass, sound-proof paints etc.; similarly, the experiments may show us the way to prepare thunder-proof metal, anti-lightning glass, etc.

Now is the era for making instruments to utilise the energy from the Sun. Solar power is known to be enormous and its utility for many purposes can be established by way of these experiments.

According to the information presented in an article entitled "Vedakaalada Vimaana Shaastra" by Sri P.K. Bangera from Bombay in the 7th number of the 4th volume of the Journal *Veda Prakasha* published from Kunjibettu, Udupi (for October, 1978), it appears experiments were conducted on the basis of these and other texts in Sanskrit on the construction of aeroplane at he end of the 19th century. It is mentioned to have been recorded on page 30 of a book *Hindu Scriptures* by Mr. Vaasudeva Visoon Doyaal of Mauritius island and published by Messrs. Macmillan & Co. One Sri Shivakar Bapooji Thalapade constructed an aeroplane on the basis of the Vedic Mantras and exhibited it at the Town Hall, Bombay, in an exhibition conducted by the Bombay Arts Society. Further experiments by Sri Talapade on the possibility of using mercury in the generation of energy for the aeroplane to fly, it is mentioned, were successful. The name of the aeroplane constructed by Sri Talapade was 'Marutsakha' and was made to fly in Chowpatty, Bombay, in the presence of a large number of spectators in 1895. It is also mentioned by Sri Bangera that the spectators included Maharaja Sayyaji Rao Gaekwad of Baroda, Mahadeva Govinda Ranade and others. Further, it is mentioned that the aeroplane was sold to a British Company by Talapade's relations, later.

Construction of aeroplanes which fly on the energy of mercury cells may be difficult to accept now. Before long, one may witness such things in the era of modern science.

Perhaps these experiments may be beyond an individual's limits of finance. But institutions which are devoted to conducting experiments in the development of technology and science specially in the branch of aerodynamics and related subjects should be able to carry them out, of course with the help of people who can lead in this line of study.

# 42

# Astrology and Abnormal Places of Birth

Some interesting observations have been made by astrologers of early times with regard to the abnormal places of birth. The abnormal places of birth are varied: Birth in ship, in the vicinity of water, in prison, in cave, in playground, in desert, in temple, in gardens, in burial ground, etc. Not verylong back a birth in aeroplane was recorded when Sri Viscount Vimana Rao was born on Sunday, 12th July 1959.

The planetary combinations which govern such births will interest students of astrology. When the Moon is strong in Cancer, Mercury is in Lagna and the other benefics, Jupiter or Venus, occupy the 4th, the birth takes place in a ship or a boat. It is also recorded that when Cancer, Pisces or latter half of Capricorn happens to be Lagna with the Moon in the 7th, birth takes place in a ship or a boat. Possibly such an observation was supported by the birth of Vyasa or Krishna Dwaipayana.

If Saturn is disposed in the 12th from Lagna and the Moon is aspected by bad planets, birth takes place in prison. From the epic *Mahabharata*, we know that Krishna was born in prison. The horoscope of Sri Krishna given by Prof. B.V. Raman in the text *Notable Horoscopes* does not, however, confirm to this rule. It may be that the Bandhana Yoga associated with birth Dasa may also indicate such a case. In this case the Navamsa Lagna lord Mercury is in the 8th aspected by Saturn and Mars.

If Saturn in watery signs as ascendants is aspected by Mercury, birth is indicated in playgrounds, by the Sun in a temple, and by the Moon in ooshara kshetra (saline land). If Saturn in Scorpio or Cancer ascendant is aspected by the Moon, birth is indicated in a cave. If the ascendant be Gemini, Virgo, Libra or the earlier half of Sagittarius with Saturn aspected by Mars, the birth is indicated in burial ground; aspected by Venus and the Moon, birth is in a lonely place; aspected by Jupiter, the birth is suggested to be near fire; aspected by the Sun, the birth is heralded in a palace, temple or cow-shed depending on the strength of the Sun and the aspect, and aspected by Mercury ina house of sculpture.

Shishuvisarjana Yoga is indicated by disposition of the Sun and the Moon together in trine to Saturn and Mars, when the baby will be parted from the mother. Perhaps this combination was present in the case of Karna, the epic hero. He was rescued by a fisherman which indicates that such a combination had the benign aspect of Jupiter.

It is stated that birth in an aeroplane was first recorded during an Air India flight from Rangoon to Calcutta on 12th July, 1959, at about 3.30 p.m. A rare case, with only two more such records later, the birth is really curious. For this one can see with advantage the chart of Sri Viscount Vimana Rao*.

The horoscope has been cast for the given time considering the longitude 92° East. The balance of the Moon's Dasa is 4 years, 4 months and 24 days at birth.

Saturn (airy planet) is in Lagna and in Navamsa, the Lagna falls in Gemini which is an airy sign. Further, the birth is in Saturn's Thrimsamsa. Since this is a rare case, it has to be observed whether the above dispositions are sufficient to indicate birth in an aeroplane.

Some of these combinations noted for abnormal places of birth are to be confirmed. Since the entire superstructure of the life has to be built by careful consideration of the birth chart, the birthplace is very important and perhaps indicates the extent of influence the particular tatwa has upon the native.-291.

**References**

*Rasi: Sagittarins - the Ascendane and Saturn; Place, Ketu; Gemini - the Sun; Cancer - Mercury; Leo - V and Mars; Virgo - Rahu and the Moon; and L Jupiter.

Navamsa: Gemini - the Ascendant, the Moon, Saturn and Venus; LibrāKotu; Capricorn - M Arios - Mars and Rahu; and Taurus - the Sun.

# 43

# The Astrological Basis of Hindu Philosophy

A Study of the reality underlying the Universe, both manifest and unmanifest, is a reward by itself and was pursued by Indians from time immemorial. Modern education, which originated in the West in recent centuries, with great stress on the material existence has been the foundation for the present thinking of mankind in terms of acquiring great possession of material things at the cost of the spiritual. Before introduction of the modern system in Universities, in the West also emphasis was laid on the study of natural philosophy, law and medicine. A study of natural philosophy would, in the least, give a comprehension of much of the universal manifestation. But, the study of disciplines like botany, zoology and the physical sciences which have now been beautifully compartmentalised to the detriment of inculcating a breadth of vision and the necessary comprehension, has caused incalculable damage to mankind. By studying or appreciating the laws of one discipline, it is not possible to have an overall picture. Nature in its manifestation appears to be full of scope and it is futile to make an attempt at getting a full picture of the nature by study of an individual disscipline. It would require appreciation of all the disciplines, of course treated in a balanced manner, to impoart a knowledge which results in the realisation of perfect interdependence of the disciplines.

Such a study was already in existence in the scripts of the Hindus. The Vedas contained profound truths of nature. Though at the superficial level the Vedic hymns look to be only prayers, they are not simple lines but codified formulae, specially of the activities of various natural agents. From such truths discussions followed to the Vedanta, and the six systems of Indian Philosophy were formulated. Finally, the *Upanishads,* the *Bhagavad Gita* and the *Brahma Sutras* resulted, the right interpretation of which would enable one to realise the truth of the reality underlying the universal existence.

The role of Jyotisha in understanding the Vedic injunctions is very well known; it was actually considered as an essential limb of the Vedas. Without the knowledge of astrology, it is hardly possible to look into the intricacies of the Vedic hymns. *Nakshatra Sookta, Navagraha Sookta,* sooktas like Soorya-Savitri and Soma, sooktas on Varuna, Mitra, Agni, Pooshan, Parjanya, night, etc. etc. are too well known to describe here, but it suffices to state that they are all codified formulae of various aspects and agencies of nature. These truths had been mastered by the diligent seers over a long time of observation and deep thinking over the behaviour and activities of various natural phenomena. With all these details, a beautiful theory of the earth and its life emerges in the context of the macro cosm. The relationship underlying between the macro and micro cosm is brought out by astrology.

The Hindu Philosophy is a dynamic school of thought. This fact is more than evident in the essence of the *Bhagavad Gita.* Lord Krishna insists that one should prefer to work in favour of getting liberation. That too one should work with an indifference to getting the fruits of the work. This status is next to impossibility, as he in a later chapter says, that it is difficult even for a moment to keep idle, and when you once commence any work, you are sure to think about its fruits. Further, it is extremely difficult to decide which is correct and which is not correct, on the path of undertaking. With these and many constraints, the truths expounded in the *Gita* become clear and will lead one to realise that it is not easy to lead a life of Nishkāmakarmayogi, the first path advised by the Gitacharya, to get out of the cycles of births and deaths.

What is the dynamism of realising the truth presented in the *Gita*? It is very clear that, if anybody suggests that one should not undertake any work to dissolve the birth/death cycle by taking to *karma sanyāsa,* he would be declared none else than a coward. This is the same condition, of course in a different context, that Arjuna took to *Shastra-sanyāsa,* from which occasion the discussion of the *Gita* starts. The Gitachārya never advocates any to enter the school of *sanyāsa* of any kind. He is a great advocate of the fact that every one should be involved. Though one is involved, he suggests that, one should not be attached to it. Non-attachment/non-involvement is a condition which comes by practice, specially with the knowledge that the doer is not the person to do the thing or cause things to be done, but he is a tool in the hands of some unknown control. This aspect becomes clear when one gets at the knowledge of astrology.

The ego that colours the person is removed by the understanding that the doer is not himself but he is only a tool in the hands of a Universal Person, or Force, call it He, She or God. Astrology helps one to know when the person is going to be put into a circumstance from where he gets name, fame, wealth, etc., or he is left as a commoner, one among the million. The other side of it, that if one is affluent, one may really come to know the bad periods for him, due to which he will be bereft of his affluence and left uncared for, even by the closest of his kith and kin. Under such circumstances, if one is having even an inkling of astrology, one will not get elated or dejected, for what has happened, but will think in terms of the eternal cycle and plan that his act has come to an end and some others have to lead the light. This is the same advice given by the Gitachārya, specially when he describes the person as *sthitapragna.* All that one boasts of one's self that he did this and he did that, carries no meaning in this context. When some of the favourable Dasas and Bhuktis with strength run in one's life span, he will automatically find himself in surroundings demanding the exercise of his decisions, which may affect all those involved. The moment this period is over, for petty reasons he mao find himself thrown out of his position, stripped off power and perquisites. Pointing any one situation as responsible for such an act is simply ridiculous in the eyes of astrology. It is nothing but one's own karma, which highlights in some parts of one's life span and keeps one in dark in other parts of the life span. The realisation that one can really do anything great or big by himself is simply baseless. Gitachārya's advocacy to involve each and every individual in the framework of manifestation is only to make one realise the extent of one's ego, which has great limitations. This limitation is not realised by most people and they will repent when things planned by them do not take shape accordingly. This also has no significance and there is nothing to be done or not to be done in the frame of the supreme manifestation and a petty human being hardly realises its limitation.

The advancement in the 20th century has been spectacular, specially due to the advancement in science and world wars. Man has been able to get over to the Moon and explorations are afoot to understand distant object including the body of Saturn. It is rather difficult to estimate the end of such adventure, specially with the powerful tools of mathematical analyses and getting at the right point by the help of monstrous instruments like the computers, but it can be surmised that all these end at the level of matter. The material philosophy is part and a very small part of the universal manifestation. It is comparable to the visible part of the iceberg, which is but in one-eighth part. There is much more in the invisible manifestation of the Universe, that is not available in the visible, which is all but the realm of modern scientist.

The theory of astrology is based upon the fundamental relationship that exists between the unit life and the whole universe at large both manifest and unmanifest. This fact has not been realised by the modern scientist, inspite of his sophistication. In theoretical astrology, for example the Moon, a celestial body, has been the representative of mind. This cannot be explained by any amount of description to the modern scientist, who was to prove it by the presence of any kind of visible connection. First of all, modern science does not know the nature and potency of mind, though psychology is a discipline of science. Further, how many human or any other kind of mind is related to the moon is another great problem. Everything on the earth or in the Universe cannot be explained. Even in science there are many realms which cannot have any description, nay definition. But this aspect that the moon is the mind of upreme Purusha is pronounced by the Veda. Purusha Sookta observes that Candrama manaso jatah meaning that the moon was born out of the mind of the Supreme or Virat Purusha. Hence, the whole of universe view in terms of human form, stands to reason that human mind is to be know from the dispositions of the moon in a horoscope i.e. heavenly chart. It is difficult to say how the author of Purusha Sookta found this truth, but considering the fact that the nature and strength of the moon in his chart, many things could be deciphered to the satisfaction of his experience, there should be no difficulty in accepting the theory put forth by the Vedic seers. It is the same case as with the theory of dynamics. So long the theory yields results which can be corroborated by facts of experience, it can be employed with advantage, while doubting thomases may continue to please themselves.

There is no place for weaklings and doubters in the Hindu philosophy. The weakness and doubt in Arjuna was at once attacked by the Gitacharya and got Arjuna convinced that he must involve himself. The dharma aspect which was troubling Arjuna at the beginning of the discourse was of weaklings and doubters. The name of killing one's kith and kin for getting the kingdom and mixing up of jatidharma (caste system) were all imperative in the eyes of the Universal Planner. Having enlightened Arjuna, when Arjuna was yet unrecovered from the shock, Gitacharya pronounces - that He had already killed all the enemies and Arjuna should only stand in the war (Nimitta matram bhava savyasachin)......

By showing Arjuna the Vishwaroopa, *i.e.*, Parama Purusha Roopa of the Universal Person, he makes Arjuna realise his utter limitation. This should be borne in mind by every VIP of today and the coming days that nobody is indispensable. If any one thinks that because of him or his great work that the world is continuing or some act is being carried out, he is utterly mistaken. A chance is given for one to exercise in a manner approved by the scriptures. It is his heaven or hell to make use of the opportunity. If he is selfish and helps a limited section of mankind, it will be returned to him no more no less. Hence unselfish act, which benefits the whole of mankind should be performed in answer to his inner person. Thus only, one will attain the status of eternal bliss:

A question arises: what is this eternal bliss and why at all one should strive to get it? When all sorts of comforts and joy are available in the world, one should strive to get the joy of a ruler of the earth, than anything else. Many have tried and caused incalculable amount of damage during the process, which has been repeated in the world history. Hindu dharma does not advocate one to live on the earnings of the others. The first sloka of *Īsāvāsyopanishad* which is given below:

*Īshāvāsyamidam sarvam yatkinca jagathyam jagat*

*Tena tyaktena bhunjeetha ma gridhah kasya swid dhanam*

means that the whole of this universe is occupied by Īsha (He who is omnipresent). By renunciation one should support one's self. One should not covet the wealth of any one.

In the context of the *Gita*, the Upanishadic statement makes it very clear that nothing belongs to any one person. The ego of a person desires to claim it. When one has no control over one's self, cannot change as he desires, cannot do as his whims and fancies, he is but a shadow of the Controller. This is brought out to an admirable extent by what can be called interpretative astrology.

The helplessness of a person is at every step he takes. One may get into a tram on a particular day with the utmost intention of carrying out all works he has planned overnight. He may just slip, he may just forget his brief case, he may just be compelled to cancel his attending to duty and apply for C.L., for no reason he could relate. He will be unable to do all he had planned. If he has to analyse in terms of astrology, he may find the day most unsuitable for undertaking any job as it may be a day of Chandrashtama, it may be a day when his natal Moon may be aspected by inimical Saturn, it may turn out to be a day ruled by Naidhana tāra. If one is acquainted with this divine science, as it is rightly called, he may for once allow his mind to think whether he can execute his plans that day. He may give a margin and when things go as per the eternal plan, he would have anticipated it and would accept it in the larger context. Then it would not be helplessness, but total acceptance, of His will.

Of all the *Darshanas,* perhaps *Poorva Meemamsa* of Jamini draws heavily upon astrology. All the *yagnyas, agnihotras* and various other rituals which actually wash the human *vaasanas* (those acquired by one's samskāras of attachment) and render the person purer to realise the truth are incorporated in this school of Hindu Philosphy. Jaimini discusses the nature of Dharma, *i.e.,* the conduct based on the Vedic edifice, which is essential to the happiness of self and community as a whole.

The other darshanas like Samkhya, Yoga, Nyāya, Vaisheshika and Uttara Meemamsa, though they do not depend on astrology much, seek its fruits for practice. In Sāmkhya system, the inactive prakriti (nature) is said to become active by coming in contact with the Purusha. This school was founded by Kapila and the theory underlying astrology has been explained in terms of Prakriti and Purusha. The whole of universe has been the interaction between these two fundamentals, the latter being the motivator. The bearing on this concept in the *Purusha Sookta* and the facts of astrological importance have been noted.

The Yoga school, propounded by Patanjali, insists on Hata Yoga and dissolution of body by practicing Hata Yoga. This may have the basis of the dynamic statement:

***Dwaāvimou purushou loke soorya mandala bhedinow***

***Parivrād yoga yuktascha rane cabhivimarditaha***

meaning that only two types at persons will be able to dissect solar ring; one, the Hata Yogi who dissolves his body by the practice of yoga and the other, one who dies in the battle-field.

For the yoga school, man appears to over-power the Prakriti by slowly acquiring natural powers by yogic practice. Finally, he rejects the body in favour of the bliss. To get at this astrology is very much necessary. The person practising yoga must know his capacity by a clear analysis of his chart and must get evaluated whether he has acquired sufficient refinement so that he will not turn back on his final journey,. Also, it is necessary to the yogis who have decided to reject their body onece and for all, to wait for 7-1/2 year period of Saturn in their chart, so that they will be able to concentrate to succeed in the project.

Nyaya school, founded by Gautama, emphasise that the way to salvation is the true knowledge of the substance or being. He goes by evidences of varied type and lengthy discussions. Here logical deduction about everything is entered upon and there is no scope for astrology in this school.

Vaisheshika school is based on pure materialistic understanding and is attributed to Kanāda. It could be a branch of Nyāya school, with special reference to matter and may be as good as modern science.

*Uttara Meemamsa* of Vyāsa lays down that the only way to salvation is true knowledge of the soul. Vyāsa, to whom the *Bhag avad Gita* is attributed, has brought out the following yogas in the *Gita*:

Karma yoga, Raja yoga, Bhakti yoga and Gnyāna yoga.



# 44

# The Astrological Aspect of the Bhagavad Gita

Bhagavad Gita is the essence of Indian Philosophy. It is also referred to as one of the cardinal texts along with *Upanishads* and *Brahma Sutras*, the interpretation of which qualifies one to be addressed as an Achārya. The Song Celestial enjoys world-wide popularity as a commendable text for one and all to be acquainted with and followed. It is composed of about 700 verses and in the span of such a close-knot text the ocean of Indian Philosophy has been distilled.

One may wonder at the title and ponder what the planets have to do with the great philosophical text, Bhagavad Gita. To hold the pride of place the Gīta should reveal the Real or the True to justify its position in the field of philosophy. A study of the other texts also reveals the Real but justify relatively leaving the student still with doubts about many critical points. The improvement over all other texts of philosophy in the Gīta is so much that a clear interpretation and exact grasp of the import, call for speical efforts and continuous thinking on concerned topics. Hence, if understood, it gives the student complete satisfaction for all the philosophical problems so that a practical approach thus obtained will secure to him realisation.

Amongst the planets saturn stands for philosophy. It is peculiear to associate philosophy with the planet which normally has been given the title of malefic, poor, dark, weak, thief, creator of troubles, dirty etc. etc. This position is not given to jupiter, virtue personified. Niether to the sun, the ātmakāraka, nor to any other. But kethu in the 12th is hailed as mokshakāraka. What makes the evil planet saturn hold this very important portfolio? Is it for his stand for justice, hard work, not to covet others possession, etc.? Then what is the exact relationship between philosophy (pursuit of truth) and saturn? Why should he hold this field of study? What dynamic or any other reason exists to support his stature? These things can be gleaned considering the point in the Gīta, the speaker of the truth and the planet saturn and his peculiar characteristics as known from astrological texts.

The *Gita*, an elaborate form of discussion between Sri Krishna and Arjuna in the battle field of Kurukshetra just before the commencement of Mahābhārata War, commends the performance of one's karma, and holds the Theory of Karma as the basis of discussion, as a means to an end. The text reveals the importance of work and work without expecting anything in return (nishkāmakarma) with the view that one is a tool in the hands of the Almighty. The existence underlined by the dynamic fact of work is revealed and most of the text supports this main point. In the view of Indian Philosophy, there is no room for inaction, inertness, blankness, weakness or staying away fom the normal creation to realise the truth. It insists that one should live a dynamic life, one should work all the life and one should be just and wise. To put Arjuna right who wanted to get away from his duty, Sri Krishna reveals the nature of work, differentiates the right from the erroneous, and induces him to work rather than renounce for by renunciation nothing will be solved. Sri Krishna tells Arjuna that it is no doubt difficult to make out the right path from the erroneous one. The revelation of karma is followed by other discussions to make Arjuna think and act in the name of the Almighty. The teacher Krishna having revealed his Viswarupa also says that the entire war was as good as already over, but the present drama should be enacted if Arjuna took to fighting, realising that he (Arjuna) was but a tool in His hands: *Nimittamatram bhava Savyasachin.*

When the Gitāchārya himself has without any doubt made it clear that work is better than sannyāsa dharma which is rather difficult for the untrained and desire-filled mind, the position of Saturn as the lord of work and lord of karmasthana, is established more firmly than the position of Ketu as mokshakaraka who would rather wind up the show of a particular life from birth-death-cycle, most probably with the rigours of sannyāsa. For a sannyāsi, the chief aim is to get out of this trap of existence, to escape from the bondage of life and death, which itself is a desire. The life of a *Jeevanmukta* is superior to the life of a *Sannyāsi* in this respect. While a *Jeevanmukha*, who has won over all desires, lives for others, works for others, does not get attached to anything, like a lotus leaf containing water but does not get wet, the sannyāsi, desirous of liberation, is a social misfit. Here lies the superiority of Saturn, as a doer who, by action, practises dettachment.

Saturn as the lord of Karma makes everyone work for life but seldom one feels the happiness of work than as a burden, a monotony, a necessary evil and obstacle for enjoyment of life. The way one fulfils his various desires by putting in necessary amount of effort may cause despair, resulting in sociological and material differences. If only one realises one's limitation-after self-evaluation-he would go a long way in knowing life better. Saturn does this job.

While carrying out work the doubt arises as to what is good and what is bad. Here Saturn or karmakaraka in modification seeks the wise counsel of Jupiter for the greater good. The advice of Venus the Sun, Mars and Mercury are not sought, because they are all limited in their outlook and egoistic. The Sun would be imperialistic, Mercury toes the line. Venus loves pomp and pleasure, Mars adds egoistic temperament, Jupiter is the planet who imparts wisdom, farsightedness and looks out for the largest good. Such a combination is ideal for the person who is a Jeevanmukta in terms of the *Gīta.* A favourable Saturn for hard and continued work, an excellent Jupiter to advise Saturn to cast away doubt and turn to do good to the large extent, are a combination better than even *parivrāja yoga.*

Even for a nishkāmakarmayogi, the favourable disposition of Jupiter and Saturn is necessary, especially a better or stronger Saturn to ensurc detachment from the results of work. This combination is probably very rare. Can we take the example of Sri Krishna's horoscope itself? This horoscope has been discussed by Prof. Raman in The Astrological Magazine, *Vol. 52, No. 11,* page 909-11 (November 1963) wherein he states that the *Gita* was taught by Sri Krishna to Arjuna at the fag end of Krishna's Ketu Dasa, Ketu having a dynamic disposition in the chart, notwithstanding the favourable dispositions of Jupiter and Saturn. To defend dharma or the righteous principle, destruction of the wicked was advocated. But the statement of the *Gīta* "Sarvadharmān parityajya" purports to a transformation of heart that would do even for the most wicked to realise truth by Bhakti.

A combination for *mukti* by *parivrajya yoga* in possible but it is for one's own escape. Hence grihastha (householder) Dharma was advised is preference to sannyāsa by great viraktas. A jeevanmukta grihastha is possibly the Gita-person and more and more number of horoscopes of such are necessary to be studied for improvement of one's own.

As Purandara Das of bhakti cult suggested in his songs of philosophy that one should swim and having swum one should attain the eternal bliss-Easabaeku iddu jaisabeku, but how? It is only with the implicit faith in Him and carrying out nishkamakarma (desireless action).

Thus Bhagavad Gita in its essence in terms of planetary values appears to be represented by an extremely favourable and mutually good saturn-jupiter combination notwithstanding the favourable disposition of other planets. The bondage of life, relations, possessions, enjoyment, etc. are so hard to get rid of that it is possible only by the grace of good saturn. Can we think of a better celestial object than saturn who indicates such a position? Is saturn bad, stubborn, steady, slow, undesirable? Are these not qualities for common practice and tapas? Was he not yogakaraka to the Gitacharya himself? Krishna with rohini star and Vrishabha (Taurus) lagna could reap the best of saturn in expounding the Gita to the world through discussion with Arjuna. It is, therefore, the spirit of saturn sung by the poet in the form of Gita.

[illegible] the internal [illegible] [illegible] the [illegible] it is only with [illegible] faith in him and carrying [illegible] for the welfare of [illegible].

Thus [illegible] of planetary [illegible] appears to be [illegible] by [illegible] favourable and [illegible] good [illegible] combination [illegible] the favourable disposition of other planets [illegible] the [illegible] the [illegible] of the [illegible] in the grace of good [illegible] object than [illegible] position [illegible] qualities [illegible]. Was he not [illegible] to the [illegible] with [illegible] and [illegible] the [illegible] of [illegible] the [illegible] to the world through [illegible] with [illegible]. It is, therefore, the [illegible] of [illegible] by the [illegible] the form of [illegible].

# 45

# The Astrology of Kundalini

That serpentine power which resides at the base of the human backbone, coiled three and half times, called Kundalini, is vested by nature with extra-ordinary qualities and is well known to the students of Hatha Yoga. According to Yoga Prakarana this power:

Moolaadhaarodgato vanhih dwādashaantamupaashritah

Peeyūshavarshapoornaatmaa kaamado na tu mokshadah

Sa eva oordhwagatah tasmāt apavargaaya sambhavet

is responsible for the existence of humanity through the carnal enjoyment when it moves downwars but the same becomes more important moving upwards for getting liberation from the cycle of birth and death. It does not necessitate any difficult performance for its downward movement. But it needs tremendous will and regular exercise under a guru to move it upward raising the same to Sahsrāra through the shatchakras recognised by yogis, when the person is known to get all the natural powers and also become one with the Universe beyond the distinctions of past, present and future. Although other yogas of karma and gnāna, etc., obtain in the world, the former without attaching any return and the latter by virtue of itself in parlance with a yogi who has his Kundalini residing at his Sahsrara, people with rājasa temperament would perhaps tend to follow the path of Hatha Yoga than the other yogas, the astrological bearing of which can be ascertained in very clear terms.

Rudra in his Vivarana on Brihatjātaka elaborates of the following terms the divisions of a Rasi a Drekkana, Hora, Navamsa, Thrimsamsa, Dwadasamsa, etc.:

Moolaadhaare drigānasyaat pitruchintā ravisthatha
Swaadhishtaanetu horāsyaat maatruchintā shashee thatha
Manipoore navaamshascha bhrātru chintā kujo api cha
Anaahate cha thrimshaamsho vaanee chintā budhasthatha
Vishuddhou dwaadashaamshasyaat putrachintā thatha guruh
Aagnyaayaam kshetramuddishtam jaayaachintā sitasthatha
Dwaadashaante shanaischaari naashachintā cha kirtita
Tatrasthaistadadheesaischa balaabalavashatphalam, etc.

This would mean:

| *Chakras* | *Divisions* | *Karakatwa* | *Planet* |
|---|---|---|---|
| Moolaadhaara | Drekkana | Father | Sun |
| Swaadhisthaana | Hora | Mother | Moon |
| Manipoora | navaamsa | Brother | Mars |
| Anaahata | Thrimsaamsa | Speech | Mercury |
| Vishuddhi | Dwaadasaamsa | Children | Jupiter |
| Aagnaa | Kshetra | Wife | Venus |
| Dwaadasaanta | | Destruction | Saturn |

From the above it can be seen that the strength of Moolaadhaara Chakra in a person can be evaluated by a study of the person's drekkana chart and similarly with other chakras also. While the horoscope can also be studied in terms of satwa, rajo and tamo gunas based on the strength of the planets, the Hatha yogic achivements of a person can also be evaluated and it appears that it will be best presented by the rajo guna charts.

One of the masters of Kundalini Vidya observed in an Indian weekly that "Man is a gorilla standing up on his hind legs to reach God. This is both the history and the mystery of evolution" and has recognised that "It is not a supernatural, abnormal or occult phenomenon as the ancients claimed but a biological mechanism, the engine of evolution, built into the cerebrospinal system and the genital region of the body" (*Kundallni Yoga* by Sri Gopi Krishna, in *Blitz* dated April 10, 1976).

Based on these observations and the rediscovery of Kundalini as has been stated, a Kundalini research project has been sponsored at the All India Institute of Medical Sciences. It appears that the project is perhaps not the first of its kind but has been already under study by the doctors at the Kundalini Research Foundation in the USA. The research project in India is aimed at identifying the Kundalini as etherial prana and determining its parameters.

As the master says not all the persons can contribute to the subject but some are chosen. What are the characteristics of such personalities? Can it be ascertained from a study of planetary positions at the time of birth of such persons? What time is conducive for the performance and detailed studies and observations? These and other similar aspects of the issue can be found out from astrology, the science ***par excellence***.

In *Sri Lalitha Sahasranama*, Sri Lalitha is described as residing at Moolaadhaara (Moolaadhaaraikanilayaa). She is also described to enter Manipoora Chakra through Brahma Granthi. Also she is described to enter Aagnaa Chakra through Vishnu Granthi. Further she is described to enter Sahasradalapadma through Rudra Granthi and cause heavenly bliss.

In the above context, it is a fundamental necessity that the person performing the shaktichālana and advanced exercises in Kundalini Yoga must have an extra-ordinary powerful horoscope, the strength being derived from favourable disposition of the Sun, the Moon, Venus and Rahu, notwithstanding the favourable set-up of other planets. After all human body is representative of the Universe in a mini organic frame, and to attain superconsciousness it needs minimum qualifications. With these minima, when once the person becomes a yogi, he may need little help from all these in later activities since he will be above time and space.

A study of horoscopes of persons who were acclaimed yogis will make the matter clear. We can study the horoscope of Sri Ramakrishna Paramahamsa as given by Prof. B.V. Raman. Lagna was Kumbha (Aquarius) and Saturn was exalted in the 9th. This disposition assured that Lagna lord was extremely favourable, hence no "nasha chinta". In any yogic study the disposition of Saturn is supreme as also of the Moon representing the mind. Sri Ramakrishna's Moon was also in the birth sigh of Kumbha, a Sthira (fixed) Rasi, Saturn holding double control. Venus was exalted and Sri Ramakrishna was said to worship Sharada Devi, his devout spouse; hence Aagnaa Chakra is free without any obstruction for the Kundalini to enter, since Venus is powerful and not aspected by malefic, as also yogakaraka for Kumbha. The 7th lord the Sun, natural Ātmakaraka, is usually favourable for the Kumbhis, owning the 7th house, and the devotion of Sharada Devi to Ramakrishna is well known. Rahu is on the meridian, the lord of which is exalted in the 12th. Jupiter is not unfavourable. However, Mercury appears to be in the arc of combustion. While the various chakras represented by the Sun, the Moon, Mars, Venus as Moolaadhaara, Swaadhishtaana, Manipoora and Aagnaa are clear and ready to receive the raising Kundalini without any obstruction, Vishuddhi of Jupiter was not unfavourable since the Moon, Lagna, the Sun and Saturn were aspected by him from a soumya's (benefic) house. The Anaahata was combust by the rays of natural Ātmakaraka, but the aspect of Jupiter on the combination rendered the same clear of its adverse effect. His discourses were something superb. The horoscope was naturally endowed with all yogic experiences.

The field of applied astrology to Kundalini Research may open up a grand field of knowledge the advantage of which is more essential to humanity in the present context of civilisation. The field of human physiology may be understood better and applied yoga may be useful to cure may incurable diseases.

While shakti chālana is performed by yogic exercises in Hatha Yoga, it is also possible to do the same by reciting certain mantras of beejaksharas, spread over a mandala of punashcharans or repetition. To clear the body of ill-effects of poorvakrama, *i.e.*, to bring favourable disposition of the planets, long yogic exercises or more periods of punascharana may be necessary. Once the Kundalini is raised by Hata Yoga, its control and its upward movement cause unusual experiences and terrible strain. Slowly the body, *i.e.*, the organic system has to be attained to the raising Kundalini, otherwise effects may be adverse. These are normally undertaken under instructions of regular teachers. Similarly the beejamantrochaaraṇa also is to be done perfectly under the guidance of gurus, when experiences of

Kundalini manifest in the person. Since the sound to uccharana commences from the nabhi moola (navel centre) the corresponding chakra has a direct control and accounts for the same as shaktichalana by praanaayaama.

One of the qualities of a yogi is the possession of knowledge of astrology, i.e. thrikaalangnaana. This is also attained by a study of astrology itself and improving one's own intuition by upaasana. Nādis are all special fields, perhaps common to super astrologers and yogis. He who knows the origin, destruction and appearance of the panchabhootas (five elements) and also what is right and wrong is addressed as Bhagavān. With the super knowledge of the universe attained by Hath Yoga or Mantragnaana or by astrology, the Universe will be realised, the be all and end all of all that is to be known-110.

# Selected Bibliography

Anon (1975) The Cultural Heritage of India IV vols. Ramakrishna Mission.

Achyuta Krishnanda Tirtha (1913) Vanamala commentary on Taittariya Upanishad.

Bhargava, M.L. (1964) The Geography of Rg. Vedic India.

Bhasin, J.N. (1984) Astrology in Vedas.

Bhat, R.K. (1987) Varahamihira's Brhatsamhita, 2 vols. MLBD.

Colin Ronan, N. (1964) The Astronomers

Dave, J.H. (1970) Immortal India, vol. I to IV.

Dayananda Saraswati (1976) Rgvedadibhāshyabhūmika.

Grifith, R.T.H. (1986) The Hymns of the Rg. Veda

Goendka, S.D. (1931) Srimadbhagavadgīta.

Harbilas Sarda (1975) Hindu Superiority.

Holmes, A. (1964) Principles of Physical Geology.

Jaggi, O.P. (1966) Scientists of Ancient India

Josyer, G.R. (1950) Āswalayana Pūrva Prayoga

______, (1966) Sanskrit Civilisation

Kapileshwara Choudhury (1946) Suryasiddhānta. K.S.S. No. 144, Banares

Krishnan, M.S. (1956) Geology of India and Burma.

Lockyer, N. (1964) The Dawn of Astronomy.

Max Muller, (1961) India; What can it teach us?

Murthy, S.R.N. (1978) Varahamihira's contribution to the Vedic Theory of the Earth

______, (1987) An Integrated Theory of the Earth

______, (1990) Gemmological Studies in Sanskrit Texts

______, (1992) Ancient Indian Theories of the Earth

Pascoe, E.H. (1973) A manual of the Geology of India & Burma, vols. IV.

Raghava Rao, N. (1949) Scriptures of the Heaven

Raman, B.V. (1958) Bhavartha Ratnakara

______, (1958) Studies in Jaimini Astrology

______, (1959) Hindu Predictive Astrology

______, (1961) Three hundred important combinations

______, (1961) Graha & Bhava Balas

______, (1962) Muhurta or Electional Astrology

______, (1963) Notable Horoscopes.

______, (1965) Astrology & Modern Thought

______, (1967) Ashtakavarga System of prediction

______, (1969) Varshaphal

______, (1970) Neelakantha's Prshnatantra

______, (1971) How to judge a horoscope

______, (1993) Astrology in forecasting weather & earthquakes

Rao, B.S. (1958) Strijataka

______, (1957) Brhat Jataka

Rebellow, R.J./Panchanga Parishkarana Samitiya Varadi (Kannada) (1971)

Sacchindananda Jois (1919) Markandeya Joutisha (Kannada)

Satvalekar, S.D. (1939) Rg. veda Samhita

_____, (1936) Samaveda Samhita

_____, (1990) Taittariya Samhita

_____, (1944) Atharvaveda Samhita

Seetharama Jha (1968) Brahtparāsarahorāsāstram

Shama Sastry, R. (1936) Vedānga Joutisha

_____, (1938) Drapsa: The Vedic cycle of eclipses.

Sontakke, N.S. (1933) Rg. Veda Samhita vol. I

_____, (1984) Rg. Veda Samhita vol. II

_____, (1978) Rg. Veda Samhita vol. III

_____, (1951) Rg. Veda Samhita vol. IV

Subbrayappa, B.V. & Murthy, S.R.N. (1988) Scientific Heritage of India.

Subbrayappa, B.V. & Sharma, K.V. (1985) Indian Astronomy - A Source Book.

Thibaut, G. & Dwivedi, S. (1968) The Panchasiddhantika of Varhamihira.

Tilak, B.G. (1972) The Orion.

# Appendix

References to the first publication of these articles in the Astrological Magazine.

| | |
|---|---|
| The Evolution of Time, | vol. 61, no. 5, pp. 475-478 |
| The Fourth Dimension | vol. 57, no. 6, pp. 552-611 |
| Rationale of Astrology | vol. 62, no. 6, pp. 544-546 |
| The Astrological Control | vol. 58, no. 11, pp. 1017 7 1020 |
| Approaching the third approximation | vol. 62, no. 2, pp. 193-195 |
| The Indian Chronology | vol. 58, no. 8, pp. 741-742 & 804-805 |
| Murdane Astrology | vol. 62, no. 5, pp. 505-506 |
| Adityachara | vol. 58, no. 12, pp. 1124 & 1145 |
| Movements of the Moon | vol. 59, no. 7, pp. 653-654 |
| Movements of Mars & Mercury | vol. 59, no. 8, pp. 745-746 |
| Jupiterian Movements | vol. 59, no. 9, pp. 840-841 |
| Venus in Marriage | vol. 58, no. 9, pp. 757-758 |
| The Planet Saturn in Astrology | vol. 61, no. 1, pp. 20-23 |
| Varahamihira & Vaiking on Mars | vol. 66, no. 7, pp. 528-529 |

| | |
|---|---|
| Is Ayanamsha Revolutionary | vol. 64, no. 3, pp. 261-263 |
| Astrology & National Crisis | vol. 64, no. 1, pp. 34-35 |
| Planets and Self-Generating Economy | vol. 62, no. 11, pp. 988 & 1052 |
| Relativity Theory and Judicial Astrology | vol. 59, no. 1, pp. 112-113 & 116 |
| The Hindu Calendar | vol. 56, no. 7, pp. 664 & 697 |
| Astrological Basis of Economic Planning | vol. 61, no. 7, pp. 653-656 |
| Planets & Environment | vol. 72, no. 1, pp. 54-57 |
| The Geological Aspects of The Brhatsamhita | vol. 57, no. 4, pp. 386 & 425 |
| The Astrological Aspects of Vastu | vol. 70, no. 1, pp. 96 & 100 |
| Importance of Vastu in Mundane Astrology | vol. 63, no. 11, pp. 833-834 & 889 |
| Astrological Indication for Ground Water | vol. 58, no. 10, pp. 937-938 & 940 |
| Astrology & Gems | vol. 59, no. 2, pp. 230-232 |
| Planets & Sound Vibrations | vol. 62, no. 10, pp. 905-906 |
| Operation Hiroshima | vol. 62, no. 3, pp. 289-290 |
| The Vedic River Saraswati | vol. 73, no. 1, pp. 102-104 & 116 |
| The Solar Control of Mountain Formation | vol. 57, no. 12, pp. 1104 & 1129 |
| Geological Veracity of Cheirós Earthquake Preicition | vol. 71, no. 1, pp. 27-30. |
| Varahamihira on Earthquakes | vol. 58, no. 5, pp. 497 |

| | |
|---|---|
| Prognostication of Earthquakes | vol. 61, no. 5, pp. 410-412 |
| Causes of Earthquakes 975 | vol. 56, no. 10, pp. 934 & |
| Planetary Purturbations and Earthquakes | vol. 62, no. 1, pp. 32-34 & 40 |
| Tides & Earthquakes | vol. 59, no. 6, pp. 568-569 & 632 |
| Forecasting Earthquakes | vol. 58, no. 1, pp. 42-46 |
| Astrological Evaluation of Personality | vol. 62, no. 7, pp. 633-634 |
| Rationale of Ashtakavarga | vol. 59, no. 4, pp. 393-394 |
| Using Divisional Charts in Horoscopic | vol. 70, no. 9, pp. 688-690 |
| The Vedic Science of Aeronautics Studies | vol. 75, no. 2, pp. 197-199 & 235 |
| Astrology and Abnormal Places of Birth | vol. 63, no. 3, pp. 262 |
| The Astrological Basis of Hindu Philosophy | vol. 69, no. 1, pp. 37-39 & 48 |
| The Astrological Aspect of The Bhagavad Gita | vol. 64, no. 2, pp. 177-178 |
| The Astrology of Kundalini | vol. 65, no. 8, pp. 597-598 & 652 |

# Index
## (of more important terms)